THE

FRENCH COURT AND SOCIETY

REIGN OF LOUIS XVI. AND FIRST EMPIRE

VOL. I.

The French Court and Society: REIGN OF LOUIS XVI. AND FIRST EMPIRE.
BY CATHERINE CHARLOTTE, LADY JACKSON

IN TWO VOLUMES
VOLUME I.

WILDSIDE PRESS

Large Paper Edition

This edition is limited to one thousand copies, of which this is Number 139

CONTENTS OF VOL. I.

CHAPTER I.

	PAGE
INTRODUCTORY	1

CHAPTER II.

A Momentous Crisis. — "*Louis Le Désiré.*" — A Royal Blacksmith. — Hopes and Expectations. — Henri IV. *Resurrexit.* — Good Wishes and Intentions. — Louis the Well-beloved. — A King without Dignity. — Vulcan and His Coiffeur. — A Heaven-born King. — A Minister of State. — Madame Adélaïde's Agent. — Machault or Maurepas? — A Victory and a Defeat. — Queens-Consort and Queens-Regent. — Her "Sacred Majesty" of Austria. — Effort to Reinstate Choiseul. — The Dauphin and the Jesuits. — False Charge of the Jesuits. — The Favourite and Her Rival. — The Duke in Exile. — A Chilling Reception 10

CHAPTER III.

Atonement. — An Effort of Gallantry. — At a Loss for Amusement. — Unattached Couples. — The Petit Trianon. — Forming a Queen of France. — The Dear, Good *Abbé.* — Guide, Philosopher, and Friend. — An Appeal to the King. — The Results of Indecision. — An Apollo Taking a Bath. — The Young Dauphine. — The Royal Bride. — The Queen's Peccadilloes. — The *Ques-a-co?* Plume. — Pleasure and Devotion. — The King's Aunts. — The Gardens of Bellevue. — The Court of Mesdames. — First Reception, at La Muette. — Fashionable Headdresses. — Senseless Mythology. — Aristocratic Privileges. — Etiquette Banished. — The Queen's Enemies . . 29

CHAPTER IV.

A New Moral Code. — *Un Vieillard Charmant.* — Louis XVI. — Governing Alone. — A Minister in Exile. — The Austrian Party. — A Frugal Minister of State. — Boucher's *Chefs-d'œuvre.* — The *Petits Appartements.* — Venus Rising from the Sea. — Removal of the Pictures. — Louis XVI. as a Patron of Art. — The Private Income of Louis XV. — The Famous Secret Diplomacy. — Treachery of Monsieur. — " Tartuffe " at Marly. — Disappointed Hopes. — A Royal Rustic Village. — M. de Maurepas's Colleagues. — *Louis Quinze* and *Quinze Louis.* — The *Système* Maupeou. — Sister Louise, the Royal Nun. — Burning the Chancellor. — A Satisfactory Beginning. — The King and His Minister 50

CHAPTER V.

A Musical *Émeute.* — Gluck and Piccini. — Grétry and Marmontel. — A *Mot* of Madame du Barry. — *Iphigénie en Aulide.* — The *Devin du Village.* — A Knight of the Golden Star. — Sophie Arnould. — *Célébrons Notre Reine.* — The King and the Comte d'Artois. — Royalty at the Opera. — Amateurs and Critics. — Head-dresses in Peril. — A Sentimental Head-dress. — A Critical Position. — The Diamond Aigrette. — The Music of Nature. — Jean Jacques at the Opera. — Quinault's " Roland." — Marmontel and Piccini. — Madame du Deffand. — Piccinites and Gluckites. — Piccini's Triumph 72

CHAPTER VI.

Monsieur and Madame. — Monsieur's *Bons Mots.* — Louis le Sévère. — A Breach of Court Etiquette. — Jupiter at Versailles. — Putting the Clock Forward. — The Royal Brothers and Sisters. — A *Fête* at Brunoy. — The Comte and Comtesse d'Artois. — Mademoiselle Bertin. — Races *à l'Anglaise.* — Hunting and Gambling. — At Heart a Rake. — A Petition to the Queen. — The Barber of Séville. — Beaumarchais's Secret Mission. — The Monopoly in Corn. — A Raid on the Bakers' Shops. — Distress and Extravagance. — " Gros Madame." — The Courtly Comte de Buffon. — A Point of Etiquette. — A Grand Fancy-dress Ball. — A Question of Precedence. — The Parisians Indignant 93

CHAPTER VII.

Which Shall It Be? — An Irreverent Proposal. — The Sainte Ampoule. — The Coronation Oath. — M. Turgot Overruled. — The Last Crowned Queen of France. — The Cost of a Queen's Whim. — The New State Carriage. — The New Crown. — Arrival at Rheims. — The Cathedral of Rheims. — Where Is the King? — "*Elle Me Gêne!*" — "*Vive le Roi!*" — Healing the Sick. — "*Le Pauvre Homme!*" — Visiting the Abbaye de Saint-Rémi. — Ungrateful Human Nature. — The Queen's Sage Reflections. — A Gratifying Reward. — Clotilde and Elisabeth. — The Royal Carmelite Nun. — Goldoni at Versailles. — The Heir-presumptive 114

CHAPTER VIII.

The *Salons;* Louis XV. — "Mother of the Philosophers." — La Marquise du Deffand. — The Walpole Correspondence. — Poor Madame Necker! — Mdlle. de l'Espinasse. — Mesdames Necker and Geoffrin. — Necker's "*Éloge de Colbert.*" — A Celestial Countenance. — M. Necker's Early Career. — A Genial Host. — An Anxious Hostess. — Madame de Condorcet. — Rival *Salons.* — MM. Turgot and Necker. — The Economist's Downfall. — Check, to the Queen. — The Higher Clergy in Conclave. — The Abbé Talleyrand-Périgord. — Presumptuous Protestants. — The Divine Necker in Disguise. — M. de Maurepas's Godson. — The Clamours of the Clergy 134

CHAPTER IX.

A Severe Winter. — Sledges and Polonaises. — Sledging on the Boulevards. — Rival Favourites. — The King's Sledges. — The Queen and the *Danseuse.* — The Dignity of the Crown. — The Kingly Halo of Divinity. — The *Maison Militaire.* — The Two "Forty-eights." — The King in His Belvedere. — The Queen's Sanctum Sanctorum. — Cæsar's Wife. — A Private Interview. — The Queen's *Gardes Malades.* — Thoughtfulness for the King. — Ethics and Sentimentality. — Strait-laced People. — The Comte de Périgord. — A Mystification. — The *Petits Appartements.* — Absolution for the Queen. — The *Vox Populi.* — Alas! Poor Queen 154

CONTENTS

CHAPTER X.

Eventful Years. — The American Colonists. — Beaumarchais's Secret Mission. — Aiding the Insurgents. — Easing the King's Conscience. — Jerusalem at Philadelphia. — The American Planter. — The "*Ragoût Philadelphique.*" — Franklin Puzzled. — The *Salon Helvétique.* — "Never Too Old to Learn." — "*Ça Ira! Mes Amis, Ça Ira!*" — Superfluous Cash. — The King's Generosity. — Lansquenet. — The "*Jeu de la Reine.*"—The *Fête* of All Saints 174

CHAPTER XI.

An Imperial Visitor. — Joseph II. — The King on His Guard. — A Diplomatic Letter. — The Emperor's Quarters. — *Mauvais Sujets* and *Polissons.* — Visiting Marly *en Polisson.* — The Queen's *Cercle Intime.* — Joseph's Opinion of Louis XVI. — A Taste for Perfection. — Pedlars' Stalls in the Palace. — Exploring Paris. — Lecturing the King. — A Changed Man. — The Archduke Charles. — An Imperial Traveller. — Mozart. — The Emperor at the Opera. — The "*Coiffure Iphigénie.*" — Speakingly Evident. — The Emperor's Sayings and Doings. — The Philosopher's Stone. — A Successful Alchemist. — A Conference with M. Necker. — The Apostle of Liberty. — A Memento of Franklin. — Bewildering Politics. — The King Taken to Task 189

CHAPTER XII.

The Théâtre Français. — The *Élite* of Society. — The Duc de Cossé-Brissac. — Alone, in his *Loge Grillée.* — The *Début* of Mdlle. Contat. — One of Nature's *Grandes Dames.*— The Lady of Luviciennes.— An Imperial Guest. — A Presentiment of Evil. — An Amiable Nation. — The Temple of Love. — Mademoiselle Guimard. — "The Incorruptible Chérin." — Terpsichorean Divinities. — Delicate Hints. — "Royally Bad." — The Fire of Love. — *Les Adieux.* — A Brother's Counsels. — It Is Time — Ah! More than Time. — Poor Marie Antoinette! . 213

CHAPTER XIII.

An Equivocal Personage. — La Chevalière d'Éon. — A Ladylike Gentleman. — A Secret of State. — The Empress Elizabeth's Reader. — The Modern Jeanne d'Arc. —

CONTENTS ix
PAGE

Jeanne d'Arc at the Opera. — M. Campan in Doubt. — "*Ça Ira! Ça Ira!*" — La Fayette's *Preux Chevaliers*. — American Independence. — The Rebukes of the Empress. — The Farce of the 12,000,000. — Birth of the Duc de Berry 231

CHAPTER XIV.

Gluck's Return. — Madame Saint-Huberti. — Gluck and Piccini. — An Iconoclast of Eighteenth Century Shams. — Misgivings. — Voltaire's Arrival in Paris. — The Patriarch's Lever. — The Benediction. — The Philosopher's Wig. — First Performance of Irène. — *La Grande Citoyenne.* — Apotheosis of Voltaire. — Glory and Literary Renown. — The Old Duc de Richelieu. — Voltaire and Jean Jacques. — In Death United 243

CHAPTER XV.

The First Hostile Shot. — The *Belle Poule* and *Arethusa.* — The *Coiffure Belle Poule.* — A British Heroine. — The English and French Fleets. — The Fleets in a Gale. — A Victory Lost. — *Lâcheté*, or Indiscipline? — Immortalised at the Opera. — Disappointed Hopes. — A Blow to the Empress-queen. — An Unsympathetic Virgin. — Better Success Next Time. — Starlight Revels. — Madame Campan. — Christening of Madame Royale. — Thirst for Military Glory. — A Swedish Hero of Romance. — Count Fersen's Departure. — American Independence. — American Gratitude 256

CHAPTER XVI.

Changes in France. — M. Necker's "*Comptes Rendus.*" — M. de Maurepas's Successor. — Death of Maria Theresa. — The Secret Correspondence. — The Emperor Francis I. — "We Will Die for Our King." — Unto France a Child Is Born. — "*Mon Dieu! que Je Suis Heureuse!*" — An Overflowing Cup of Bliss, — Privileged People. — Sobering Down. — Mocking Tongues 274

CHAPTER XVII.

Under New Guidance. — A Change for the Worse. — The Queen's Expectations. — The Queen and the Duchess. — A Transfer of Privileges. — The Fall of a Brilliant

x   CONTENTS

PAGE

Meteor. — An Expensive Luncheon. — A Reasonable Husband. — The Indignant Confessor. — The Palais Royal *Salon*. — Madame de Sillery-Genlis. — A Deep-rooted Aversion. — Excuses of Madame de Genlis. — The Favourite Winter Games. — Dissipation and Luxury. — A Severe Winter. — Misery and Starvation. — Bonaparte's First Siege. — Liberty and Equal Rights. — A General Promotion. — M. de Calonne. — *Vogue la Galère* 285

CHAPTER XVIII.

Mariage de Figaro. — Private Readings. — "*Détestable! Injouable!*" — Determined to Vanquish. — The Comte and Comtesse du Nord. — "*Le Frère Charmant.*" — "Figaro" at St. Petersburg. — Defying the King. — "Oppression and Tyranny." — The King Consents. — The New Censor's Opinion. — "Much Ado about Nothing." — Untrustworthy Memoirs. — A Picture of the Manners of the Day. — First Performance of "Figaro." — A Galaxy of Talent. — A Trying Occasion. — A Charitable Project. — Inaccessible to Reason. — Vanquishing Lions and Tigers. — Beaumarchais at St. Lazare. — Release of the Prisoner. — The King's Atonement. — A Second Triumph. — Causes of the Revolution. — Mirabeau. — An Affair of Time 304

CHAPTER XIX.

Birth of a Second Son. — Dazincourt. — Arrest of Cardinal de Rohan. — The Mystery of the Necklace. — The Château of St. Cloud. — Jeanne de Saint Rémy-Valois. — Jeanne's Patrons. — Presented to the Queen. — Unfortunate Concealment. — Cagliostro. — The Alchemist's Portrait. — The Comtesse Cagliostro. — The Cardinal's Trial. — The Cardinal Acquitted. — The Sister Superior. — The Queen's Dissatisfaction. — Poor Marie Antoinette. — M. de Bréteuil. — "The Excellent *Abbé*" . . 327

CHAPTER XX.

The King Buys Rambouillet. — "*Le Déjeuner de Chasse.*" — "*Il est Ivre Mort.*" — Dining in Public. — "The Queen's New Domain. — *De Par la Reine.*" — Mdlle. Necker's Suitors. — The Accepted Suitor. — Count Fersen Released. — Madame Lebrun's *Étrennes*. — An Ineligible

CONTENTS xi
PAGE

Ami Intime. — An Invitation to the Ball. — M. de Calonne's Last Remedy. — Death of M. de Vergennes. — A Lost Friend 343

CHAPTER XXI.

A Lifelong Wish. — The Queen's Advisers. — The New Minister of Finance. — Struggling with Difficulties. — Shovels and Tongs. — M. Necker's Return to Paris. — Paying Court to the Queen. — Agriculture in France. — The Three Estates of the Realm. — The "Plebeian Count." — The Dawn of the Revolution 356

LIST OF ILLUSTRATIONS

VOLUME I.

	PAGE
MARIA THERESA	*Frontispiece*
LOUIS XVI.	16
DUC DE CHOISEUL	26
MARIE ANTOINETTE	42
NECKER	140
VERSAILLES	206
LA FAYETTE	238
BEAUMARCHAIS	304
CAGLIOSTRO	336

THE FRENCH COURT AND SOCIETY

REIGN OF LOUIS XVI. AND FIRST EMPIRE

CHAPTER I.

INTRODUCTORY.

"YET forty days and Nineveh shall be overthrown." Such was the text of the last Lenten sermon preached in 1774 before Louis XV. at Versailles.

Truly, the mantle of a Bourdaloue, Fléchier, or Massillon, had not fallen on any of the court preachers of that day. Rarely, very rarely, was then heard the stirring pulpit eloquence which, during the former reign, and in the earlier years of that of Louis XV., so often awakened terror in the accusing conscience of the king, and thrilled with fear and trembling — passing though the emotion may have been — the fashionable assemblages of courtly sinners who thronged the gilded chapel of Versailles. The philosophy of the *salons* had invaded the pulpit. Preaching had lost much of its influence. Strife and ill-feeling prevailed among the dignitaries of the Church, the "bishops, both pious and philosophical," being alike contentious and intolerant.

Nevertheless, a few truly devout and earnest-minded men still fearlessly denounced the vices of the age, and proclaimed aloud to that corrupt and sceptical generation that its cup of iniquity was full and retribution at hand. Amongst these the Abbé de Beauvais, Bishop of Senez, was conspicuous, — no less for his zeal than the general impressiveness of his oratory. It was he who was appointed to preach before the court on the above named occasion. Addressing the king, as at that period was customary, the *abbé* slowly and solemnly repeated his text. "Yet forty days," Sire, "and Nineveh shall be overthrown."

It was remarked that the king turned pale. And as it was usual with the obsequious congregation to arrange their faces according to the expression observed on the king's, many were no doubt much mortified that they could not in this instance follow suit, and show pale faces also. But all were not affected by the text as the king had been; for on his ear it had fallen as startlingly as though a prophetic message were specially sent to him. And as the preacher — growing more fervidly eloquent as he developed his subject — compared Paris to Nineveh, the infidelity of the age to "the sin of that doomed city," and urged on all the necessity of repentance, "that perchance the evil, otherwise too surely coming on France, might thus be averted," Louis listened with ever increasing uneasiness.

The solemn tones of the *abbé's* warning voice ceased. His sermon was pronounced both eloquent and edifying. Most persons present then gave no further thought to it. But there remained with the king a vague sense of uneasiness, of some peril near at hand, — personal peril he fancied, therefore to him the more afflictive. On his return from the chapel he was moody and melancholy in the extreme. Even the *bons mots* of the old Duc de Richelieu failed to rally him. "Only could his mind," he said, "be at ease again when those forty days should have expired." Yet when the solemnities of the Holy Week were concluded, and the *grandes chasses* resumed, his dreary forebodings seemed gradually to fade away in his keen enjoyment of the chase.

One morning, however, towards the end of April, as the king was strolling in the gardens of the Petit Trianon he was seized with a giddiness and pains in the head. In great alarm he returned to Versailles, and sent off immediately, at Madame du Barry's suggestion, a sum of 200,-000 *francs* to the Curé of Ste. Geneviève, accompanied with a request that prayers might be made to the saint on his behalf.

His physician meantime having arrived, the

king, who grew worse, was recommended to take to his bed; while, to prevent the recurrence of a scene like that which once took place at Metz, a message, at his desire, was conveyed to Madame du Barry, praying her to retire to Ruel, and spend some days there with the Duchesse d' Aiguillon.

It is the 10th of May, 1774, — a lovely evening following a genial spring day. The sun already is sunk below the horizon; the brilliant hues of the western sky are fading into the dusky tints of advancing night; and the Château of Versailles in its sombre grandeur looms larger in the increasing gloom.

There are saunterers on the terrace in earnest conversation; carriages and horses and a throng of attendants in the courtyard. A group of impatient pages; *écuyers*, booted and spurred; an escort of household troops, eager for the order to mount, are watching with anxious eyes the flickering glare of a candle that faintly illumines the window of a chamber in the château. In that chamber lies "Louis, the Well-beloved," at the point of death.

Suddenly the feeble flame of the candle is extinguished, and instantly all is movement and animation in the courtyard; for it is the concerted signal by which those who are on service within that pestiferous royal dwelling inform those who are waiting without to accompany the young royal family to Choisy, that the vital spark is extinct — the king is dead! Yes, Louis XV. has breathed his last. His ignoble career is unexpectedly brought to a close by a virulent attack of small-pox, — just, too, when, his vigorous constitution flattering his hopes of life prolonged for yet many a year, his mind was bent on following the example of his predecessor by contracting a left-handed marriage in the evening of his days, if the Pope could be prevailed on to sanction the divorce of Madame du Barry.

Heavy clouds were then gathering on the political horizon, and great social changes were impending. But Louis firmly believed that the existing state of things would last his time, while the inevitable storm he foresaw was destined to burst only on the head of his successor. He, therefore, was safe. Indolence and ease and the enjoyment of the passing hour alone concerned him. "*Mais, après nous le déluge,*" he had long been accustomed to explain. In his later years he would sometimes add, with a sinister smile: "I should like well to know how Berry will contrive to weather the coming storm."

It was always "Berry." The fat, ungainly, heavy-looking youth who was to succeed him was no favourite with Louis XV. "Berry," he said, "was an ill-omened name." When he spoke of him it was usually in a tone of contemptuous pity, and he never gave him his title of dauphin. Even after his marriage with Marie Antoinette, the king would often refer to the youthful couple as "Berry and the little archduchess." But this, probably, may have been but the unconscious echoing of Madame Adélaïde's usual way of mentioning the dauphin and dauphine. It arose from her extreme and not unnatural vexation at yielding to a girl of fourteen — so ignorant and ill-mannered that her proper place was the schoolroom — the position at court which she herself had filled since the death of Marie Leczinska. Ruled by his aunt, who for some years past had stood towards the young princes in the place of their mother, Berry sympathised with Madame Adélaïde in her grievances, real or fancied, and viewed with suspicion, and repelled by coldness, the many attempts made by Marie Antoinette, under maternal guidance, to gain an influence over him. Poor, ill-fated Berry!

Now, however, he and the dauphine — who, in a remote apartment of the château, have for several hours been awaiting the expected announcement of the king's death — are surrounded by courtiers, officers of state, and princes of the blood. Scarce an hour since they thronged the antechamber of the dying monarch, eagerly or languidly inquiring, as interests prompted, of the fluctuations in his condition, and his possible chances of life. But "the king is dead! Long live the king!" And homage is now eagerly paid to the new sovereign. But an air of condolence gracefully blends with congratulation, as they salute the youthful royal pair as king and queen. This is naturally but a brief and hurried ceremony; for all are prepared for immediate flight. All are alike anxious to escape from the infectious air of the *petits appartements* and *grande galerie* of the château, whose fetid, deadly atmosphere claims yet a whole hecatomb of victims.

Three hours after the king's death Versailles was a desert. The lives of two or three under-servants of the household and as many priests of the "inferior clergy" were sacrificed to the fatal duty assigned them of remaining to pray by the body, and to accompany it to the Abbey of St. Denis. Thither, put into a box filled up with quicklime, and hastily thrust into a hunting carriage, it was conveyed with all speed, and almost secrecy, on the following night — just as fifty-nine years before the mortal remains of the immortal "*Grand Monarque*" had been — in order to avoid the taunts and insults of the populace. The only voluntary mark of respect paid to the memory of the "Well-beloved" was the solitary salute of a Fontenoy veteran, who, inspired by memories of other days, rushed forth and presented arms as the scanty funeral *cortège* of the once vaunted hero of a brilliant fight passed through the gates of Versailles. And this, as the superstitious remarked, was the fortieth night from that on which the Abbé de Beauvais had preached the Lenten sermon that had caught the conscience of the king.

The filial devotion of Mesdames, in their close attendance on their father through his terrible illness, resulted, as was to be expected, in an attack of smallpox of the most malignant type. Their lives were spared, but their persons were hideously disfigured. The king and queen, and the younger part of the royal family, retired to La Muette, and, with the exception of the queen, were immediately inoculated for the smallpox by the surgeon Jouberthou.*

As soon as it became known that the king, the princes, and princesses, had determined to avail themselves of this method of avoiding the usually more severe and dangerous results of chance infection, it occasioned considerable consternation. "The imprudent and perilous step," as it was termed, was greatly censured. None but the "Autrichienne," it was urged, "would have had

* Vaccination as a preservative against that fatal disease, from which the French people long suffered even more frequently and with greater virulence in its attacks than others, was not then introduced. It is asserted, however, that both French and German physicians were acquainted with it long before Jenner made it publicly known, and its value became generally recognised. The physician Chaptal wrote a pamphlet on the subject in 1781. Jenner's first published work on vaccination bears date 1798; but the efficacy of his discovery had then been proved by a series of experiments extending over several years.

the temerity to suggest it." On the young queen, then, the blame of it was laid (happy indeed would it have been both for her and for France had she been always as little deserving of blame as then), and curiosity was eager among all classes to ascertain its result. All fears, however, as regarded its effect on the king and royal family were speedily dispelled. The operation was entirely successful. The short period of convalescence was spent at Marly — and spent rather gaily, it seems, for a period of supposed sickness and mourning. The nine days, then believed to be a safe interval against the danger of infection, having elapsed, the king and queen returned to La Muette.

But it was necessary, before Versailles was again inhabited, that it should undergo thorough purification. The Château of the Tuileries, so long out of favour as the residence of the sovereign, was then in too dilapidated a state, as well as too scantily furnished, to receive the young king and his court. Royalty's abode, therefore, for the first few months of the new reign was alternately at Marly, Compiègne, and La Muette.

CHAPTER II.

A Momentous Crisis. — "*Louis Le Désiré.*" — A Royal Blacksmith. — Hopes and Expectations. — Henri IV. *Resurrexit.* — Good Wishes and Intentions. — Louis the Well-beloved. — A King without Dignity. — Vulcan and His Coiffeur. — A Heaven-born King. — A Minister of State. — Madame Adélaïde's Agent. — Machault or Maurepas? — A Victory and a Defeat. — Queens-Consort and Queens-Regent. — Her "Sacred Majesty" of Austria. — Effort to Reinstate Choiseul. — The Dauphin and the Jesuits. — False Charge of the Jesuits. — The Favourite and Her Rival. — The Duke in Exile. — A Chilling Reception.

IT was at a momentous crisis in the life of the nation that Louis XVI. ascended the throne of France. The time had arrived when the abuses of the old *régime* could no longer be tolerated, and sweeping reforms were demanded. The philosophic tenets of the age, which for years past had formed the chief subject of discussion in the *salons*, and thence were diffused through all classes of society, had gradually developed a new power in the state, — public opinion, whose voice, in its strength and vehemence, already defied every effort of the government to stifle it. The nation, hitherto politically a nullity, had awakened to a sense of its rights; while absolute sovereignty, with its arbitrary dictum, "*L'état c'est moi*," and its right divine to govern wrong, had lost its prestige, and had apparently no prospect of regaining it.

Notwithstanding, the attitude of the people towards their sovereign was not then a menacing one. For the French Revolution, which may be said to have actually begun with the reign of Louis XVI., was in its origin and objects essentially domestic. Its political character was developed later on, and was the natural result of the abuses of power disclosed during the struggle of certain classes in the state to obtain the social recognition so long denied them. The people, indeed, regarded the young monarch as "the hope of the nation," and named him "*Louis le Désiré*," a testimony to the ardour with which they had looked forward to his accession, and their reliance on his justice for some alleviation of the burden of taxation so ruthlessly laid on them, and from which the wealthy and depraved aristocracy were wholly exempt. Under such auspices, a great career was undoubtedly open to the successor of Louis XV. And it is probable that had a more able pilot—"a king more a king," than that feeblest of monarchs, Louis XVI.—been called to the helm at that period, the vessel of the state might have been safely guided through the shoals and quicksands surrounding her, and the eddies of that devastating moral whirlpool in which she was eventually engulfed been avoided.

Little was actually known by the nation at large of the mental or moral qualities of the young king. He was now in his twentieth year, and continued to lead the same isolated life as when under the control of his governor, the Jesuitical Duc de Vauguyon. Unlike his brothers, the Comtes de Provence and d'Artois, he was extremely diffident in manner, and at ease only with persons of inferior position. Except in his devotion to the chase — his sole amusement — his time had latterly been chiefly employed in perfecting himself in the blacksmith's art. His industrious pursuit of this grimy craft was the cause of much annoyance to the dauphine; and while it gave rise to many stormy ebullitions of temper on her part, was no less the subject of many a satirical jest in court circles. Much restraint had, however, been imposed on the young princes by the conduct of Louis XV. towards them and their girlish consorts. He held them aloof, as it were, influenced probably by Madame du Barry, who had a jealous dread of her circle of flatterers being diminished by the attractive gaiety and noisy mirth of the court of the youthful dauphine. When the king's death removed this restraint from the royal brothers the remarkable difference in their characters became speedily apparent.

It had been bruited about among the people that the heir to the throne had inherited all the virtues attributed to his father, "*Le Grand Dau-*

phin;"* and that while systematically kept in the background by the vicious Louis XV., and all knowledge of state affairs withheld from him, he had turned his forced seclusion to account by acquainting himself with the condition of the country and the needs of the people he was one day to rule over. The young king was, in fact, credited to a considerable extent with giving promise of ruling his subjects with the same prudence and thoughtful regard for their welfare that had so eminently distinguished Louis XII., surnamed "the father of his people." He possessed in no less a degree, it was also reported, the frugal tastes, the genial temper, and air of *bonhomie* to which the gallant Henri IV. owed so much of his popularity.

No wonder, then, that the accession of Louis XVI. was hailed throughout France with a hearty expression of general delight; or that the enthusiastic people — their many expected reforms in imagination already conceded — should have written in conspicuous characters, "RESURREXIT," beneath the statue of the heretic monarch whose jovial humour and pliant conscience enabled him to gratify his Catholic subjects with his presence at a *Te Deum* and celebration of grand mass when the gates of Paris were opened to him. Some simple country folk, as we learn, were so sanguine as to the results of the new reign as

* The second prince, so named by the Jesuits.

actually to look forward to the realisation of their Gascon king's well-known wish; and to expect ere long, instead of fattening their pullets to meet the exactions of the relentless tax-gatherer, to make savoury meat of them in their own *pots-au-feu*. But hope, as too often she is wont to do, told them but a flattering tale.

When the young king made his public entry into the capital, the joyous demonstrations of the Parisians affected him deeply. "What had he done," he inquired, with tearful emotion, "to deserve so effusive a display of attachment to his person and confidence in him." Truly, he had as yet done nothing; but much, very much, was expected from him. And if sincerely wishing to see his people prosperous and happy could have made them so, France would have had no more beneficent ruler than Louis XVI. But his good wishes and intentions were rendered nugatory by his utter want of energy and ability to carry them out. Infirm of purpose then, so he remained to the end. The decree, "Let there be light," unhappily, never went forth to quicken his mental faculties, whose torpid action was but too plainly evidenced by the sluggish inactivity of his heavy, ungainly frame.

In their eagerness for reforms the Parisians perhaps displayed unreasonable impatience. For when but a few weeks later their young monarch again passed through Paris, he remarked — though, unfortunately, the lesson was lost on him — that the acclamations of the people were far less frequent and fervid than on the former occasion. And his eyes were once more suffused with tears when he perceived that the conspicuously displayed RESURREXIT was transferred from the statue of the gallant Henri to that of the slothful Louis Quinze. But, with all his vices, Louis "the Well-beloved," on those rare occasions when he appeared in public, had always commanded the respectful homage of his subjects, simply by the dignity of his bearing. By the same means he imposed silence on his courtiers — the companions of his orgies — when, in license of speech, they infringed the limits within which, when a fit of piety was on him, it was sometimes his good pleasure to restrain them. Occasionally, too, when the Parliament opposed his edicts, or the dissentient opinion of a minister in matters of special interest to him roused him from his habitual indolence, he could at once assume the arbitrary tone, the "*je le veux*," of the absolute monarch, and carry out his purposes with a very high hand. And it is probable that his handsome person and majestic air — for whatever may have been his shortcomings in other and more essential qualities, in appearance he was every inch a king — may have gone far in preventing the utter extinction of the enthusiastic affection which on several occasions during his reign the people so singularly, yet so generally, expressed towards the royal *debauché*. A lingering spark of that once ardent feeling must have smouldered on in their hearts to the end. For grievously oppressed though they were, and vicious as they knew him to be, they still toiled on under their burdens, — not exactly uncomplainingly, yet in a spirit of toleration towards him ; while the yearned-for relief was, as if by the tacit consent of his subjects, to be claimed only from his successor. Truly, indications were not wanting that a storm was brewing, and that Louis XV. was fully aware of it, his oft-repeated "*Après nous le déluge*" sufficiently testified.

Unhappily, his successor possessed not the shadow of a shade of the kingly quality of dignity. Notwithstanding his acknowledged virtues and his professed desire to redress, to the utmost of his power, the grievous wrongs of his subjects, and to initiate useful reforms, he yet failed — both in his domestic circle, as head of the family, and in his public capacity, as head of the state — to inspire the respect and to command the deference which naturally, and by right, were due to him. He was shy and reserved, and as dauphin had made but a poor figure amidst the brilliant cavaliers of the court. His voice was harsh, his manners abrupt, — an apparent want of culture the more remarkable from its contrast with the excessive politeness on which the court

Louis XVI.
Engraved by W. Wellstood.

circle then piqued itself. Courtesy was cherished by the aristocracy as the one remaining and invisible barrier between them and the "*égalité et fraternité*," then advancing with rapid strides and menacing the overthrow of all social distinctions.

Slight, very slight, was the attention that the princely Vulcan gave to his *toilette*. Memoir writers inform us that he occasioned many an agonising pang to his *coiffeur;* for that his hair, however careful its daily arrangement by that clever and, at the period in question, all-important *artiste*, was generally in such wild disorder, from continually passing his hands through it, that it looked as if it were constantly the sport of the four winds of heaven. This, trivial as it seems, was in fact no small matter. Royalty was associated in the minds of the *belles dames,* and gay courtiers of Versailles, and even in the memory of some two or three veterans — the old Maréchal Duc de Richelieu, for instance — with the stately figure, rich costume, and awe-inspiring peruke of the magnificent Louis Quatorze; and later on with the satins, the velvets and embroidery, perfumes and powder, of the indolent and handsome "Well-beloved." Royalty sat uneasily on poor Louis XVI. even when he was only heir presumptive;[*] but he seemed oppressed and over-

[*] Mesdames were greatly desirous that Louis XV. should contract a second marriage, and suggested several princesses whom they thought eligible for the honour of becoming Queen

whelmed by his *rôle* of monarch. And oppressed by it he doubtless was, until, sinking gradually under his burden, he at last became its victim. The popular voice, however, now proclaimed that "a king so frugal in his habits, so simple in manners, so pious, so just and good, had been formed by heaven less for his court than for his people," and that with his reign they looked for the beginning of a new era of universal prosperity.

The dauphin, father of Louis XVI., from the infirm state of health he fell into, was precluded from any expectation of reigning over France. But he had a presentiment that his son would be called to the throne at an early age. Therefore, together with many written counsels, warnings, and suggestions as to the course he would have him pursue, he left for his guidance in the formation of his council a list of the ministers whose principles he then disapproved, and another of the men he himself would have appointed to fill the great offices of state. Chief among the latter was M. de Machault. He had been minister under Louis XV., or, more correctly, perhaps, under Madame de Pompadour. To her he owed his elevation. But, on the occasion of Damiens's attempt on the king's life, Machault, too hastily

---

of France. They probably feared he would marry Madame du Barry, but certainly hoped to disappoint the expectations of the much disliked "Autrichienne" by the probable birth of an heir to the throne.

concluding from Louis's urgency in summoning his confessor that the favourite's reign was ended, assumed towards her a supercilious tone and air, suggested that she should *"prendre le parti noble"* and voluntarily withdraw from the court, to avoid, as he said, an ignominious dismissal. A few days after a *lettre de cachet* ordered him to retire forthwith to his estates at Arnouville. The indignation of the favourite and the displeasure of the king secured for him the favour of the dauphin. But this favour availed him nothing. He had long been forgotten by the court — having remained in exile for seventeen years — and now, at the age of seventy-four, and under the changed aspect of public affairs, had probably little desire to begin anew a ministerial career.

The young king, however, reverently obeying his father's injunctions, though contrary to the advice of Mesdames, and especially of Madame Adélaïde, who then seemed disposed to take a prominent part in directing the affairs of the kingdom, wrote a letter to M. de Machault, desiring him to repair to Choisy without delay, "to advise and assist him in the discharge of the arduous duties of government; for which, with his barely twenty years and his utter inexperience in state affairs, he was himself so little qualified." Mesdames, though shut up in their apartments lest they should spread the infectious smallpox, yet kept a strict watch on the king, one of his personal attendants being Madame Adélaïde's trusted agent. This Argus duly informed her that a letter was about to be despatched to Arnouville; that, in fact, it was already in the hands of a page, with orders to the Chevalier d'Ulzac, chief officer of the royal stable, to send off a courier with it immediately.

With her usual energy and promptness of decision, Madame Adélaïde rose from her couch, and rapidly penned an epistle to her nephew. She reproached, entreated, counselled, commanded, well knowing how to take advantage of his weakness, and to gain her point. Vexation added vehemence to her demand, for she had resolved that the old friend and favourite of her youthful years — the gay, the evergreen Comte de Maurepas — should quit the shady groves of Pontchartrain, where, in expiation of some coarse jokes on Madame de Pompadour, for near twenty-seven years he had vegetated, or rather flourished, in spite of the henpecking of his fretful-tempered wife.

"Unstable as water," the poor young king could not resist the strongly worded appeal of his strong-minded aunt. Of the two exiled ministers, he would have preferred to recall M. de Machault, whose grave character was more in harmony with his own, and who was as severe in his manner as he — "Louis, le Sévère," as he wished to be surnamed — believed himself to be. On the other hand, M. de Maurepas, though of the same age as M. de Machault, still retained the sprightly temper and keen, sarcastic wit that had brought him into disfavour with the reigning Sultana in his earlier days. But to yield was natural to Louis XVI.; and, besides, the manly minded Madame Adélaïde had been his oracle from boyhood.

"Haste, then! haste!" exclaims Madame. "Let a second courier be instantly despatched in pursuit of the first, and let him not fail to overtake him, even should he break his own and his horse's neck in the chase."

Luckily, however — or it may have been, designedly — some sort of *contretemps* had delayed the departure of the courier. For his foot was in the stirrup, and he about to set out only when the order was issued to bring him back. He delivers up the letter of which he was the bearer, and it appears that it need not be rewritten. Only a new cover and new address are required for its new destination, when it is handed again to the courier, who is ordered to proceed with the speed of the wind to Pontchartrain, to summon the Comte de Maurepas to the council-chamber of his sovereign.

Madame Adélaïde's victory was a crushing defeat to the hopes of the Choiseul or Austrian party. It proclaimed to anxious courtiers how small was still the influence that Marie Antoinette had acquired over the king. She, indeed, —

engaged in a round of frivolous pleasures, and sharing with childish eagerness and as little dignity as any Parisian grisette of that day, in the *escapades* of the dissipated and arrogant young Comte d'Artois,—probably would not at that period, but for the promptings of interested persons, have sought to interfere in political and state affairs. It was, besides, contrary to all the traditions of the court of France that the queens-consort should do so, except in those instances when, during a minority, they had been in their widowhood invested with power as queens-regent. So long, too, as pensions and places solicited for her favourites were granted, Marie Antoinette had appeared satisfied.

But as dauphine, her solicitations, or rather demands, were so frequent that the minister, M. d'Aiguillon, was sorely perplexed by them. Anxious to conciliate the good graces of the future queen, he made a point of complying with her wishes to the full extent of his power. Yet at times her inconsiderate and persistent applications on behalf of persons for whom it was far easier to show why they should not, than why they should be thus favoured by the state, were so extremely embarrassing that on more than one occasion he prayed her, before submitting them to him, to refer her requests to the king's decision. This displeased her greatly, and drew forth her usual menace, "*Je m'en souviendrai.*"

It is the Comte de Mercy-Argenteau who relates these things in his secret correspondence with her "sacred majesty" of Austria. The wily empress-queen had evidently expected, when the "amiable and excellent friend, father, and monarch, Louis XV., for whom she had so sincere an affection," had shuffled off his mortal coil, that the policy of France would be regulated by the cabinet of Vienna, then as insidious and corrupt as any in Europe. Austrian interests and views were to be furthered and upheld by her daughter's looked-for ascendancy over the timid and irresolute young king. From her suggestions and counsels on public affairs to that butterfly queen of eighteen summers, it would seem that the empress regarded her daughter's position as resembling her own, when, united to the easy-going Francis Joseph of Lorraine, the husband of her choice, and a prince as indolent as Louis XVI. himself, and a libertine to boot, she became, with the advantage over Marie Antoinette of a few more years, the reigning sovereign of two kingdoms.

The king's incapacity for governing was soon patent to all who approached him. In every respect he was far below the level of his position. Who, then, should take up the reins of power and rule in his name and through his weakness? "It must be the queen," replied Maria Theresa. "She must allow none to supplant her. M. de Choiseul should be her minister; the worthy Abbé Vermond her secret counsellor, and M. de Mercy, who has played so ably the part of social mentor," will inform me minutely of what is going on in the council-chamber, and also give full details of the private life of the king and queen and the princes.

It was difficult, if not almost impossible, at that time, and for many years after, to induce Marie Antoinette to give five minutes' attention to anything but dress and amusement. Greatly urged, however, by the count and the *abbé*, and Choiseul being also of the number of her favourites, she no doubt did her best on this occasion to prevail on the king to recall the duke from exile, and to reinstate him in the ministry. But Louis for once was immovable. "Choiseul should never be a member of his council." He had given credence to the absurd story, set afloat by the Jesuits, of the dauphin, his father, having been poisoned by persons employed and paid by the Duc de Choiseul. It was owing to the efforts of the duke and Madame de Pompadour that the decree for the expulsion of the Jesuits from France was obtained from Louis XV. Naturally, therefore, the Jesuits were his enemies, and the dauphin, being entirely under their influence, became his enemy also when deprived of the services of his spiritual advisers.

On the first opportunity that presented itself the dauphin spoke to Choiseul on the subject, and in no measured terms. The haughty minister was then in the plenitude of his power, high in the favour of his sovereign, and with an overweeningly high opinion of himself. His temper was quick, and as he very lightly esteemed the dauphin — whose mental calibre was about on a par with that of his unfortunate son — he braved him to his face, reproached him with conduct unworthy of a prince in his abject slavery to a set of artful, intriguing priests, and, he added, as his friend M. de Besenval relates, that "although it might happen to him one day to become his subject, he would carefully avoid the further misfortune of ever becoming his servant." The dauphin complained to the king, who excused M. de Choiseul, and told his son that he had given his minister great provocation for the hasty words he had used.

The dauphin was enormously corpulent, as were all his children, with the exception of the Comte d'Artois. With the view of reducing his size he took acids, we are told, in large quantities, and thus injured his health. When about thirty years of age he had an attack of smallpox, which left a train of ills behind it, and eventually the dauphin wasted away and died of decline. His wife's grief for her loss was so excessive, so strangely exaggerated, and was kept alive by so many singular devices, that scandal declared half of it, at least, was for the loss of the crown she had hoped to wear. It, however, brought her to an early grave, for she died in the following year.

The hope of the Jesuits expired with the dauphin, who was bound by vow to bring them back to France. But, according to their account, their enemy Choiseul, being determined to prevent the realisation of this vow, succeeded in doing so by means of poison, administered in small doses by some secret agent among the attendants of the prince. The Duc de Vauguyon affected to believe this story, and impressed it on the minds of the dauphin's three sons. Louis XVI. certainly gave credit to it.

When urgently appealed to by the queen in favour of M. de Choiseul, he, without refusing her request, answered her evasively. At length, however, he consented to relieve the duke from his nominal sentence of banishment to Chanteloup —a princely estate where he had resided during the past three or four years when it was not his good pleasure to be in Paris. With remarkable audacity, he had frequently visited the capital; but as he did not venture to appear at Versailles, Louis XV. took no notice of Choiseul's contempt for his *lettre de cachet*. In this he showed his decided leaning towards his late minister, who may be said to have braved the king as well as the dauphin; in ordinary cases, incarceration in the Bastille would have been the consequence of his act.

Duc de Choiseul.
Photogravure by Goupil and Company from an
Old Portrait.

ETIENNE FRANÇOIS DUC DE CHOISEUL
Pair de France, Chevalier des Ordres du Roi et de la Toison d'Or,
Colonel Général des Suisses et Grisons, Lieutenant-Général des Armées
de S. M. Gouverneur et Lieuten.t Général de la Touraine &c. &c. &c.
Ministre et Secretaire d'Etat de la Guerre et des Affaires etrangeres, Grand-
Maitre et Surintendant des Postes &c. &c. &c.

He had been dismissed from his office of First Minister, and ordered to retire to his estates, for insolence to Madame du Barry, whose post of *maîtresse-en-titre* had been anxiously coveted by the Duchesse de Grammont, his sister. But the old *debauché* king was frigidly insensible to her wiles, and avoided falling into the snares she spread for him. Urged on by her, the duke made a point of continually saying offensive and insulting things to her rival, while the duchess took her revenge for the king's indifference towards her, in inventing and circulating infamous stories respecting his favourite.

To lessen in some degree the mortification of dismissal and disgrace, Madame du Barry, being a generous enemy, prevailed on the king to grant him a retiring pension of much larger amount than it had been intended to give him, as well as to increase considerably the sum he was to receive *en argent comptant*. This assisted M. de Choiseul — who was rich, but excessively extravagant, also immensely popular in society, a hero of the *salons*, and friend of the philosophers — to keep open house in exile, and to give a round of entertainments and *parties de chasses* at the Château de Chanteloup, at which all the *beau monde*, the *noblesse*, and the *haute bourgeoisie* of Paris and Versailles assisted.

A brilliant reception in society awaited M. and Madame de Choiseul on their return from exile to take up their residence again in Paris. But on paying their court to the king and queen at La Muette, Louis, though as usual greatly embarrassed, received the duke with such extreme coldness that the easy, nonchalant air habitual with the latter momentarily forsook him. He saw in the young king's chilling constraint and gloomy countenance that his star would no more be in the ascendant. The queen, however, with difficulty concealing her vexation, was profuse in expressions of delight at the return of the exiles.

"It gives me great pleasure," she said, "to have contributed towards it, and thus to have been able to acquit myself of one of the many obligations I owe you."

The duke's friends and *protégés*, who had hoped for places and pensions when the reins of power were again in his hands, were also wofully cast down. But Marie Antoinette bade them hope. She knew that the king believed he would be insulting his father's memory should he reinstate Choiseul in the ministry. But time — and a short time, too — she vainly fancied would suffice to banish the "poor man's" scruples.

CHAPTER III.

Atonement. — An Effort of Gallantry. — At a Loss for Amusement. — Unattached Couples. — The Petit Trianon. — Forming a Queen of France. — The Dear Good *Abbé*. — Guide, Philosopher, and Friend. — An Appeal to the King. — The Results of Indecision. — An Apollo Taking a Bath. — The Young Dauphine. — The Royal Bride. — The Queen's Peccadilloes. — The *Ques-a-co?* Plume. — Pleasure and Devotion. — The King's Aunts. — The Gardens of Bellevue. — The Court of Mesdames. — First Reception, at La Muette. — Fashionable Head-dresses. — Senseless Mythology. — Aristocratic Privileges. — Etiquette Banished. — The Queen's Enemies.

THOUGH the king's pious horror of the infamous deed and the infidel philosophy attributed to the Duc de Choiseul had inspired him with courage and firmness to refuse to accede to the wishes of the queen, and to reject advice to the same effect from the empress, he yet lost no time in seeking to gratify the whims of his flighty young consort in another direction. Within three weeks after his accession, "Madame," he said, addressing the queen, "you have often expressed a desire to have a pleasant and pretty country house for yourself, of which you would be the sole mistress, and where, subject to no will but your own, you could banish etiquette and live entirely as you pleased. I am now able," he continued, "to realise that wish, by offering you the Grand and the Petit Trianon entirely for your own private use. There you may reign sole mistress; for the Trianons really belong to you, having always been the residence of the favourites of the Kings of France."

For Louis XVI. this speech was a great effort of gallantry. It delighted Marie Antoinette; for it inspired her with hope that "her god, Vulcan," would in due time become civilized. She replied that "she accepted only a part of the present the king offered her. The Petit Trianon was all she desired." But, with a smile and a very low curtsey, she added, she "would consider it so much her own property that his majesty must never think of visiting it, except by special invitation."

In former reigns the court had invariably followed the example of its sovereign. It had renounced open profligacy for piety, or, at all events, its outward show, when the *Grand Monarque* became devout; and, for the same good reason, when the opera airs of Rameau and Paisiello were no longer in favour at Versailles, had taken to singing with edifying zeal the solemn chants of the Church. Some sort of change — similar in kind, if less rigid in degree — had apparently been looked for at the beginning of the new reign. For Louis XVI. ascended the throne with a great reputation for piety, and had he been capable of taking the lead in his court, and asserting his will as its sovereign, he might, at the least, have purged his youthful consort's intimate circle of the titled courtesans and libertine *grands seigneurs* of whom it was chiefly composed.

Madame Campan relates that, on the court retiring to Choisy immediately after the decease of Louis XV., the young king — prevented by the court mourning from indulging in his one favourite amusement of the chase — proposed to the queen to explore together the gardens and grounds of Choisy. Arm in arm, then, and accompanied but by two or three persons of their retinue, the royal pair set out for a quiet rural walk, and continued this exercise daily, without intermission, during their stay at Choisy.

Such was the force of this excellent example that it was immediately followed by the courtiers and their wives, who, though generally, and, as Madame remarks, for excellent reasons wholly unattached couples, were, as etiquette required, invited to court together when forming part of the royal suite. Though so long estranged, they now, in Darby and Joan fashion, began to stroll in the park or on the terraces for hours at a time; enduring, like loyal subjects, the almost insupportable *ennui* of a long conjugal *tête-à-tête*, in order thus flatteringly to pay court to the king and queen. But the king and his consort were themselves an uncongenial pair. And when, after their short sojourn at Choisy, they proceeded to Marly, and the daily walks which had served as a *pis aller* to pass away time came to an end, doubtless to both them and their court it was an immense relief. Again the king assumed the air of reserve and the cold and churlish manners habitual to him; and the desire he had momentarily exhibited of living on more united and confidential terms with the young queen passed away with the arrival of M. de Maurepas.

Yet it was probably at the Comte de Maurepas's suggestion that the Trianons were offered to the queen. It was providing her with what, as he perceived, she needed, — occupation and amusement, — while serving as a check to an inclination she began to evince to interfere in public affairs. It could not of course be foreseen that the comedy of rural simplicity, to be afterwards performed at the Petit Trianon, or Kleine Shœnbrunn, would lead to so many ruinous demands on the already impoverished state treasury.

The Petit Trianon was then but a small pavilion in a secluded spot at the further end of the great park. It was surrounded by very fine gardens. The trees, having escaped the formal clipping then so much in vogue, grew with untrained natural grace, their luxuriant foliage affording shady retreats, impervious to the sun's rays, in many a nook and corner of the grounds. Louis

XV. had built an orangery and hothouses there, and sometimes spent a day or two at the pavilion.

Another concession to the wishes of the queen, when at this time her household was formed anew, was the fatal one of allowing the Abbé Vermond to retain the post he had held — *soi-disant* of secretary and reader — while she was only dauphine. Actually, however, he was the most intimate confidant of her acts and thoughts, her sole guide and counsellor, — a sort of priestly Mephistopheles, whose evil influence determined her every action and urged her on to her ruin. This "philosophical *abbé*" was a man of humble birth, who had obtained the favour of the dissolute Archbishop of Sens — Loménie de Brienne — afterwards Minister of Finance, a prelate of the same theological school. He had strongly recommended the Abbé Vermond to M. de Choiseul when the latter was in quest of a clerical tutor for the future queen of France. Several ecclesiastics had declined the post, being unwilling to accept the double responsibility of tutor and confessor. No scruples of this kind troubled the Abbé Vermond; and as his remarkable ugliness was considered another desirable qualification for his office, he was forthwith despatched by M. de Choiseul to Vienna.

To aid him in forming a queen of France he was accompanied by a skilful French *coiffeur* and two clever *modistes*, — *artistes* of distinguished excellence in those professions being rare at that period in the Austrian capital. The *abbé* was most graciously received by the empress-queen; for the dearest wish of her heart was secured by this French matrimonial alliance. To accomplish it she had stooped very low, but, having conquered by stooping, was gracious to all concerned.

Puffed up with conceit by his sudden elevation, the Abbé Vermond made it his business to play the courtier rather than the tutor. He succeeded so well in ingratiating himself with the devotee-empress, who thought this renegade *abbé* almost a saint, that when he returned to France with his pupil, scarcely less ignorant than when he undertook her instruction, though perhaps a little more artful, she was greatly alarmed lest "the dear good *abbé*" should resign his post, feeling that the dissipated court of France was no place for him. It was true he often threatened to withdraw the light of his handsome countenance from it; for his vanity suffered, and both he and his office (he was fond of magnifying both) lost, he conceived, some of their importance when the dauphine, who was lamentably wanting in reticence, and was restrained by no delicacy of feeling as regarded the nature of her *confidences*, would impart her secrets to any one of her attendants who chanced to please her, or, as frequently happened — poor little *ingénue* — to some favourite young noble of her rather libertine circle. Then the secretary's righteous soul was vexed. And his displeasure was shown after the manner of the old Cardinal Fleury towards the youthful Louis XV. But having no Issy to retire to, he shut himself up in his apartment until his absence was noticed, and it was announced that he was preparing to depart.

The penitent dauphine — who on such occasions was always severely lectured by the empress, and solemnly warned of the terrible consequences that would ensue from the loss of so faithful and valuable a friend — would then hasten to pacify the much aggrieved *abbé*. Petted, flattered, coaxed to his heart's content, he would graciously condescend to forgive, and to forego his threatened resolve of resigning his post. It would, however, have been a terrible blow to him had he been taken at his word and allowed to go his way, as he ought to have been. But year after year he was permitted to stay on, and was still, at the accession of Louis XVI., the guide, philosopher, and friend of the young queen, and as such the chief cause of her unpopularity.

The Duc de Vauguyon abhorred the Abbé Vermond almost as much as he abhorred his patron, M. de Choiseul. The *abbé* and Marie Antoinette reciprocated this feeling to the fullest extent: the former would often amuse his fair pupil with sarcastic remarks on the strait-laced manners of the duke and his duchess; and generally he had many satirical anecdotes to relate of the elderly *débris*, including Mesdames, then remaining of the pious court of Marie Leczinska and the dauphin, her son. The young king shared so deeply his governor's aversion to the *abbé*, that during his four years' residence at Versailles he had never been able sufficiently to overcome his repugnance even to speak to him.

The time is however arrived when, if the Abbé Vermond is to be retained in the queen's household, it must be by the king's consent. To put an end to suspense and to compel the king to a decision, Vermond resolved to write to him. He vaunted the confidence placed in him by Louis XV.; the continued favour of the empress; the faithful service he for five years past had rendered the dauphine, and which he hoped further to render her as queen. Poor Louis would have been supremely happy could he have plucked up a resolution and said, as he longed to say, "Her majesty had no further need of the Abbé Vermond's services." But he hesitates. Courage to do the deed fails him. The opportunity he has so longed for of dismissing the *abbé* is slipping away from him, and the fat, burly youth suffers a martyrdom from the necessity of making up his mind.

Again he reads the *abbé's* epistle; then snatching up a pen, writes on the blank side of the paper: "I consent that the Abbé Vermond should continue in the discharge of the duties of his office in the queen's household." The letter is then returned to the sender. But never again, except on one occasion,* does Louis XVI. address a word, either written or spoken, to the Abbé Vermond during the fifteen years he remained at Versailles, but always studiously avoided him. Secure of his post, his boastful conceit at once put forth new vigour. He was constant in his attendance at the queen's *toilette*, where he assumed very grand airs, and treated all present, even those of most elevated rank, as scarcely his equals — rather, indeed, with a condescension that bade them, as inferiors, be at ease in his sublime presence. Ministers, dignitaries of the Church, and *grands seigneurs*, who sought to curry favour with the queen, often paced the anteroom of this lofty-minded *abbé* until patience was well-nigh exhausted. At times he would do them the honour of admitting them to a sort of *petit lever*, and afford them the gratifying spectacle of an Apollo taking a bath.

The king's brief but decisive reply to Vermond's letter was no less satisfactory to the queen than to the *abbé*. She would not have permitted her spiritual adviser to dictate to or thwart her in the

---

* It was at the death of the empress-queen. The king, thinking that the *abbé* could better than himself break the intelligence to the queen, sent his *premier valet de chambre* to request him to do so. The next day the king visited her majesty. The *abbé* was leaving her apartment. The king (says Madame Campan) turned towards him and said: "I thank you, M. l'Abbé, for the favour you have done me," and passed on.

choice of her amusements, had it ever occurred to him to do so. But as her secretary the *abbé* was necessary to her. Who so well as he could write or dictate her letters, or cajole the inquisitive empress into the belief that his pupil was going through a course of history and other serious and edifying reading? Truly the office of reader to Marie Antoinette was no very onerous one. Only to reading of the most frivolous kind would she give the slightest attention, and she cared for very little of that.

The idealised portraits of this unfortunate queen usually describe her, on her arrival in France, then a girl of fourteen, as beautiful in person, refined in manners, and possessing education and accomplishments that would have been remarkable indeed in a young woman of twenty. But the fresh, clear German complexion, bright fair hair, and youth, were poor Marie Antoinette's sole claims to beauty. The long, narrow Hapsburg face, with its small eyes, thick under lip, and projecting chin, was never deemed beautiful. It may have been a pleasing, expressive countenance when lighted up by gaiety and wreathed with gracious smiles; but its plainness was striking when, as too often happened, it was clouded over by vindictive feeling and ill-temper. From indulgence in lounging habits, it became necessary for a time carefully to bandage her back and right shoulder, lest, as she took a fancy to learn music and to play the harp, she should grow up awry and her figure be spoiled. With much pains, and much talking to (of which she complains in her letters), she was brought into shape. Her figure was slight and not ungraceful. She had a long, thin neck, and a habit of tossing her head. Her friends called it dignity, her enemies, arrogance.

Her manners on her arrival in France caused many a cynical smile. Yet notwithstanding the disfavour with which in some quarters the Austrian marriage was viewed, her rather forward and hoidenish air, and the evident self-satisfaction with which she went through her part of royal bride and future queen, might surely in so young a girl have been pardoned. She seems in the short space of two or three years to have entirely forgotten her mother-tongue; and it is asserted that although she afterwards took lessons in German she never regained more than a very slight knowledge of that language. This, if true, is indeed remarkable, and the more so, as she did not speak French with facility until some years after — her fluency in the language being then acquired more from studying the parts she performed in a variety of plays than from other reading or actual instruction. Only shortly before Marie Antoinette became queen, Maria Theresa — herself far from having attained proficiency in the French tongue — complains to the Comte de Mercy-Argenteau of the faulty orthography, hasty, illegible scrawl, and slovenly diction of her daughter's letters. She speaks of her also as "untruthful," and says "she will turn and turn again to compass her objects." Sometimes, too, she suspects the more carefully written letters she receives to be productions of the *abbé's* pen in a feigned hand.

"Try to furnish your head" ("*tapisser votre tête*"), writes the empress to the dauphine, "with some solid ideas, by good and serious reading. Reading is a resource which you especially need, having acquired no other; neither music, drawing, dancing, painting, nor any pleasing accomplishment. Therefore, do not neglect it."

Many are the excuses which the count, while revealing greater indiscretions, makes for the queen's negligence and deceit, and the numerous peccadilloes noticed by the empress. Marie Antoinette had developed a strong passion for gambling; for bestowing gifts on her favourites with a very lavish hand; and for introducing fashions—in head-dress especially—of the most *outré* kind. The empress—to whom the affairs of Europe and their bearing on Austrian politics had ever been the chief subjects of thought, fashion and dress having at no time occupied much of her attention—lifted her hands in amazement when she received the portrait of the degenerate daughter of the Cæsars decked out in her "*Ques-a-co*" plume.

This strangely absurd head-dress was forty-five

inches in height from the roots of the hair on the forehead to the top of the feathers. It was composed of several yards of gauze and riband, from among the folds or plaits of which sprang bunches of Provence roses — the entire edifice being surmounted by a full, waving plume of white feathers. It derived its name from Beaumarchais having used satirically the term " *Ques-a-co?* " (in the Provençal dialect, *Qu'est que cela?*) in one of his famous memorials addressed to his judges during the celebrated "*procès* Goezman." Marin, one of the witnesses, and a native of Provence, in giving his evidence, exhibited extreme malignity towards Beaumarchais, who, in his rejoinder, cast so much ridicule on his adversary that all France, and, indeed, all Europe joined in the laugh against poor " *Ques-a-co.*" Any passing event was at that period seized upon to give a name to a new fashion. The court milliner appropriated the term "*ques-a-co,*" and the dauphine appeared in the preposterous *coiffure* thus named at about the time of the death of Louis XV., and it became the favourite *mode* of the day.

"This is no daughter of mine!" exclaimed Maria Theresa; "some mistake has occurred; it can only be the portrait of an actress."

But such covert remonstrances were of little avail. To more direct ones, Marie Antoinette replied that "she had not then time to attend to them, not having a moment to spare from her amusements; but that all omissions and shortcomings she would promise to repent of and atone for when the Carnival ended — though she took cold much more frequently," she declared, "at the Lenten devotions than at masked balls or plays." Monsieur l'Abbé, doubtless, laughed heartily, as on such matters he was accustomed to do, and promised the fair penitent absolution, with plenary indulgence in the interval. Such was Marie Antoinette — vain and frivolous, fond of admiration, and lending a willing ear to all the flattery, fulsome compliments, and unwise counsels of her favourites — when she became, in her nineteenth year, Queen of France.

"I regard her brightest days as past," wrote Maria Theresa, at this period; "ended at an earlier age even than my own happy time. She must now be very great or very miserable." (The empress seems never to have divested her mind of the idea that the government of France rested on the shoulders of her daughter.) But the happiest days of Marie Antoinette were now to begin, and for the next ten years she enjoyed life, probably to the fullest extent of which she was capable. If evil reports were abroad concerning her, and calumny already sought to blur her fair fame, such things passed her by unheeded; or, if their echoes ever faintly reached her ear, they had lost much of their menacing sound ere they penetrated the charmed circle of courtly incense and flattery

Marie Antoinette.
Photo-etching from an Old Print.

with which feigned friends then surrounded, and lulled into false security, their brilliant but thoughtless young queen.

At the same time that Le Petit Trianon was presented to the queen, the king's considerate, almost filial, regard for his aunts led him to offer them also an establishment of their own. These elderly princesses had grown gray in the *mesquin* apartment allotted them when children in the Château of Versailles. Louis XV., on the marriage of his grandsons, had been unnecessarily lavish of the public money, it was generally thought, in appointing separate households, at enormous expense, for two so very young princes. But it seems never to have occurred to him that one of the many châteaux and estates he possessed might be an acceptable present to his daughters, now no longer young, to retire to occasionally from the gaieties and busy life of the court. Very great, then, was their satisfaction when the young king offered them, as a separate residence, the magnificent domain of Bellevue, with its handsome château, fine gardens, and extensive range of greenhouses, built for Madame de Pompadour. In the time of the marquise, the choicest exotics were reared there; and soon after the princesses made Bellevue their home the greenhouses were refilled; again the air was full of sweet odours, and the parterres of the garden brilliant with blossoms of every hue. For Mesdames Victoire and Sophie had a passion for flowers, and had found at Bellevue ampler space for its gratification than when they attempted, with but little success, to cultivate a few choice plants in the narrow balcony of their boudoir at Versailles.

Even Madame Adélaïde — the master-mind of the group of sisters — appeared to be sufficiently pleased with Bellevue quietly, ere long, to settle down there as *dame châtelaine.* Perhaps her recent and very severe illness, and the repulsive traces it had left behind, had subdued in some degree her natural energy of character. Or she may have been satisfied with the mortification she had caused the Austro-Choiseul party, by the famous stroke of diplomacy that brought M. de Maurepas in his old age from exile at Pontchartrain to end his days at Versailles as First Minister. Certain, however, it is that the domineering part she had seemed disposed to play, in counselling the king on affairs of state, ended with her possession of Bellevue.

There she had her own small court, which was decidedly hostile to the queen. It was chiefly composed of discontented, elderly courtiers of the former reign, and *grandes dames* who had then figured as *belles* of the court, but whose hey-day was long since past, — the wrecks, in fact, of the old *régime.* A few old Jesuits, friends of the late dauphin and his wife, and a venerable Polish priest or two — to whom Marie Leczinska had left pensions, and whom she had recommended to the care and consideration of her daughters — completed the intimate circle of Mesdames. The queen's many indiscretions were duly reported at Bellevue, and were the subject of frequent censure, — too often, indeed, fully deserved: as, for instance, the queen's reception at La Muette of the ladies, some of them very aged, who came from the provinces during the period of deep mourning for the late king to do homage to the new sovereign, as then was the custom. What a lamentable want of self-respect she evinced! And what an unpardonable want of respect for the feelings of others!

Madame Campan's account of this ceremony, intended to excuse the queen, represents her with her fan before her mouth, like a tittering schoolgirl, trying to conceal her laughter at the silly and ill-bred behaviour of one of her ladies, whom she should rather have put to blush for her ill manners by the more becoming dignity of her own. As a further excuse, we are told that these venerable dowagers, in their provincial caps and costumes, making their deep curtseys in the old-fashioned style to the queen, — some with tottering steps, others with palsied heads, — formed a very grotesque spectacle. But one that with more propriety might be so called, and which the old ladies themselves probably thought grotesque, was the queen herself, in her wonderful *panier*, with her ladies, their petticoats inflated to the same size, forming a sort of bulwark around her. The *panier*, however, had been so long in vogue, passing through the many vicissitudes of fashion, from small beginnings until it had attained to its then magnificent proportions, that it might, in more moderate degree, have been not unfamiliar to those ancient dames. But what could they think of the monstrous *coiffure*, rising up like a tower from the centre of each round-about petticoat?

It was no longer the nodding plume of the " *Ques-a-co.*" That for the moment had given place to two other new and equally artistic designs, named respectively, "*coiffure de l'inoculation,*" and "*coiffure mythologique.*" The scaffolding on which the gauze, crape, lace, and other materials were spread was higher by five inches, for both these head-dresses, than that of the *Ques-a-co.* The "inoculation" was decorated with "*ornaments de circonstance,*" — representations of the rising sun, a serpent, a club, and an olive-tree. It was a sort of pictorial enigma. In a small daily paper of the time, edited by Métra, it is thus explained: "The rising sun represents Louis XVI., towards whom all hopes are turned; the serpent is the smallpox; the club, the art of the physician which has overthrown the monster; and the olive-tree symbolises the peace and happiness with which the successful inoculation of the princes has suffused all hearts." The mythological head-dress was ornamented on one side with a cypress, denoting the mourning of the nation for Louis XV. On the other was a cornucopia overflowing with every good gift, and emblematical of the good time coming.

The circumstances of the moment made it *de rigueur* that every woman of distinction should appear in one or other of these elegant concoctions on occasions of ceremony, such as that referred to above, called the "*reception de grand deuil.*" The poor old *dames de province* appear to have been ignorant of this. And they may have considered their ignorance bliss, as they gazed with awe on those lofty edifices; wondering, perhaps, that heads so weak could carry such monstrous burdens. "The few that remain of the old school," says a French writer of the time, "have indeed great reason to say that good taste is in all things departing from us. To my mind, nothing proves it so much as this kind of senseless mythology, which our women of highest rank, following the example of the queen, now carry about piled up on their heads."

But both the wide-spreading *panier* and monumental head-dress were destined shortly to be cast aside — at least by the milkmaids and shepherdesses of Le Petit Trianon, where also *liberté* and *égalité*, under the auspices of Marie Antoinette, were to begin their reign in France. For it was there that the first blow was aimed at certain aristocratic privileges, possessed by a portion only of the ladies of the *haute noblesse*, and especially that of the *tabouret*, or the right of being seated in the presence of the queen or king. What jealousies, what heartburnings had not the right of the *tabouret* caused! To what intrigues had not noble ladies descended in order to obtain the coveted distinction! Imagine, then, what a thrill of malicious pleasure must have passed through the breasts of those ladies who had it not, and the mortification of those who plumed themselves on possessing it, when the queen, seating herself, requested, in a lively nonchalant manner, the whole of the ladies, without distinction, who formed her intimate circle at "le petit Schœnbrunn," to seat themselves also!

It was then she began to give effect to the oft-repeated menace, *"je m'en souviendrai,"* — a menace first uttered on her arrival in France, and on a question of etiquette: when the *haute noblesse* declined to accede to the discourteous request of Maria Theresa to Louis XV. that the Prince and Princess of Lorraine, who accompanied the young archduchess, should take precedence of them in the dauphin's marriage festivities. Etiquette, therefore, should now be banished, and princes and princesses, and both *la haute* and *petite noblesse*, in spite of their cherished distinctions, all sit down together. The French nobility were, she said, a *parvenu* race compared with the Austrian; and, doubtless, this contempt for the conventionalities was a terrible blow to those who valued the privileges they derived from any distinction of office or superiority of rank. Poor, thoughtless Marie Antoinette! It was an ill-advised step on her part; but it had the Abbé Vermond's approval, and probably was suggested by him.

But she proposed to reign at Trianon, it may be urged, not as Queen of France, but simply as a lady of the manor, surrounded by her friends. This descent from the throne, however, was not only loudly condemned at Bellevue, but was disapproved by many of the court circle and professed friends of the queen. By her enemies — and she had none more inimically disposed towards her than the Comte de Provence and his Italian wife, who had once looked to sit on the throne of France herself — it was very severely commented upon. Generally it occasioned much scandal, and laid the queen open to the charge of throwing off the dignity of her position, in order more freely to indulge in the dissipation to which she had already shown herself naturally inclined.

CHAPTER IV.

A New Moral Code. — *Un Vieillard Charmant.* — Louis XVI. — Governing Alone. — A Minister in Exile. — The Austrian Party. — A Frugal Minister of State. — Boucher's *Chefs-d'œuvre.* — The *Petits Appartements.* — Venus Rising from the Sea. — Removal of the Pictures. — Louis XVI. as a Patron of Art. — The Private Income of Louis XV. — The Famous Secret Diplomacy. — Treachery of Monsieur. — "Tartuffe" at Marly. — Disappointed Hopes. — A Royal Rustic Village. — M. de Maurepas's Colleagues. — *Louis Quinze* and *Quinze Louis.* — The *Système* Maupeou. — Sister Louise, the Royal Nun. — Burning the Chancellor. — A Satisfactory Beginning. — The King and His Minister.

LOUIS XVI. had drawn up for his guidance in the government of his kingdom a sort of ideal moral code, consisting of maxims extracted from Fénelon's "Telemachus" and the ethical writings of Nicole, a theologian and moralist of the seventeenth century. He had vowed never to swerve from the principles inculcated therein. And he had no doubt — their truth and excellence being to him so self-evident — of their ready acceptance in his council-chamber, as the basis of an improved system of government. But after despatching his letter to Pontchartrain he gathered from various sources (he was fond of gleaning, indirectly and obscurely, for odds and ends of information) that the ineradicable levity of the Comte de Maurepas's character would be likely to clash with his views and with his own sedate and serious temperament. He had too readily yielded, he reflected, to the wishes of Madame Adélaïde in calling to power a long-exiled and, though aged, inexperienced minister. But as reflection came too late to be of any avail, Louis looked forward to M. de Maurepas's arrival with a sort of vague apprehension; tempered, however, by a determination he had come to of governing alone, — aided, indeed, by the advice of his council, but submitting to the control of no First Minister.

M. de Maurepas had the reputation among the ladies of "*un vieillard charmant.*" He was received by Mesdames with warm congratulations, as one who in bygone days had won the favour of Marie Leczinska, but by the king with the timidity and reserve that were natural to him. This reserve was, however, but of short duration; for the old count, notwithstanding the airiness of his manners and the quips and cranks he delighted in, was not merely an inveterate jester, but a man of considerable intelligence and discernment. He was supple and insinuating, and, says a contemporary, "had the eye of a lynx for detecting the weak or ridiculous side of a man's character, with consummate art for leading him imperceptibly to the point he desired." It needed no great facility of perception to penetrate the character of Louis XVI. He had his full share of the dissimulation that formed so distinctive a quality of the Bourbon race; but it was tempered in him by a lesser degree of selfishness, which made him sincerely desirous of carrying out reforms for the benefit of the people, even at the cost of personal sacrifices that his predecessors would certainly have shrunk from.

All this M. de Maurepas clearly perceived in his first conference with the young monarch. Nor less manifest to him was his want of the inflexible sovereign will which alone could accomplish the vast changes aimed at by the spirit of the age, and could remove the yoke of bondage from the people while yet maintaining the dignity of the throne.

"Your majesty then would have me understand," said the count — after Louis had explained to him his views on the critical state of public affairs at that time — "that you honour me with the post of First Minister?"

"By no means, M. le Comte," replied the king, somewhat testily; "I presumed you would comprehend that I propose to govern alone."

"Ah! truly, Sire," replied the wily count, "but that you look to me to instruct you how to do so."

This point conceded, M. de Maurepas announced that he would on the morrow develop in council his views on the existing state of things.* Nor was he wanting in ability to do so; for he is said to have possessed in an eminent degree the art of simplifying the work of the cabinet, and of setting before the Council of State a clear and concise exposition of the most complicated affairs. And he was not so entirely inexperienced as rival candidates represented him. At the age of sixteen, and in the full swing of the regency, M. de Maurepas had entered on an office — that of Minister of Marine — which had long been hereditary in his family. The French navy was then at its lowest ebb; but, in the face of every possible discouragement, the count, as long as he held his post, had at least endeavoured to get the few ships of war that were rotting in the harbours repaired and manned, and to raise the naval forces of the country from the state of neglect and ruin they had fallen into.

When dismissed by Louis XV. after thirty years' residence at court, it was entirely against the king's wish. Wit and good temper had

* Whether, as some writers have confidently asserted, it would have been more advantageous for the court and the nation at large, and have afforded a chance of saving the monarchy, if either M. de Machault or M. de Choiseul had at this juncture succeeded to the direction of affairs, must be left to the historian to descant on and decide. It is without the province of the writer of these pages to touch on political questions further than in their bearing on the social life of the court and the Parisian *salons* of the day.

made him a favourite; but Madame de Pompadour was inexorable. His exile, however, like M. de Choiseul's, was almost nominal; though, his estates being smaller, and his income increased by no pension, he had lived in greater retirement than the duke, and with less attempt at *éclat*. But he had been a diligent observer of passing events, and well understood the times he lived in. He was also an enlightened patron of the arts, and took much interest in the progress of science. His manners were courteous, and he was polite to all, after the fashion of the old school; amiable, affable, and with a lively *bon mot* ever ready for all occasions; yet prudently reserved where he was not on terms of intimacy. As minister, the old count was declared to be "*très séduisant;*" very easy of access, and on the whole — except by the queen and the Choiseul faction — generally much liked by the court.

With the king M. de Maurepas grew rapidly into favour. He could talk with him sentimentally of the dauphin, his father, whom he had known, and whom he professed to have loved, and deplored with real or feigned interest his and the dauphine's early and mysterious death. He was not one of those who affected to believe that M. de Choiseul had had aught to do with that event. But, as it was necessary to crush the hopes of the queen and the Austrian party, — who, relying on the vacillating character of the king, were yet in expectation of succeeding to power when the new minister's presumed short tenure of office was at an end, — he would give no opinion, either to confirm or dispel the suspicions yet current in some quarters, and which the king had a strong conviction were thoroughly well founded.

One great merit of unusual rarity at that period M. de Maurepas undoubtedly possessed, — that of not seeking to enrich himself at the nation's expense. His great probity in monetary transactions was generally acknowledged; perhaps no minister except Cardinal Fleury had been so moderately remunerated for his services. Certainly there had been none who, with the sole control of the government in his hands, to turn to account for his own and his *protégés'* benefit, if it so pleased him, had, like the Comte de Maurepas, refrained from doing so. With his elevation to power he retained the same simple habits and unostentatious style of living to which for years he had accustomed himself in retirement. This harmonised well with the frugal tastes of the king, who, on ascertaining that his minister's former residence — the Hôtel Phélippeaux, in the Rue de Grenelle — had become much dilapidated from damp and neglect during its owner's long absence, and that the furniture, from the same cause, needed to be entirely renewed, offered him a suite of apartments in the royal château, in close communication with his own.

It was on the occasion of a visit of inspection to the Château de Versailles, after it had undergone purification, and immediately before the return of the court, that M. de Maurepas chanced to enter the late king's private apartments. Amongst other cabinet pictures collected there were several of the choicest productions of Boucher's pencil. The count being a man of much artistic taste, was probably no great admirer of the usually meretricious style of Boucher's painting. But he was also a connoisseur, and at once perceived that the artist had expended unusual pains on these pictures; that they were, in fact, his *chefs-d'œuvre*, — gracefully composed, harmonious in colouring, and as charming groups of flowers and fruits, Venuses, Cupids, loves, and doves, as had ever left the easel of the *premier peintre du roi*.

Louis XV. had never admitted his grandsons to this sanctum of the fine arts. But the young king was introduced to it by his minister soon after his arrival at Versailles. Aware that his tastes were not in sympathy with the refinements of art, M. de Maurepas was prepared to point out to him the artistic cleverness with which the painter disguised defects that he was himself, perhaps, more conscious of than the unsparing critics who so constantly sought to convict him of them. Except in very rare instances Boucher's drawing of the human figure was extremely faulty. And the demands of his courtly patrons were so numerous and pressing that no leisure was left him for correcting or retouching what, once hastily sketched out, was handed over to his assistants for completion. His goddesses were partially enveloped in flowing diaphanous draperies, wreathed about with garlands of flowers, or fanned by zephyrs with waving plumes. These he painted rapidly and exquisitely; and similar accessories in the way of *toilette* formed the chief, if not sole, merit of his portraits.

But his majesty is coming to look at these pictures. Fancy the fat young king, with his serious countenance, pacing heavily along the narrow corridors leading to the *petits appartements*, and conducted by the jesting, smiling, lightly stepping elderly courtier of the old *régime* — in his youth a sprig of the regency. They enter the luxuriously furnished sanctum sanctorum of "the Well-beloved," and proceed to inspect his collection of cabinet paintings. They are not all Bouchers. There are pictures of much greater merit among them, — the works of artists of far higher excellence and less licentious taste. But Louis XVI. has no feeling for art. Of drawing he knows nothing but the drawing of maps, with which he sometimes amuses himself when not employed with his workman, Gamain, in forging his famous locks and keys.

He gazes around him with a sort of bewildered air; glances hither and thither; then peers for a minute or two (he was very near-sighted) at a "Venus rising from the sea"—a picture that M. de Maurepas considers a perfect gem. He smiles therefore approvingly, supposing that the delicacy of treatment and exquisite finish remarkable in it have actually attracted the king and roused his admiration.

What then is his surprise when Louis, abruptly turning his back on the Venus, inquires whether it is not in one of these apartments that M. de Maurepas and himself are together to examine the late king's private papers. Being informed that it is in the one immediately adjoining the room they are in, Louis, with as much asperity as he is able to assume, replies: "M. le Comte, before beginning that work I desire to have all these pictures removed."

"Where would your majesty wish to have them placed?"

"Anywhere, anywhere, out of sight. In some remote and unused loft of the château, or out of the château entirely." M. de Maurepas lifts his eyebrows in unfeigned astonishment. The king continues: "You did well, M. le Comte, to let me know that such things existed here; I am sorry to have looked on them. But I trust to you to have them removed, and that I may see them no more."

A strange smile passes over the old count's face. The pictures forthwith are carefully removed, and the remote destination assigned them is out of the château, as the king wished, and in the remotest apartment of the minister's own suite of rooms, — his private cabinet, in fact, — in the Hôtel Phélippeaux, now under repair. There, concealed from general view by closely drawn silk draperies, it is only an appreciative connoisseur or two that occasionally obtains permission from the *rusé* guardian of these treasures of art to gaze on and admire them, as he shrugs his shoulders and exchanges with his old friends well-understood glances, strongly expressive of pity and contempt.*

Had things gone on smoothly in France, — that is, had the French nation, though fretting under its galling yoke, yet continued to bear it during this reign, — some future minister might have been desired to restore these pictures to their places. An order for two or three designs, for reproduction in the Gobelins tapestry, was the extent of royalty's patronage of the painter's art (the portrait-painting of Madame Vigée Lebrun excepted) during the reign of Louis XVI. But the king's tastes might possibly have changed ; for

---

* These pictures were removed from France to Amsterdam at the time of the Revolution, — whether by order of the heirs of M. de Maurepas or of other persons does not appear. The Revolution ended, they were brought back to Paris and sold for very large sums. The finest of the Bouchers are said to have been purchased eventually for the Hertford collection.

at the age at which he ascended the throne his predecessor was no less pious than he, and would not have missed repeating his prayers to save anybody's life, for he might have missed saving his soul. He amused himself, too, no less innocently and usefully, though his occupations were less laborious and much more cleanly. He did a little amateur delving, had his embroidery-frame, his omelette pans, and his turning-lathe, and from roots of trees made very nice boxes, which, as presents, were prettier and more acceptable than locks and keys. The circumstances of the period, therefore, one may conjecture to have been the cause of the parallel going no further.

However, to return to the *petits appartements*. M. de Maurepas having duly obeyed his sovereign's commands, nothing further remained to offend the eye or distract attention in the cabinet where Louis XV. had been accustomed to conduct the business of his secret diplomacy, and the monetary and commercial affairs in which, as Louis de Bourbon, he sometimes largely engaged. Without delay, then, the king began the examination of his royal grandfather's private papers. On the day of the king's death, a portion of them had, with his nephew's consent, passed into the hands of Madame Adélaïde, and were, of course, not likely to be restored. Whatever of importance they contained, if they reflected unfavourably on their father's memory, Mesdames were sure to destroy them.

Those that remained in the bureaux and cases, upon which seals had been placed, did not reveal the king's possession of the enormous wealth he was supposed to have hoarded up.

His cash-box contained but seventeen hundred *louis d'or*. But documents relating to his interest in several financial speculations showed that from these and similar sources he had realised a large private income. This he disposed of partly in secret-service money to the political agents he employed at foreign courts, and partly — probably the greater part — in his *menus plaisirs*. He had a floating capital of twenty-one millions of *francs*, employed in a variety of speculative affairs, when, in 1766, after the death of his son, he made his will. During the eight following years the amount of capital had greatly increased. It was well that it had, as a sum of from thirty to thirty-five millions of *francs* was required to pay the legacies left to his numerous illegitimate family. However, compared with his predecessor, he was moderate in this respect. He gave them neither titles nor estates; and the sum distributed amongst the whole of them, once for all, would have been considered by the magnificent Louis XIV. a very paltry endowment indeed for even one of his legitimised princes.

Certain shares in financial companies remaining undisposed of by will, Louis XVI. gave to the late king's *premier valet de chambre*, M. de Ville d'Avray.

The secret diplomatic correspondence, according to the order then given, should have been entirely destroyed. Nevertheless, a part of it found its way into the national archives, and the aimless secret diplomacy of Louis XV., which then was no secret to any of the European cabinets, has since, in several published collections of letters, etc., been made known to France and the public generally.

Amongst his numerous papers was a number of letters, written by the Comte de Provence. Probably the young king was not wholly a stranger to the artful, intriguing character of Monsieur (the count's title after his brother's accession). But if he was, he had the fullest testimony to his perfidy in the series of cynical epistles that now came into his hands, and whose object was further to depreciate him in the king's esteem, he already having but little regard for the dauphin. The dauphine, too, was by no means spared; Madame's opinion of her conduct being also given. What effect these treacherous reports had produced on Louis XV. could not be known. It did not appear that he had sought such information, but it was clear he had not objected to receive it.

The discovery of his brother's deceit was a shock to poor Louis' XVI., — for Monsieur made a point of putting on the mask of a very fair face in his social relations with his family. He was even obsequiously attentive to Marie Antoinette, both before and after she became queen, — writing verses in her praise, or appropriating those that others had written; for he had little imagination, but a most remarkable memory; while he at the same time was setting afloat many of the most scandalous reports that were in circulation amongst the people respecting her. His disparaging letters were probably destroyed. The only notice taken of his treacherous act was when, a short time after, Monsieur — who was full of vanity and pedantry, and plumed himself on the universality of his genius — undertook to play the leading part in Molière's "Tartuffe" at the court theatricals at Marly. The king, who rarely attended them, by chance was among the spectators, and applauded his brother continually. "Remarkably well done," he said, when the performance was ended; "remarkably well done, indeed. One may say, a character played to the life by an actor made for the part."

Many of the young king's greatest foes were doubtless to be found among his near relatives, — a selfish, extravagant set, the gratification of whose whims increased the financial difficulties of the almost bankrupt state. Even Mesdames were dissatisfied with the annuity of 200,000 *francs* which their father left to each of them, in addition to the income they already possessed. Madame Adélaïde had looked for a large immediate bequest in money, besides the annuity. In accordance with her great expectations (like the rest of her family she was disposed to be lavish) she had announced gifts to the amount of 80,000 *francs* to the nurses and servants who had attended in her illness. Disappointed in her hopes, she at once threw on her nephew the onus of supplying the whole of the funds for her largesses. He — poor, weak youth — not only readily complied with this very reasonable demand, but further, to console the disappointed ladies, and to enable them befittingly to support their new dignity at Bellevue, he made some addition to their already ample means, increased the number of their household, and undertook to defray a large part of their expenses.

The queen naturally expected to be as liberally dealt with. Marie Leczinska's pin-money had been fixed at an annual sum of 200,000 *francs*, and that pious queen had found it enough and to spare. Louis XVI. increased the amount for Marie Antoinette to 300,000 crowns or 900,000 *francs;* nearly the half of which she immediately expended in purchasing from Boëhmer a pair of magnificent diamond earrings that had been ordered by Louis XV. for Madame du Barry. At the same time, on her sole authority, she desired the architect, M. Hubert, to furnish plans for transforming the domain of the Petit Trianon into a Swiss village. It was to consist of a moderate-sized rustic dwelling, with twelve smaller cottages grouped around it, windmills, dairies, a river, an island, and a bridge. M. Laurent de Jussieu, one of the family of celebrated botanists of that name, was also summoned to superintend the replanting of the gardens, and to select for that purpose the choicest and most suitable trees. Thus, with projects for throwing away millions of *francs* of the public money on the carrying out of childish fancies, began the reign of the pious and frugal Louis XVI., and the thoughtless, extravagant Marie Antoinette.

The treasury was nearly empty. The Abbé Terray was Contrôleur-Général. M. de Maurepas recommended as his successor the economist, Turgot; to whom the king objected that "he was informed he never attended mass." "Sire," replied M. de Maurepas, "the Abbé Terray attends mass every day." Nevertheless, the coffers of the state had become empty under M. l'Abbé's control. His majesty therefore consented to try the other extreme, and M. Turgot — destined to succeed in a few weeks to the controllership of the finances — entered the council, *pro tem.*, as Minister of Marine. An entire change of ministry was intended. But, as it was difficult to find the right men for the vacant posts, M. de Maurepas took time to look leisurely around him for eligible colleagues. The late king's minister of war, the Duc d'Aiguillon, at once resigned, opportunely making way for the nomination of a minister, — the Général Comte de Muy, recommended to Louis XVI. in the memorial left to him by his father. M. de Vergennes — exiled under the Choiseul ministry, and opposed to the Austrian marriage and to the Jesuitical policy of the empress-queen — was recalled by his friend, M. de Maurepas, to fill the post of Minister for Foreign Affairs; and this in spite of the intrigues of the queen, directed by Baron de Besenval, the Duc de Choiseul's bosom friend.

However, Marie Antoinette continued to have very little influence generally as yet with the king, and in state affairs none. He seemed in such matters to be on his guard against her. M. de Maurepas was his guiding star, and kept the queen, the Abbé de Vermond, and Comte de Mercy, at a safe distance from the concerns of the government; he attributed to the counsels of the latter and those of Maria Theresa the queen's frequent attempts at interference.

On the 24th of October the new ministry was complete. It included the celebrated jurisconsulte, M. Lamoignon de Malesherbes. This appointment gave satisfaction to most of the politicians of the philosophical *salons*. He replaced in the Departement de Paris the old Duc de la Vrillière, who for fifty-five years past had allowed his mistresses, in lieu of pin-money, to enrich themselves by the sale of *lettres de cachet*, complacently issued by him on the slightest pretence. M. Maupeou received his *congé*, and the new Parliament, known derisively as "le Parlement Maupeou," was abolished. The "*grand citoyen*," Beaumarchais and his famous *procès*,— originating in the misappropriation of *fifteen louis d'or* by the counsellor Goezman's wife,— doubtless contributed greatly towards it. For the people who laughed so long and so heartily at Beaumarchais's scathing wit, and his defiance of the order of his Maupeou judges that his cause should be pleaded with closed doors, had declared, with their usual love of a *calembour*, that as *Louis Quinze* had abolished the old Parliament, *quinze louis* would abolish the new.

But it was not without many misgivings and much fear and trembling that the young king signed the edict that reinstated the refractory Parliament which, with its right of remonstrance so freely used, had proved such a thorn in the flesh to Louis XV. M. Maupeou, a man of determined will, undertook to free his sovereign from their humiliating domination; "to snatch," as he said, "the crown from the Record office." In the place of the old hostile assembly, all whose members were banished, he substituted a magisterial body devoted to the king and to the upholding of the royal authority. And it was not the Parliament of Paris only that was dispossessed of its functions. The provincial Parliaments having strenuously opposed many edicts of Louis XV., the *système* Maupeou was also applied to them. The *coup-d'état* was general, and was generally disapproved.

It was an agitating moment, then, for poor Louis XVI., when required to recall the rebellious Parliament and to reinstate it in its former privileges. It was but an act of justice; and, as some persons thought, one that had been already too long delayed. Exile had brought distress on many of its members; and poverty, sickness, and in some instances death, had fallen on the families of those whose means were solely derived from the offices they held. Anxious to do right, but fearful of doing wrong, the king sought in all quarters, from friends and foes alike, for opinions and advice on the subject. Unfortunately, none of the carefully selected maxims of his private code seemed to apply to this case. Monsieur — a profound politician in his eighteenth year — was so violently menacing towards all who proposed to undo the work of the " Well-beloved," that the king was truly alarmed.

Mesdames of Bellevue also opposed "an act so disrespectful to their father's memory," while Madame (now " Sister Louise "), the Carmelite nun, loudly raised her voice against it, as a " sacrilegious attempt to restore to office the persecutors of the clergy." (They had dared to direct public attention to the abuses in the Church and to the dissolute lives of several of its prelates.) Sister Louise was in the habit of falling into holy ecstasies. On the present occasion, while in that state of hysterical excitement, she prophesied, " Woe, woe," to all concerned in the recall of the old Parliament. But the popular voice called louder still " Woe, woe," to all who supported the new. To that voice M. de Maurepas gave more heed than to the cry from the cell of the royal·nun.

The queen, for once, was on the popular side; also the Ducs d'Orléans, d'Artois, and de Chartres, the Jansenist clergy, the philosophers of the pulpit, and philosophers of the *salons*, and ultimately — at the triumphant nod of M. de Maurepas — so was the king. In this downfall of the new Parliament some writers have seen the triumph of those long proscribed opinions that eventually overthrew the monarchy.

The seals of the chancellorship were delivered to M. de Meromesnil — another returned exile — and the old Parliament was forthwith reinstated. The populace were so extravagantly enthusiastic in the expression of their joy, that, after lighting a bonfire in the middle of the Place de Grève, they, with loud acclamations, consigned M. Maupeou and his colleague, l'Abbé Terray, to the flames, dancing frantically around them, singing, laughing, and shouting gleefully, until not a trace of their ashes remained. Happily, this was only in effigy; for the ex-Chancellor and the ex-Contrôleur-Général, while being thus extinguished in Paris, were in person quietly rolling along in their carriages on their way to their estates.

Public opinion thoroughly approved these first acts of Louis XVI. and his minister. The people's confidence in their young king revived; for they had been inclined to murmur at his tardiness. They now looked on the new reign as at least satisfactorily inaugurated. M. de Maurepas, preparing for as long a term of power as, at his age, he could reasonably expect, selected for the ministry men who had secured a share of popular favour. He encouraged economical reforms, and recommended the king to make many concessions he considered desirable, both for the welfare of the people and the security of the tottering throne. This brought on him from his opponents the charge of too readily falling in with the opinions of the time, and of floating on carelessly with the stream, more mindful of his own personal ease than of the prosperity of the nation and the dignity of the crown.

But, at all events, under a king mentally and bodily inert, and pitiably insensible to the dangers that gradually, but too surely, were on all sides hemming him in, M. de Maurepas contrived to stave off for some years the evil days coming on France. He could not impart to her sovereign the qualities needful for the times his lot was cast in, and which nature had wholly denied him; but he yet constantly strove to veil from others' eyes those lamentable deficiencies of character that were so plainly apparent to his own.

CHAPTER V.

A Musical *Émeute*. — Gluck and Piccini. — Grétry and Marmontel. — A *Mot* of Madame du Barry. — *Iphigénie en Aulide.* — The *Devin du Village.* — A Knight of the Golden Star. — Sophie Arnould. — *Célébrons Notre Reine.* — The King and the Comte d'Artois. — Royalty at the Opera. — Amateurs and Critics. — Head-dresses in Peril. — A Sentimental Head-dress. — A Critical Position. — The Diamond Aigrette. — The Music of Nature. — Jean-Jacques at the Opera. — Quinault's "Roland." — Marmontel and Piccini. — Madame du Deffand. — Piccinites and Gluckites. — Piccini's Triumph.

NEITHER Paris nor Versailles was so entirely absorbed by the changes then occurring in the ministry, and the expectation of reform in the system of government, but that both the court and the public, with that facility so characteristic of the French, could also give eager attention to a sort of musical *émeute*, and enter with ardour into the feeling of partisanship then agitating the *salons* respecting the rival claims to preëminence of the German school, represented by Gluck, and the Italian, represented by Piccini.

The Royal Academy of Music, from the falling off of patronage, was overwhelmed with pecuniary difficulties that menaced the directors with ruin. The former constant frequenters of that courtly

Grétry, he attributed its success to the words he had furnished rather than to his collaborator's music; and as the lion's share of praise was never awarded him, though he thought it his due, he would often allow his dissatisfaction to appear.

Madame du Barry fairly expressed the general opinion concerning many of Marmontel's operettas when — on hearing to whom the marquis had applied to furnish the Italian composer with a libretto — she exclaimed, "Poor Piccini! He gives me the idea of a lark required to sing and to soar aloft with a tortoise attached to its claws."

While arrangements were in progress for the reintroduction of Italian music, it happened that Gluck, the German composer, having finished his opera of "*Iphigénie en Aulide*," with a French libretto (a detestable one, according to Grimm), prepared by Du Rollet from Racine's tragedy, was desirous of producing it in Paris. To further his views, his patron, the Emperor Joseph II., wrote to his sister strongly recommending the composer to her favour and protection. At the urgent request of the Comte de Mercy, supported by the dauphine, the directors of the Royal Academy sent proposals to Gluck for the production of his opera. But it formed no part of Gluck's plan to appear eager to treat with the directors. In his overweening vanity he chose to put them aside, as it were, and to condescend to the wishes of royalty ; so that, although invited to Paris in 1772, he did not set out on his journey until late in the following autumn (1773). In the meantime, however, probably to keep expectation alive, he wrote to the "*Mercure de France*," saying, "he had in view the establishing of a system for abolishing the ridiculous distinctions of national music, by providing music of a character suited to all nations. He hoped to succeed in this scheme with the aid of the celebrated M. Rousseau of Geneva, whom he proposed to consult on the subject. The study of his works on music," continued Gluck, "having convinced him of the sublimity and accuracy of that great man's taste and knowledge." Rousseau's operetta, the "*Devin du Village*," he regarded as a model which hitherto none had successfully imitated, and from which he had learned that the language of nature was the universal language.

This letter to the "*Mercure*" was to many persons a subject of mirth ; but, generally, it merely raised public curiosity respecting Gluck; yet it kindled, in Rousseau's mind, vague suspicions of Gluck's sincerity, and also set to work the pens of many essayists who had never before given a thought to music.

In due time the Chevalier Gluck, Knight of the Papal Order of the Golden Star, made his appearance in Paris. He was then sixty years of age, of common demeanour, unpolished manners, and much disfigured by the scars and seams of that frightful disease, smallpox. He was arrogant and insolent in the extreme; the consciousness of his musical talent finding expression in airs of insufferable self-conceit. Piccini was in his fortieth year, and in character and appearance the very reverse of Gluck. The former, declining the offer of a home in the house of the Abbé Morellet and of other wealthier amateurs, was modestly lodged with his wife and children at Passy, — the chevalier in a dwelling of some pretension (he piqued himself not a little on the dazzling rays of his golden star) in the Faubourg St. Maur.

But before either *artiste* had been heard disputes ran high as to their respective merits — the numerous partisans on both sides supporting each his candidate for public favour with extraordinary vehemence. Gluck was honoured with a very flattering reception by the dauphine and her circle, and the *entrée* to her *toilette* was immediately granted him. He was a constant attendant, it appears, at this ridiculous ceremony, and talked to Marie Antoinette so unceasingly, and was so grandly affable to all present that he succeeded in throwing into the shade the pompous Abbé Vermond himself.

Piccini was introduced by the Italian ambassador to Madame du Barry; also to the Abbé Morellet, at one of his famous weekly *matinées musicales*, where Piccini's compositions won great applause. But while Gluck's "Iphigénie" was in preparation, and he storming and raving at refractory singers under his training, and while Piccini was diligently working at his opera, and learning French from Marmontel,—all Paris at the same time on the tiptoe of expectation,—Louis XV. was taken ill. Six weeks of suspense, of hopes, and fears, were followed by the announcement of his death. Then came the period of deep mourning, during which all public amusements must be suspended. So that not until the 4th of August, 1774, did "Iphigénie" appear on the operatic stage.

The orchestra no less than the singers had given the composer much trouble. It had even been rebellious, almost in open revolt against "German drill." But Gluck was inflexible; and had so well taken advantage of the delay that had occurred that, on the evening his opera was produced, the orchestra was perhaps more efficient than any the frequenters of the Royal Academy of Music had hitherto heard. The overture was played with remarkable precision — Gluck conducting — but the audience at the first were chary of applause. The *rôle* of Iphigénie was assigned to Sophie Arnould, who murmured a little at the overwhelming accompaniments. Her delicate organ had even then — though she was but thirty — lost much of its original power and sweetness, and was rapidly becoming what the Abbé Galiani not long after termed "a very fine asthma." Larivée was Agamemnon, and by his fine singing elicited applause from all parts of the theatre. This had an animating effect on the performers, both vocal and instrumental; and the result was a triumph for Gluck, and a triumph for those who had so ably interpreted his music.

It was also a triumph for Marie Antoinette on her first public appearance as queen. Hopes and expectations were then very generally cherished, outside what was called her "*cercle intime,*" that with her new dignity she would adopt a new line of conduct, one more suited to the elevated position of Queen of France than that she had hitherto so thoughtlessly pursued as dauphine. When, therefore, the grand chorus, "*Chantons, célébrons notre reine,*" first burst on the ear, all eyes instantly were turned towards the royal box. The audience rose, and, with enthusiasm as spontaneous as it was general and intense, saluted the young queen in the words of the chorus, "*Chantons, célébrons notre reine.*" The choir, with the principal singers then occupying the scene — Iphigénie herself, forgetting her *rôle*, even as it was momentarily by all forgotten — followed the example of the audience, bowing to the queen and singing with an energy that must have delighted Gluck even as this impromptu ovation may have been gratifying to the queen.

The king, too, had made a point of being present, though his custom of being in bed by eleven and up again at five, in order to transact the business and get through the various avocations he daily marked out for himself, did not allow of his wasting much time on operas, balls, and plays. The opera began early — at five o'clock; but there was the journey back to Versailles. However, from Paris to Versailles was a well-kept road. And of the immense number of horses in the royal stables, half a dozen were always fresh and in trim for the journey at any hour of the night or day. The Comte d'Artois was constantly in the habit of returning to Versailles after the opera, opera ball, or Comédie Francaise, usually to escort the queen. After supping with his family he would return to Paris to promenade in the gardens of the Palais Royal, or to spend the night in dissipation with wild companions; again, between four and five in the morning, returning to Versailles to begin his night's rest when his staid eldest brother was about to rise to begin his day's work.

Of course the young count witnessed the first representation of "Iphigénie." He and his tiny, long-nosed countess, the intriguing M. and Madame de Provence, the Duc and Duchesse de Chartres, the Princesse de Lamballe, with other princes and princesses of the blood, the ministers, the ambassadors, and in fact the entire court, had assembled to do honour to Gluck and to please his royal patroness. But amongst all this brilliant company, whose eyes seemed to wait on the queen as on a divinity, to obtain from her a smile or an approving glance, there was none, it may be confidently said, with the exception of the king, and possibly the Comte d'Artois, to whom the homage publicly paid to her was not as much a mortification as a surprise. For she did not divide honours with the king. He, "*pauvre homme*," as she was accustomed to call him, seems to have had neither part nor, lot in this burst of enthusiasm. He was merely a passive, yet no doubt much gratified, spectator of an incident unexpectedly developing the apparent popularity of the queen.

At the second representation of the opera, the audience was even more numerous than at the first. It was indeed a less courtly one; but the opinion of amateurs and *artistes* respecting Gluck's music was then more decidedly expressed, and notwithstanding the strong feeling of partisanship then existing, was certainly favourable. Some few grumbling critics there were who complained that it was noisy. Yes — "Gluck's sweet music" was far too noisy. But none had then dreamed of the "music of the future," and the mercilessness with which the ears of future generations were doomed to be assailed. The enthusiasm of the general public, however, is said to have reached actual frenzy,— the men stamping, waving hats, and shouting as if delirious, "*Vivent*

Gluck et Iphigénie." Soldiers were placed at the entrances to restrain the energy of those who were determined to wedge their way in, though they should be suffocated themselves or suffocate others in the gallant attempt to find room where there was not the fraction of an inch of space unoccupied.

Women — after the manner of the excited *bella donnas* at Spanish bull-fights — threw their gloves, fans, and laced handkerchiefs on the stage. Others, in more tender emotion, sighed, sobbed, and fainted; but this may have been due to the uproar and confusion around them, even more than to the charm of the music; for however beautiful it may have been, who that had music in his soul could enjoy its beauties amidst so demoniacal a scene? Under any circumstances a number of ladies gathered together, each carrying on her head the lofty structure then the *grande mode* for all who had any pretension to rank as members of the *beau monde*, must have been a very singular spectacle. But when these ladies, unmindful of their highly plumed "*Ques-a-cos;*" the race-course, the jockeys, the dogs, and the five-barred gates of the "*coiffure à l'anglomanie;*" the turnips and beet-root, the carrots and cabbages of the "*belle jardinière,*" etc., took to fainting with emotion, or to hysterical sobbing, and the scaffolding and various appurtenances of these yard and a half high edifices came tumbling down, what a pretty scene that must have been to witness.

This is said to have occurred in several instances, and necessarily must have occurred, if it be true, as stated by contemporary writers, that the audience on the second night of Gluck's opera carried their enthusiasm to such frantic excess. Something of the kind even happened on the first night in one of the royal boxes. But accident, not emotion, was the cause of it.

The Duchesse de Chartres had determined to surpass the queen in the height of her head-dresses. It was owing to this laudable spirit of rivalry that they had attained their monstrous elevation; for on the other hand the queen had determined she would not be surpassed, and as the ladies of the court and the *beau monde* strove to follow her lead she still rose inch by inch above them. Aided by the fertile fancy of the celebrated *coiffeur*, Léonard, the duchess had invented, exclusively for herself, a head-dress, which she christened "*le pouf sentimental.*" The scaffolding was two inches higher than that of the head-dress worn by the queen, and which was also invented for the occasion, and named "*coiffure à loge d'opéra.*" It was composed of numberless plumes, waving at the top of a tower. Léonard had used fourteen yards of gauze or lace for the duchess's "*pouf*" and folds and plaits surrounding it. The ornaments employed were two waxen figures, representing the little Duc de Beaujolais (afterwards King Louis Philippe) in his nurse's arms. Beside them was placed a parrot pecking at a plate of cherries; and reclining at the nurse's feet was the waxen figure of a black boy. On different parts of the edifice were the initials of the Ducs de Chartres, de Penthièvre, and d'Orléans, formed with the hair of those princes — the husband, father, and father-in-law of the fair wearer of the sentimental *coiffure*.

Forgetting the height of her "*pouf*," the duchess in the course of the evening leaned forward to speak to the Duc de Penthièvre, when her head-dress became entangled in the ornaments of a girandole on the opposite side of her box. On resuming her upright position the girandole remained firm, but drew out a long piece of the gauze and displaced the parrot and the cherries. Luckily they fell on the duke, who caught them, and, with great presence of mind, prevented a further fall into the *parterre*, — thus saving his daughter from becoming an object of mirth to the audience, and perhaps saving also Gluck's opera; but the incident occasioned much merriment among the royal party.

To Louis XVI., the queen's lofty head-dresses, and the forest of gigantic plumes that daily dazzled his limited vision as they waved to and fro in the grand gallery of Versailles, were the constant cause of much chagrin. Timidity restrained him from remonstrating with the queen on carrying folly to such amazing heights. But he now availed himself of the accident to the duchess's "*pouf*" to have a quantity of diamonds, inherited from the dauphine, his mother, made up into a splendid aigrette, which he presented to the queen, at the same time venturing to express a hope that, being so fond of simplicity, she would wear it in her hair, and allow it to supplant those complicated arrangements of feathers, flowers, and lace, that had already too long retained their vogue. He did not forget to impress on her also that, economy in his private expenditure being then imperative, he had not been so thoughtless as to purchase those diamonds.

"I have had them mounted only," he said. "It will, I feel sure, give them additional value in your eyes to know that many years ago they were paid for."

Poor Louis! did he really believe that his present would be more acceptable to his queen on that account, or did he mean to be sarcastic? At all events the diamond aigrette was graciously received and greatly admired. And if it did not immediately supplant the tall feathers of which Marie Antoinette was so fond, it formed, as long as its novelty pleased her, the principal ornament of a new *coiffure*, epigrammatically named "*À l'économie du siècle.*"

But we must return for a moment to the Salle

de l'Opéra. A celebrated amateur was there on the second night, who has not yet been mentioned. It was the great man who was to assist Gluck in establishing in France — whence it should spread throughout the world — that one universal language, the Music of Nature; a grand project, of which nothing more was heard, though the composer and *l'homme de la nature* had several interviews; each with his harsh, croaking voice singing his compositions to the other, "to the accompaniment of a cracked spinet."

Refusing the more convenient place that Gluck had reserved for him, Rousseau squeezed himself into a niche at the further corner of the *salle*. Those who observed him closely and saw the enthusiasm with which he applauded, were of opinion that he actually did, for awhile, forget the existence of that interesting person Jean Jacques, to revel in a dream of music. Hitherto his *beau idéal* of the "divine art" had been the music of Italy. But it had been Gluck's good pleasure to flatter him extravagantly, and to talk and write in the same exaggerated strain of his musical talent. As soon, therefore, as Jean Jacques was recognised, he had the gratification of hearing his name coupled with that of the famous German composer — " *Vive Rousseau!* " "*Vive l'auteur du 'Devin du Village!'*" " *Vivent Rousseau et Gluck!* " " *Vive l'Iphigénie.*"

Recalled to himself by these unwonted acclamations, Jean Jacques, apparently much mortified, made a hasty retreat. Doubtless he thought it a conspiracy to deprive him of the pleasure of hearing the opera to the end; and "*Chantons, célébrons notre reine*" — received as enthusiastically as on the previous evening — favoured his exit unperceived.

The completion of Piccini's opera was considerably delayed through the composer's ignorance of French. The directors of the Royal Academy had suggested to him as a subject the story of the famous paladin, Roland, and previous to Gluck's arrival had made the same suggestion to him. But as the latter brought with him to Paris his "Iphigénie" ready for production, and "Roland" had yet to be written, they appear to have transferred their request for that opera to Piccini, and without mentioning to Gluck that they had done so. This may have been with a view of keeping up, for their own possible benefit, the heated discussion in the *salons* on the respective merits of the rival composers, who themselves took no active part in the dispute.

Marmontel, whom Gluck afterwards contemptuously spoke of as "a dramatic author of operas supposed to be comic," distrusted his powers, he tells us, in lyrical tragedy. "Lofty language," he says, "lends itself less readily to musical expression than does the language of comedy." The happy thought, however, occurred to him of revising and remodelling Quinault's lyric poem of "Roland," which Lulli had set to music. Its many episodes and superfluous details were omitted; the terribly long recitatives shortened; some expressions modernised — the poem being then above a century old — and the five acts reduced to three, as had been done with "Iphigénie." Thus far Marmontel's task had been comparatively an easy one, and he was as much pleased with his improved arrangement of Quinault's poem, he says, as though he had written it wholly himself. It now only remained to make Piccini comprehend it.

Many weary days and weeks the musician and the poet spent together over the poem — the one labouring to explain the sense of every line, and almost word for word; the other intently gazing at him, eager to understand. When he had thoroughly seized the meaning of a passage, Marmontel slowly declaimed it, while Piccini, with painful earnestness, listened for the accents, and noted down in accordance with them his own musical phrases. And his ear was so sensitive, so true, that when the morning's work was finished, and Piccini opening his piano to play over to his friend the music he had written, "it rarely happened," says Marmontel, "that a single note needed correction." This laborious method of composing his opera became a jest among the "Gluckites," who confidently prophesied a failure; but on the other hand, though Piccini was not the court favourite, his pretensions were supported by a powerful party of private friends and connoisseurs.

Gluck meanwhile had gone off to Germany. The queen had obtained for him a pension of 6,000 *francs*, besides a gratuity of the same amount for every new opera he should produce in Paris. The directors of the Royal Academy of Music had also treated him with a liberality of which there had been no previous instance. But their receipts were then large. The *salle* was nightly crowded. All Paris wished to hear "*Iphigénie en Aulide*," and many of the public were desirous of knowing in what the new school of music so far excelled the old. Some old opera-goers were even unwilling to acknowledge that Lulli, Compra, and Rameau were excelled by Gluck. Madame du Deffand is said to have been extremely annoyed at the idea of those old favourites being dethroned.*

This musical fray was at its height when Gluck returned. A large part of "Roland" was then

---

* Madame du Deffand, it appears, could neither appreciate Gluck's music nor the sparkling dialogue of Beaumarchais's *spirituel* comedy, "The Barber of Seville," which was attracting all Paris to the Théâtre Français, at the time Gluck's "Orphée and Eurydice"—dedicated to the queen, and produced for the marriage *fêtes* of the Princesse Clotilde—was delighting the opera-goers. She writes to Horace Walpole, in 1775, that both opera and play had been so extravagantly praised that she was

written; but as soon as Gluck learned that Piccini was engaged on the same subject, he burned all he had composed for that opera. "There," he exclaimed, in a voice the reverse of calm, "I leave the ground free to the Italian and his French *collaborateur*." Piccini, however, was warned that the "Gluckites" would not allow his opera to proceed. A cabal was already prepared to hiss the overture and to prevent the singers from being heard. Piccini's family were so much alarmed for his safety, when the first performance was announced, that they endeavoured to prevail on him to remain at home.

"My dear children," replied Piccini to his imploring wife and daughters, as he was about to set out, "bear in mind that we are residing amongst the most polite and generous-natured people in Europe. Should they think it right to reject me as a musician, yet be assured they will do me no personal harm, but will respect me as a man and a foreigner." Whether the "Piccinites" had assembled in sufficient force to overawe the "Gluckites," or that some curiosity to hear Piccini's music silenced the hostile

compelled to go and see them, and that she was wearied to death by them. Madame du Deffand was then nearly eighty; her hearing was very defective, and she had been blind for nearly thirty years. Therefore, the criticism on acting and music of that once famous "*monstre d'esprit*," like many other things that form the subject of these latter-day letters, are little to be valued or relied on.

band, certain it is that the overture was played without opposition to a crowded and attentive audience, and elicited immense applause. As the opera proceeded, it was evident that "Roland" had nothing to fear from "Iphigénie;" and Piccini was rewarded with the brilliant success due to his perseverance and his genius. His opera ended, he was carried in triumph by his friends to his anxiously expectant, and now delighted family.

Italian music became the rage. "The ladies declared it full of sweetness, charm, and grace" — just as when, twenty years before, Pergolese brought his "*Serva Padrona*" to Paris, and gained a convert in Rameau, who said, "had he been forty years younger, he would have gone off instantly to Italy to study his art, and have taken Pergolese as his model." Piccini's triumph, however, in no way prejudiced Gluck's; the Italian himself was one of the foremost in acknowledging his rival's great musical ability. Gluck was far less generous. He said that the Neapolitan ambassador would give dinners and suppers to three-fourths of Paris to win applause for the opera of "Roland;" and that Marmontel, so skilful a writer of tales, would tell a tale to the whole kingdom concerning the great, the exclusive merits of that distinguished composer, Piccini.

But throughout this musical hubbub, which with

more or less vigour continued for several years, the Opéra Comique experienced no falling off of public favour, — Grétry's charming music, tender, mirthful, grave, or gay, sustaining, undiminished, its high reputation.

CHAPTER VI.

Monsieur and Madame. — Monsieur's *Bons Mots*. — Louis le Sévère. — A Breach of Court Etiquette. — Jupiter at Versailles. — Putting the Clock Forward. — The Royal Brothers and Sisters. — A *Fête* at Brunoy. — The Comte and Comtesse d'Artois. — Mademoiselle Bertin. — Races *à l'Anglaise*. — Hunting and Gambling. — At Heart a Rake. — A Petition to the Queen. — The Barber of Seville. — Beaumarchais's Secret Mission. — The Monopoly in Corn. — A Raid on the Bakers' Shops. — Distress and Extravagance. — "Gros Madame." — The Courtly Comte de Buffon. — A Point of Etiquette. — A Grand Fancy-dress Ball. — A Question of Precedence. — The Parisians Indignant.

F the numerous enemies of Louis XVI. and Marie Antoinette, none were more persistently insidious than Monsieur and Madame de Provence. Under the specious exterior of politeness, deference, and the affectation of studious habits, and a taste for *les belles lettres*, Monsieur was animated by a restless spirit of malice and intrigue, the more revolting from its strongly marked development in a youth of his age — he was then but in his nineteenth year. An instance of so total an absence of generous instincts in one so young, and the presence of selfish ones overpowering the ties of nearest relationship, has indeed very rarely been met with.

And the boyish husband found a sympathetic helpmeet in his girlish Italian wife, — so far as regarded her ready appreciation of his views and the means adopted for their attainment.

The crown was, doubtless, the object of his longing aspirations; and, bearing in mind the miserable weakness of Louis XVI., and the more than indiscreet folly of the queen, it was not an unreasonable expectation that sooner or later voluntary, or more likely compulsory, abdication might place it on his head. Though he did not affect in his *toilette* the lavish *recherche* of the Comte d'Artois, he yet carefully avoided the undignified slovenliness that so unpleasantly distinguished the king; his obesity, which even exceeded his brother's, was therefore less unfavourably noticed by the public eye. He was also more condescending in manner, and not so ungainly; and, on the whole, to a certain extent, Monsieur, a professed *esprit fort* and *homme de lettres*, secured the kind of popularity he sought among the philosophers of the new school.

Many of his *bons mots* were current in the *salons* of Paris. They were not remarkable for refinement, and were more frequently told in a whisper than repeated aloud. But Parisian society laughed at their piquancy, and the cleverness with which certain persons at Versailles were indicated under a *double entendre*. He had none of the king's strange nervous timidity, or the overbearing arrogance of the Comte d'Artois. When displeased he was sarcastic, or took his revenge in a scurrilous epigram; while the king — his reserve once thrown off — became not only *brusque* in manners and rough in speech, but almost brutal.

It was on these occasional bursts of "coarse and aimless anger" that the king founded his claim to the surname of "Louis le Sévère." They gained him enemies, however, amongst the courtiers, and as they occurred when least expected, most persons preferred to communicate with the king on business of a public nature through the intervention of M. de Maurepas, who was always much amused by his sovereign's explosions of severity. At this early period of the new reign, domestic squabbles, in which strong hints of an impending divorce were thrown out, and harsh and vehement language was used, were of frequent occurrence in the young royal family, — Marie Antoinette vigorously retorting on her sisters-in-law the accusations they brought against her. While Louis XV. lived, though aware of this scandal, he would never interfere to put an end to it, and Louis XVI., though inclined to do so, had not the power.

On coming to the throne, he refused to receive from his brothers and sisters the title of "Majesty." This was communicated to Maria Theresa by Comte de Mercy. The empress replied: "He has followed the example of my son, the Emperor Joseph; but it is to be hoped that his complaisance will not go beyond this one change in long-established court etiquette." It was, however, followed by the refusal of Monsieur and Madame, and the Comte and Comtesse d'Artois, to pay their court daily to the king and queen, as had been "from time immemorial" the custom. They were supported in their refusal by Mesdames of Bellevue; and it was intended as a mark of disrespect to the queen, who, on questions of etiquette, was constantly endeavouring, in pursuance of her vow, "*Je m'en souviendrai*," to humiliate the princes of the blood and the *haute noblesse* of France.

But the king of course shared with the queen the disrespect that Mesdames were desirous should rest on her alone; and the conduct of his brothers was well calculated further to debase him in the eyes of his courtiers, and in public opinion. When the court circle assembled in the Grand Gallery of Versailles — where once the *Grand Monarque* held his *réunions*, called "*appartements*" — "a stranger would have found it difficult to recognise the king from any particular attention or any deference paid him." What, then, must have been the agonised sensations of the perturbed spirit of the superb Louis if ever, to look on his degenerate posterity, he revisited, on such occasions, the scene of his former greatness and grandeur; where once he sat enthroned, like Jupiter among the inferior deities, and where all around him were but too willing to fall down and lick the dust of his godship's feet, had it been his "*bon plaisir*" that they should do so. Changed — changed, indeed, is the scene!

Monsieur, though he paid no court to Louis XVI., was not openly disrespectful. Full of dissimulation, politeness was a part of his *rôle*, and of Madame's also. But the haughty young libertine, the Comte d'Artois, made a point of publicly insulting the king. "On occasions of great state or solemnity," says an eye-witness (the Comte de Mercy, quoted above), "he will pass before the king twenty times, push him aside, tread on his feet; and this, apparently, without any thought of apology or excuse being necessary for behaviour that pains and shocks every one present."

Yet the Comte d'Artois was the queen's chevalier *par excellence*, — the champion ready at all times to defend her reputation against the many aspersions cast upon it. He accompanied her to masked balls and other amusements, while the king was fast asleep and perhaps was snoring. Sometimes the clock was put forward to send off the poor drowsy man to his slumbers at half-past ten, instead of eleven. While he, *en revanche*, that his slumbers might not be disturbed, would order the gates of the courtyard to be locked when he went to bed; so that when her majesty came home at two, three, or four in the morning, she would have to go round to the back of the château and slip in at the servants' entrance. "Manners had indeed undergone a change without undergoing improvement."

The change, most decidedly, was for the worse. For, as somebody remarked, — and it may have been Madame du Barry, who certainly ought to have known, — "in the former reign it was the king who roamed about at night, and being sometimes locked out, slunk in in disguise at a side door." But now the king stays at home and sleeps, while the queen is gadding about with the count, and meeting with all sorts of strange adventures. The little Comtesse d'Artois had her own private distractions, — sentimental flirtations, which were well known to the count; and this "*vrai chevalier francais*" had many a hearty laugh, we are told, at his wife's *légèretés*. Monsieur and Madame, meanwhile, were shut up in their study (they were not accustomed to take part in the nocturnal escapades of their royal relatives), composing scraps of trustworthy information for the "*Mercure de France;*" stinging epigrams, mysterious *on dits*, and writing anonymous letters to be put in circulation the following day. The Comte de Mercy-Argenteau told the empress-queen he was "overwhelmed with such missives, — scandalous, audacious, or absurd, and some of them horribly defamatory."

Whence a large and the more infamous part of

them came was more than suspected. At times an effort was made to trace out and punish the author of some unusually offensive *chanson* or pamphlet; when suddenly the lieutenant of police would bring his quest to a close. A name would be whispered to M. de Maurepas, who did not exactly repeat it to the king, but would recommend that the inquiry be pursued no further; Louis would then understand that, to spare "Tartuffe," the lieutenant's search had come to a standstill. The king had a strong feeling of aversion towards Monsieur le Comte de Provence, and certainly with excellent reason. Yet no *fête*, given in honour of Marie Antoinette when she became queen, approached in magnificence, or in the gallantry of the idea that pervaded the general arrangements, that grand tournament which Monsieur prepared at his favourite estate of Brunoy to dazzle the court, and to astonish and delight its young sovereign.

Monsieur had a decided taste for luxury and splendour. His household was numerous, and kept up in the princely style in which it had first been lavishly appointed for him by Louis XV. There was none of the disorder that prevailed in that of the Comte d'Artois, who, however popular among the libertine set of the Duc de Chartres, and in the greenrooms of the Opéra and Comédie Française, was detested by the whole of his domestic establishment. The tone of authority and disdain in which he gave his orders; the extraordinary violence of his conduct at the slightest omission in executing them — which by his own fault, for he was much inclined to intemperance, sometimes happened — disgusted all who served him. He showed consideration for none; and strongly resenting this, all regarded him with feelings of utter dislike.

His insignificant little countess had neither distinction in her manners nor qualities of mind or disposition to counterbalance the evil effect of her husband's domestic tyranny. But he did not interfere with her amusements, nor she with his; so they, at all events, lived together in harmony. It was evidently, however, an object with Monsieur that his own and Madame's retired and busy mode of life, as well as their extreme courtesy, should present a striking contrast with the arrogance, frivolity, and dissipation of the Comte d'Artois and the queen.

The Duc de Chartres was not at this time on unfriendly terms with the king and queen, but was rather disposed to pay the latter considerable attention. The Duchesse de Chartres was distinguished above all the ladies of the court for the elegance and expensiveness of her *toilettes*. It was she who first introduced the jeweller Boëhmer, and the extravagant *modiste*, Mademoiselle Bertin, to the queen's apartments at Marly. This was contrary to all precedent. But Mademoiselle

Bertin, — who was, in fact, madame ; but no woman below the rank of the *haute bourgeoisie* had then the privilege when she married of passing in name from mademoiselle to the dignity of madame, until the Revolution abolished this stigma on women of her position, — Mademoiselle Bertin, then, would remain closeted for hours together at Marly, and afterwards at Versailles, in consultation with royalty in person on the fascinating subject of new fashions.

The invention of new costumes and head-dresses *de circonstance* of course required infinite thought for their appropriate adaptation ; for instance, to the *jeux de bagues*, — a revival, by the Comte d'Artois, of the games in vogue when Louis XIV. was young ; the queen, who presided, distributing the prizes. Or, again, for the English races ; introduced into France by the Duc de Chartres, who often crossed the Channel to purchase highbred racers. The English as a nation were detested by the French ; the king hated them as intensely as he hated the Austrians, and the queen loved them as little as she loved the French. But the young *noblesse* of the period, following the example of the duke, who was deeply bitten with Anglomania, entered eagerly into the spirit of this new amusement.

The races took place in the Plaine des Sablons, with, for the most part, "gentlemen riders," who had acquired their skill in this kind of horsemanship by training in England, or from two or three professional jockeys who rode the race with them. A sort of grand stand, elegantly decorated, was prepared for the queen, who attended with other ladies to animate by smiles — as in a tournament — the gay cavaliers who wore their colours. The favourite *coiffure* on these occasions was " *à l'anglomanie.*" But the people, though they assembled in crowds to see the races, looked with disfavour on the duke's fancy for English sports and fashions, and still more on the countenance given to them by the queen's presence. The libertine duke, who aped the notorious regent in all that was vilest in his conduct, lost some of his popularity with the Parisians on account of his Anglomania, and the queen was received by them with extreme coldness. Again, there were the hunting parties in the Bois de Boulogne (quite an innovation), which the queen joined, wearing a picturesque riding-costume, and a number of flying plumes in her mousquetaire hat. Her donkey promenades had been given up since that fatal day when, after a fall, she begged that "Madame Etiquette" — Madame de Noailles — might be asked how a Queen of France was to get up again, — an indiscretion that gave a new ally to the Bellevue circle.

Marie Antoinette had become a skilful horsewoman. She liked riding as an exercise, and persisted in it in spite of the unceasing remonstrances of the empress, who would have had her entirely refrain from attending the hunt, or be content to see the sport from her carriage. Very gay *petits soupers* followed these hunts, and Marie Antoinette enjoyed them amazingly. Later in the evening, she would contrive to lose five or six hundred or a thousand *louis d'or* at lansquenet, or other game of hazard. This, with her fondness for billiards, troubled Maria Theresa exceedingly. Reproach on reproach was constantly arriving from Vienna; threats of writing to the king to urge him to exert his marital authority and keep his wife in better order; prophecies of impending ruin, and long tirades on political events. But Marie Antoinette regarded them not. She was truly "at heart a rake," as woman in general has been accused of being, and warning voices were powerless to arrest her progress in that giddy whirl of dissipation which she so thoughtlessly had ventured to enter.

In the winter following the period of mourning for Louis XV., the young nobility, headed by the Comte d'Artois, made an attempt to bring again into vogue, as a court dress, the costumes of the reigns of François I. and Henri IV. To obtain the queen's sanction, says a contemporary writer, the Comtes de Provence and d'Artois; the Ducs de Coigny, de Lauzun, and de Durfort; the youthful **Marquis de La Fayette**; the **Comtes de la Marck**, de Noailles, and de Ségur; the Baron de

Besenval, no longer young, but full of *esprit* and vivacity, still handsome, a bachelor, too, and immensely rich, naturally, therefore, in high favour with the ladies ; and lastly, the handsome Édouard Dillon, between whom and the queen there was a sort of sentimental flirtation,— conjointly addressed a facetious petition to her majesty. They prayed to be allowed to appear at her balls in the old picturesque costume, and with plumes of feathers in their hats. "It is with a feather," said the petitioners, "that your majesty's humble slaves crave your permission to wear feathers. Should you graciously deign to accede to their request, this same feather with which they now write to you shall be employed, as long as their fingers are able to hold it, in celebrating your majesty's gracious condescension." Of course the request was granted.

The magnificent dress of the Comte d'Artois, and his tall plumes, rivalling the queen's in height, became him exceedingly well. His little countess is said to have actually fallen desperately in love with him then, to the court's very great amusement. To some other of the above named gentlemen the rich and picturesque costume was also highly advantageous ; but beyond the queen's intimate circle its attempted revival found no favour. The elderly courtiers were decidedly against it, and the spectacle presented by Monsieur and the king — whom the queen with some difficulty had prevailed on to wear it — waddling about, like two Falstaffs, in plumed hats, trunk-hose, etc., was much too grotesque to find imitators in men far less remarkable for *embonpoint* than were the fat royal brothers. However, this caprice of fashion continued to be more or less general that year at the carnival balls.

The carnival of 1775 was more brilliant than any that had for some years preceded it. Beaumarchais's play, "The Barber of Seville," was produced at this time, before an audience larger than any ever before assembled in the Théâtre Français. No production had been so vehemently opposed by the partisans of the Parliament Maupeou, who dreaded the satire, and the allusions the play was said to contain to Beaumarchais's late celebrated *procès* against the counsellor Goezman. Many omissions and alterations were insisted on by the government; but the play was immensely successful, and was performed without intermission to crowded houses until the close of the season, — an unusual thing at that period. The queen was present on several occasions. Indeed, not only into the gaieties, but into some of the rougher carnival amusements of the people she entered heart and soul; even, as she declared, enjoying greatly the disorderly Shrove Tuesday Saturnalia at Ramponneau's Courtille. Thus she already played, as it were, into the hands of her enemies, and gave colour to the strange reports then circulating in Paris respecting her. Libels were printed in England for transmission to the continent, and while all Paris was flocking to see Beaumarchais's play, he was secretly employed by the king to purchase and destroy a large edition of a scandalous book, then printing in London, to be forwarded to Amsterdam, and thence introduced into France. In the main, the charges therein brought against her were no doubt false. But to those who could test them only by appearances, they seem to be confirmed by the queen's open disregard for the *bienséances* which all women of rank were accustomed to observe, dissolute as the private lives of most of them were.

Try as we may to find excuses for her at this time, — in her youth, in the depravity of the court; her want of early moral training; in the bad advisers by whom she was constantly surrounded, and in the uncongenial nature of the king, — it must yet be confessed that her conduct was highly reprehensible. It is not surprising that the respect of the people should have been withdrawn from their queen, whom they continually recognised entering with highest zest into noisy public amusements, at places frequented by the disreputable of both sexes, and where it would have been thought degrading to the *maîtresse-en-titre* of the late king to appear.

In the spring of 1775 there occurred a serious

émeute in France. It began in the southern provinces; spread northward, and reached Versailles and Paris. It was caused by the high price of bread. Acting on the advice of M. Turgot, the king had abolished the monopoly in corn, and proclaimed the trade in it free. The agents of this monopoly resisted the decree. The peasantry, therefore, destroyed their mills, and committed other outrages. When the disturbance extended to Versailles, the king was advised to leave for Chambord. But he declined to do so, and endeavoured to address the assembled multitude from the balcony. Unable to obtain a hearing, he succeeded in calming the people by ordering the price of a loaf of bread to be reduced to two *sous*. But both at Versailles and Paris the bakers' shops were pillaged.

The mousquetaires were ordered out to guard the road to Versailles. The peasantry attacked them with stones. They replied with a volley of musketry, and twenty or more of the assailants were killed. Two of the ringleaders in this fray were afterwards tried, and were hanged on a gallows forty feet high. The rest then fled, some to Lille, others to Amiens, where, for a time, they continued their depredations. Paris had known nothing of public disturbance in its streets since the time of the Fronde. The Parisians were even disposed to make light of the present one. The police, however, were charged to protect the bakers' shops, in the event of any further attempt at a raid on them, and the bakers were ordered to sell their bread in accordance with the current price of corn. As soon as the incursive peasantry took their departure the people of Paris calmed down, and *chansons* and ironical epigrams appeared, addressed to the "brave mousquetaires" and their commander; while giddy fashion, utilising even this event for a new name to a head-dress, christened her latest creation the "*chapeau à la révolte.*"

It was then that M. Necker's name came prominently before the public, by means of the wide circulation of his pamphlet opposing M. Turgot's views on the corn trade. Those were trying times for a ministry of professed economists and philosophers, such as MM. Turgot and Malesherbes; for it was as difficult to carry out useful reforms as to continue the abuses of the old system. It was necessary that the head of the state, as M. Mignet observes, should have been powerful enough either to compel the privileged classes to submit to the reforms, or the nation to go on bearing its burdens, and Louis XVI. was neither a reformer nor a despot. But while the starving peasantry were crying for bread, millions of *francs* were being lavished at Versailles on *fêtes* and balls; and while the lower employés of the state, receiving then only half their salaries, and often none at all, were reduced to the greatest straits, the scanty resources of the treasury were at that time largely absorbed by the carrying out of the queen's frivolous fancies in the alterations at Trianon.

Another event that gave the mind of the economist minister many an anxious thought was the forthcoming coronation. Nothing definite was yet agreed on respecting it; but Louis declared that until he was crowned he should not consider himself actually king. *Fêtes* on a liberal scale were also in contemplation to celebrate the marriage of Madame Clotilde, the king's sister. She had been betrothed to the Prince of Savoy at the time the two princesses, his sisters, had married the Comtes de Provence and d'Artois. Being now in her thirteenth year, Madame Clotilde — or "Gros Madame," as she was familiarly called, from her extraordinary *embonpoint* — was to leave France for the court of Savoy soon after the coronation. Meanwhile, she and her younger sister, Elisabeth — who had an ample share, it appears, of her family's wonderful obesity — were receiving lessons in Italian from Goldoni.

The preparations for the above auspicious events were not yet complete when the young Archduke Maximilian, brother of Marie Antoinette, paid a visit to Versailles. He was travelling *incognito*, as Comte de Burgau, and was accompanied by the minister, Count Rosenberg, and his governor, the Count Lamberg. One object of his travels was his installation at

Brussels as coadjutor of the Grand Mastership of the Teutonic Order. After this ceremony he was to proceed to Cologne to be received there as Prince-Elector. As regarded the important sayings and doings at the court of France of this heavy German boy of fourteen, the empress desired that the Counts Rosenberg and Lamberg would so guide the royal youth that he might not be politically misinterpreted; and that to enable them to do so they should seek counsel from Marie Antoinette. But Maximilian was not a youth of sufficient promise to inspire any interest at the French court. His manners were awkward, and his acknowledgments of the attentions shown him were repeated in the *salons* with much laughter.

His well-known reply to the courtly Comte de Buffon, who received him when he visited the Jardin du Roi, amused all Paris. On taking leave M. de Buffon presented the young archduke with an elegantly bound copy of his works. Maximilian, putting it from him, said: "I should be sorry, Monsieur, to deprive you of it." What an astounding rebuff for the *écrivain, grand seigneur!* and how it must have diverted the *beaux esprits* of the *salons*. Yet these boyish mistakes, though at the time occasioning some mirth in court circles, and causing some slight vexation to the queen, with Maximilian's departure would have been speedily forgotten.

Unfortunately, however, the visit of Maximilian was destined in its results to be a lasting misfortune to the queen. Travelling *incognito*, the young archduke should, on his arrival, have paid a visit to the princes of the blood. This was the etiquette, even in the case of crowned heads. But Marie Antoinette, with her accustomed disdain of the conventionalities of the court of France, absolutely refused to allow this, and expected that the princes of the blood should waive their right to this courtesy, and hasten to pay their respects to her boy brother. The princes declined; and their conduct was approved even at Vienna, where it was generally thought that the archduke should have accepted what was offered, but exacted nothing, being *incognito*. So writes the empress, though she does not say that she also approves. But the queen, with her usual vehemence, expressed to the Comte de la Marck her astonishment at the conduct of the Princes d'Orléans, de Condé, and de Penthièvre. "She not only expected their visit," he writes, "but *fêtes* to be given by them in honour of the archduke."

Perceiving how much she was disappointed, says the count, the court proposed to the young nobles of the queen's private circle that they should conjointly give a *fête* to the archduke. Monsieur and the Comte d'Artois having been prevailed upon to place themselves at the head of it, the rest soon consented. The royal riding house was prepared for the occasion, lavishly decorated, and a theatre and temporary rooms erected around it. A grand fancy-dress ball was given; and Flemish and Hungarian quadrilles were arranged. After the ball there was a play, then a grand supper, and a little gambling by way of a *finale*. It was a brilliant affair, we are told, kept up with much spirit until break of day.

The princes of the blood were excluded, and considered themselves pointedly insulted, — the Duc de Chartres more strongly than others expressing this feeling. Hitherto he had rarely let a day pass without paying his court to the queen. His courtesy and deference towards her were exceeded by none in her circle. He now refrained from appearing at Versailles until after the departure of the archduke. The queen then received him with very great coldness, and on an explanation taking place gave way to her temper, while M. de Chartres insisted that the *incognito* of the archduke fully justified the course he and the other princes had taken. But the queen chose rather to infer that the French princes were too arrogant to condescend, as they thought, to pay the first visit to an Austrian archduke. Assuming a haughty tone, she said: "The king received him as a brother, and he supped in private with him and his family — an honour to which, I presume, you do not pretend." The duke made no reply — merely bowed and withdrew. Other circumstances afterwards added rancour to the ill-feeling then inspired on both sides; but from that time there was enmity between the Duc de Chartres and Marie Antoinette. It does not appear that the king was appealed to or that he interfered in the matter at all.

Every detail of this occurrence was soon known throughout Paris; and the Orléans family being resident in the capital, their influence there was great. Indignation consequently was general among the Parisians when they heard that "the Autrichienne had insulted the first prince of the blood." Even the court openly expressed dissatisfaction with the queen and the archduke. And it was asserted that the real motive of his visit was to conceal the object of Count Rosenberg's mission, — to ask money and men from France to aid the empress in her struggle with the Moldavian provinces.

CHAPTER VII.

Which Shall It Be? — An Irreverent Proposal. — The Sainte Ampoule. — The Coronation Oath. — M. Turgot Overruled. — The Last Crowned Queen of France. — The Cost of a Queen's Whim. — The New State Carriage. — The New Crown. — Arrival at Rheims. — The Cathedral of Rheims. — Where Is the King? — "*Elle Me Gêne!*" — *Vive le Roi!* " — Healing the Sick. —" *Le Pauvre Homme!* " — Visiting the Abbaye de Saint-Rémi. — Ungrateful Human Nature. — The Queen's Sage Reflections. — A Gratifying Reward. — Clotilde and Elisabeth. — The Royal Carmelite Nun. — Goldoni at Versailles. — The Heir-presumptive.

REAT curiosity prevailed in Paris and Versailles, and indeed throughout France, concerning the ceremony to be observed at the approaching coronation. Was there to be any departure from the ancient rites? Was it to be a splendid ecclesiastical service and state pageant, or, as nearly as possible, a mere official ceremony? Both these courses found advocates — the former in the court and clergy, the latter in the economists and philosophers.

M. Turgot proposed first that the coronation, in order that, as a spectacle, it might be more imposing, should take place in the capital, and the king be crowned at Notre-Dame, giving as a further reason for preferring Paris to Rheims, that it would be a saving of two millions to the state.

Crowned at Paris! and that the treasury might economise two millions!

The clergy raised their eyes and hands to heaven in deprecation of the audacious irreverence of such a proposal. The king was also much startled by it. Under the guidance of MM. Turgot and Malesherbes he was becoming imbued with philosophical views, and, as those ministers explained them, desirous of seeing them carried into practice. But, yielding as he was, he on this point entirely dissented from them. For it appeared to him that a King of France not crowned at Rheims could hardly be recognised by the French nation as its crowned king. It also clashed with his devotional feelings to be crowned elsewhere. An expenditure of two millions on the ceremony was indeed most grievous to him. Still, he determined to follow the custom of his ancestors. From Clovis to Louis XV. there had been but a solitary instance of departure from it,—that of the heretic monarch Henri IV.

With the grand old cathedral of Rheims many of the great historical souvenirs of France were also closely associated. And greater than all, as regarded the question of the coronation, was it not there that angel hands had delivered to the holy archbishop, Saint Remi, the sacred phial or Sainte Ampoule, brought by them direct from heaven for the anointing of Clovis; and whose miraculously inexhaustible supply of holy oil was to serve for all time for the anointing of that most Christian king's successors?* It was definitively decided then that no change should take place, the king should be crowned at Rheims. The first thing to be done was to repair the roads throughout the route to be taken by the royal procession; and this could be done only by the "*corvée*," or forced and unpaid labour of the peasantry, — a cruelly oppressive system, which M. Turgot was anxious to abolish. However, on this occasion, it was rigorously enforced, and the work urged on with much speed. It being early spring when the unfortunate people were called on to perform this labour, their own farming and field work and other agricultural employments were of course wholly neglected. But the roads and the bridges being put into good order, the poor wretches were free to return home and starve; for as no crops had been sown they had none to reap. Half famished already, some of them perished on the roads they had repaired. The greater number plodded wearily back to their homes, begging alms as they went of the great grandees they met on their way to the *fêtes*. Poor people! they will some day have their re-

---

* Ruhl, who in 1793 was the representative of the people of Rheims, seized the Sainte Ampoule, when the cathedral was pillaged, and, dashing it on the ground, broke it to pieces.

venge; but the poor and oppressed are always long-suffering.

The indignation of the clergy towards M. Turgot was further excited by his strongly expressed objection to some portions of the formula of the coronation oath, as well as of the ceremony itself. That the king should solemnly declare he would never pardon duellists appeared to M. Turgot's philosophical mind absurd. "That he would use every means in his power to put an end to the practice of duelling," he suggested was preferable. Again, he considered it shocking to every feeling of humanity that the king, on receiving the holy oil, should vow to exterminate a portion of his subjects — the heretics. "Should not the monarch's protection be extended to all peaceable and industrious citizens, even should their religious faith differ from his?" He was of opinion, too, that the dignity of the crown suffered by the excessive homage paid to the Church, in the king being required to remain for a considerable time kneeling beside the archbishop. But the philosopher smiled at the idea of the dissipated young men, as, for the most part, were the peers of the realm of 1775, placing their hands on the crown when put on the king's head, to indicate that they, like the rough and ready followers of Hugh Capet in 987 — when this part of the ceremony was introduced — were its stanchest and strongest supporters. But M. Turgot was overruled in all his suggestions. The preparations went on, and, in spite of his efforts, lavish expenditure rather than economy was the order of the day.

The Empress Maria Theresa was extremely anxious that Marie Antoinette should be crowned at Rheims with the king. The reason then given for the queens of Louis XIII., Louis XIV., and Louis XV. not having been crowned was that the coronation of those kings had taken place before their marriage. But the last crowned queen of France, Marie de' Medici, married Henri IV. several years after his accession; and she had been ten years his wife when her coronation took place with great state at St. Denis — the king assisting only as a spectator. He had given his consent to it from the double motive of deferring to the queen's oft urged wishes on the subject, and his intention of appointing her regent of the kingdom during his projected absence in Belgium. But on the following day he was assassinated.

Marie Antoinette was singularly indifferent to the wishes of the empress on this occasion. She evinced not the slightest inclination to be crowned; and indeed, it was only at Vienna that such an event seems to have been expected or desired. A priest of the Oratoire, after examining several old records, had written a pamphlet on the coronation of the queens of France. As it was favourable to the empress's views, it was presented to the king by the Duc de Duras at the Comte de Mercy's request. Nothing, however, resulted from it. M. de Maurepas and M. Turgot probably saw no reason for offering the crown to a queen who showed no desire to wear it.

But as soon as it was finally determined that Rheims was to be the scene of the coronation, she announced her intention to be present. A complete suite of apartments for the queen, her ladies, and her retinue, had therefore to be temporarily erected, nothing suited to the purpose being available on the spot. M. Turgot's righteous spirit groaned within him. The two millions at which he had estimated the cost of the king's obstinacy, and which for months had danced like a hideous spectre before his mind's eye, were joined by another two millions,— for he laid at no less a sum the cost of the queen's whim. Rheims, it seems, could furnish for the occasion nothing but a swarm of priests. Both workmen and building materials must be sent from Paris. Night and day couriers were travelling between the two cities carrying orders and messages to and fro. Numberless wagons, following each other in quick succession, were laden with splendid furniture, mirrors, lustres, services of porcelaine, plate, etc. Relays of *fourgons* carried to Rheims for the queen's apartments a varied collection of richest materials, for draping the walls, covering the floors, for window and door hangings, bed-curtains, etc.

The new state carriage was building in Paris. Its ample interior was furnished with luxurious lounges and cushions of satin and gold, for the repose of the weary limbs of the wayworn travellers. The panels were elaborately painted, and the height of this costly vehicle, with its figures and ornaments, was eighteen feet. An unusual elevation of the roof was requisite, that the queen might, without inconvenience, sit upright in order to allow the admiring or astonished multitude to gaze on her wonderful head-dress. The coronation afforded a very wide scope for the display of Léonard's great talent. And he was most anxious to acquit himself well, that the queen might be visibly justified in a matter for which she had been blamed, — the banishment of her *coiffeuse.* For before Marie Antoinette became queen-consort, masculine hands were not permitted to touch the heads of the queens of France.

At Soissons, one of the old towns on the route, the royal carriage had a narrow escape from being brought to a standstill. The ancient gateway was much too low to admit it. Happily this was observed on the morning before the expected arrival of the royal party. The top of the gateway was hastily taken down and put out of sight *pro tem.;* while to supply its place a framework of wood was run up to the required height and covered with flags or other coloured materials. This had a far more festive appearance, the town-people thought, than the old low gray gate of Soissons.

The making of the new crown, or a new arrangement of the jewels composing it — in which were comprised the twelve Mazarin diamonds and the Sancy and Regent — was entrusted to Aubert, the crown jeweller at that time. The Parisian public were for a day or two gratified with the sight of this fine jewelled cap, which poor Louis XVI. found so heavy. It was valued at 20,000,000 *francs* (£800,000).

The two months preceding the coronation were sorely trying ones to Mdlle. Bertin and her workwomen. But at last, as nearly as possible, the queen's toilets were completed and forwarded to Rheims in the charge of a numerous staff of *conturières*, *coiffeurs*, and tiring-women. The journey from Versailles to Rheims was to be a royal progress, of which the particulars were made known to the people by public proclamation. On the 5th of June the royal pageant set out from the château on its way to Compiègne. There it rested for a day; thence proceeded to Fismes, and arrived at Rheims on the 9th, when the keys of the city were presented to the king on a golden salver by the Duc de Bourbon, Governor of Champagne. Salvos of artillery, the pealing of bells, and the acclamations of the people, announced their majesties' arrival, as they had accompanied them throughout their journey. This was according to order certainly, yet acclamations would have been freely forthcoming though no commands for them had been issued. True, the country people were too generally starving, and indications of deep and widespread distress continually met the eyes of the young king and queen. But "good Louis XVI." once crowned, they said, the looked-for blessings of his reign would begin, and the *poule-au-pot* soon follow.

Having made this entry into Rheims, the king's first act, according to the programme, is to alight from his carriage and fall on his knees at the grand gate of the cathedral. The book of the Gospel is then handed to him to kiss. This done, there is brought from the king's carriage a splendidly wrought gold cup, or chalice, as an offering to God, to be preserved in the cathedral of Rheims, which he is now permitted to enter that he may place his gift on the altar. In the evening the king attends vespers, and on the following day (10th of June) the ceremony of the Sacre is to take place.

The coronation is doubtless a grand and imposing spectacle. The cathedral is draped with crimson cloth of gold. On the right of the altar, arrayed in their red and violet robes, point lace, gold crosses and chains, and wearing their mitres, sit the ecclesiastical peers, — the great grandees of the Church. On the left, in their mantles of state, stand the temporal peers of the realm. The masses of gold and brilliant colours are relieved by the long white surplices, laced or otherwise, of the clergy of lower rank — their stoles more or less ornamented, according to the degree of precedence they take. Then there are the uniforms, naval and military, various in colour, and most of them richly embroidered in silver or gold. As early as break of day the old basilica begins to fill with a brilliant crowd. The tribunes and galleries of the nave are occupied by ladies in full court dress. Their pearls and diamonds, gold and precious stones, together with the splendid *toilettes* of the queen and her retinue, their lofty plumes, their powder and rouge, rich velvets and lace, form no mean part of the show. The *corps diplomatique*, headed by the nuncio, are there; and in the choir, ranged one above another, in the form of an amphitheatre, are six hundred seats, occupied by the invited guests.

But amongst this glittering throng one descries not the king. He waits in the sacristy, whither two of the dignitaries of the Church proceed to lead him to the front of the high altar. A scene then ensues in some respects resembling that of a bishop refusing at his consecration to be made a bishop. The two dignitaries knock loudly at the door of the sacristy. The door is not opened, and no inquiry is made as to whom they seek or what they want. After a while, they knock again, and with the same result. Louder, they make their third appeal, and this time with a demand for "Louis XVI., whom God hath given them for king."

The door forthwith flies open and Louis XVI. appears. He wears an ecclesiastical vestment called a *dalmatique*. It is of violet velvet embroidered in gold with *fleurs-de-lys*. He has velvet boots and gold spurs. The heavy velvet mantle of state is placed on his shoulder. The archbishop anoints him with the seven unctions of the Sacre, and cries aloud : " *Vivat rex in æternum.*" The sceptre and hand of justice are then presented to the king. It is a hot June day. He is ready to sink under the weight of these trappings of royalty, though the pages that attend him do their best to relieve him of a portion of his burden. The grand old organ peals forth as he approaches the altar. The fresh young voices of the choristers thrilling through the cathedral and rising up to heaven, as it were, above the deep-toned basses, as they sing the impressive choral service, might well fill with emotion and overpower a stronger mind than the young king's. How startling, too, must have been the effect when, during a *sotto voce* passage of the service, the archbishop placed the crown on the king's head, and he, suddenly raising his hand, thrust it aside, exclaiming aloud, " *Elle me gêne !*" And truly he was destined to find it *gênant* in every sense. Henri III. had said, " *Elle me pique !*" All knew what had been his end.

allowed to receive M. de Choiseul, with whom she had a private conversation that lasted two hours." Her letter was read by both Maria Theresa and the Emperor Joseph, who were alarmed both at her want of discretion and at the epithet "*pauvre homme*" applied to the king, and as ironically used by the French, quoting from Molière's "Tartuffe."

The queen's interview with M. de Choiseul occasioned a great commotion among the ministers. This amused Marie Antoinette, who encouraged the report that she had prevailed on the king to send M. d'Aiguillon into exile, to displace M. Turgot, and to give him a successor of her naming. But unfortunately it was circulated amongst the people that the queen was striving to overthrow the ministry, because of its liberal views, its anti-Austrian sentiments, and the restraint it imposed on her extravagance. The Choiseul party were extremely annoyed by the queen's imprudence. They considered their interests compromised by it; and it was the duke's advice, transmitted to her through the Comte de Mercy (for when put out of temper he still spoke his mind very freely), that she would do well, both for her present advantage and with a view to what might possibly happen in the future, to abstain from some of her pleasures and amusements and seek to gain the favour of the people. The king was made aware of this little episode, not included in the general programme, but towards which he had unwittingly contributed on the day allotted to repose. But it formed no part of his system to remonstrate. When displeased he was only rather more cold and churlish than usual.

A grand cavalcade to the Abbaye de Saint Remi took place on the following day, and, for the time being, all complaints and dissatisfaction were laid aside, to be reproduced at a more convenient season. On the morrow the *Fête Dieu* was celebrated with unusual pomp, forming a magnificent *finale* to the series of coronation ceremonies. One departure, however, from the customary observances of this *fête*, and which in some degree marred the splendour of the scene, was made at the king's request. The ancient tapestries, splendid carpets, and silk and gold hangings, always forthcoming at the *Fête Dieu*, to decorate the fronts of the houses, and which give a quaintly picturesque and festive appearance to a fine old continental town, were omitted on the present occasion. The king thought they would deprive him of the sight of some of his subjects; and, worse still, that some of his loyal lieges might be deprived by them of the sight of him.

How ungrateful is human nature! With shame be it said, that, as the procession dragged its slow length along on that hot summer day, the fat young monarch was often saluted with shouts of laughter and the exclamation: "*Bon gros papa!*" and even far less complimentary epithets, — Monsieur also coming in for an ample share of these liberally bestowed salutations. But most of these ill-bred hilarious persons were not aware that those two fat youths, who might have been exhibited at a fair, were actually the king and his brother, the heir expectant, — so little divinity seemed to hedge the former, or royal dignity the latter. But Louis XVI. took these mistakes of the people in good part; Monsieur was considerably annoyed.

Of fêting and feasting there had now been more than enough, so that all were prepared to take flight the next day, — all except workmen and workwomen, couriers, etc.; for Rheims had been so thoroughly upset that it took a fortnight or more to restore it to its wonted quietude and religiously peaceful aspect. Meanwhile, the royal party arrived at Compiègne, where a grand ball was given.

From Compiègne the queen wrote to the empress: "Throughout the journey I did my best to acknowledge the eager acclamations of the people, and although the heat was intense and the crowd great, I do not regret the fatigue it caused me, as my health has not suffered from it. It is really astonishing, and a happy thing too, to have been so well received only two months after the revolt, and notwithstanding that bread is still dear. It is a remarkable trait in the French character that it allows itself to be carried away by bad suggestions and returns immediately to good ones. For my part, should I live for a hundred years, I shall never forget the coronation day."

A more circumstantial account of the ceremony was soon after forwarded to Vienna. It was from the pen of Marmontel, who had attended at Rheims in virtue of his office of *Historiographe de France*. Both king and queen were so well pleased with his narrative that he thought himself on the highroad to favour. The queen ordered his operettas of "Sylvain" and "*L'ami de la maison*" to be performed at Trianon, and on passing him after the performance said: "*Marmontel, c'est charmant!*" But from that time she seemed to have forgotten both the historiographer and his plays, and never again noticed him, — even when on one occasion she expressed in his presence her admiration of the music that Grétry had composed to Marmontel's libretto. Grétry, much flattered by being thus publicly complimented by the queen, turned towards the poet.

"Ah, my friend," he said, "what a gratifying reward for composing a few pleasing pieces of music!"

"Yes," replied Marmontel, "and for having written the detestable words to them."

On the return of the court to Versailles, a

series of balls, operas, plays, ballets, and other festivities took place, in honour of Madame Clotilde, who, poor child, enjoyed them not at all. Clotilde had a great affection for her family, and was overwhelmed with grief at the idea of leaving her relatives and her country. Between her and her younger sister, Elisabeth, there was a very strong attachment, and while others were dancing the two girls sat together embraced, weeping at their approaching separation. The royal marriages of that day were indeed cruel, — mere children being unscrupulously sacrificed to the political or ambitious views of their parents; while, as often as not, unforeseen events thwarted, or entirely upset, the objects for which these repulsive child-marriages were arranged. Marie Antoinette was far more the victim of her mother's unscrupulous ambition and political intrigues to accomplish her views on France, than of her own follies and gross indiscretions.

Clotilde was now thirteen, Elisabeth eleven. The despair of the latter when she was told that Clotilde had left — for the precise moment of departure was concealed from her — was so great that it was found difficult to console her. Brought up by Mesdames, the two girls had imbibed their aunts' prejudices against Marie Antoinette. It was therefore suggested that instead of remaining at Versailles with the queen, Elisabeth should be placed for a time with Madame Louise, the Carmelite nun. But the king interposed and forbade this. He probably thought one Carmelite nun in the family even more than enough. For Madame Louise troubled him exceedingly, and would have had him guided by her in all matters concerning the Church, she being directed, of course, by her spiritual pastors and masters, — zealous fanatics, wild for the overthrow of MM. Turgot and Malesherbes. Yet Madame, or rather Sister Louise, whatever may have originally been her motive for taking the veil, had found convent life agree so remarkably well with her that, from a poor little thin withered thing when she entered the convent, she had become, in the course of the five years spent there, as fat and rosy as some others of her family. She was able too, and with much enjoyment it appeared, as a congenial occupation, to take her turn at the washing tubs of the convent laundry.

Rescued from this fate, but reserved for a worse, poor little Madame Elisabeth, by the king's order, made her home at Versailles. Young companions were found for her, and Goldoni continued to amuse her with Italian lessons. "This princess," he says, "was gentle and amiable, but of an age disposed rather for amusement than study." She rebelled against his attempt to introduce declensions and conjugations into her studies. So Goldoni did his best to entertain and instruct his royal pupil by striving to make her comprehend short, lively passages from Italian plays, which they performed together, aided by the young lady in waiting. For a time, he says, she was pleased and amused. But Goldoni himself was not.

He had his apartment at Versailles, but did not like it. The winds he found unusually violent there, and they entered the château, he says, from all quarters, giving him pains in the head, affecting his nerves, affecting his temper, and, in short, making him very desirous of finding a more cosy abode in his old age than the comfortless upper chambers of the royal château. By and by Mesdames obtained for him an increase of pension, — he had taught them Italian in their youth, — and Goldoni retired to Paris, where, as he relates, both the atmosphere and the society were far more congenial to him.

Soon after these events the little Comtesse d'Artois presented her husband with a son (the Duc d'Angoulême). On being informed of the sex of her child, she exclaimed with much vehemence, for a lady in her interesting position, "*Bon Dieu! que je suis heureuse!*" the queen being present and ready to exclaim, "*Ah, Dieu! que je suis malheureuse!*" The sum of a thousand *louis d'or* and a pair of handsome diamond bracelets were the reward of the countess for presenting France with the first heir presumptive to the throne.

CHAPTER VIII.

The *Salons;* Louis XV. — "Mother of the Philosophers." — La Marquise du Deffand. — The Walpole Correspondence. — Poor Madame Necker! — Mdlle. l'Espinasse. — Mesdames Necker and Geoffrin. — Necker's "*Éloge de Colbert.*" — A Celestial Countenance. — M. Necker's Early Career. — A Genial Host. — An Anxious Hostess. — Madame de Condorcet. — Rival *Salons.* — MM. Turgot and Necker. — The Economist's Downfall. — Check, to the Queen. — The Higher Clergy in Conclave. — The Abbé Talleyrand-Périgord. — Presumptuous Protestants. — The Divine Necker in Disguise. — M. de Maurepas's Godson. — The Clamours of the Clergy.

THE Parisian *salons* of the reign of Louis XV. enjoyed a so wide-spread celebrity that foreigners of highest distinction, and even crowned heads, when visiting the French capital, sought introduction to them as a privilege. But in 1776 those *salons* for the most part were either wholly extinct — as that of Madame de Tencin and some others — or their glory had waned, if it had not entirely departed, and their career, like that of the ladies who so gracefully had presided over them, was hastening to a close.

Such were the *salons* of Madame Geoffrin and Madame du Deffand, — for both were supposed still to receive. But what a falling off from the days when brilliant conversational talent, liveliness, and wit, with that perfect observance of the usages of *la bonne compagnie* which made these *réunions* so delightful, and drew together the *élite* of society and the leading members of the world of art and of letters! The convivial weekly dinners to the *gens de lettres* had long since been given up; and the gay *petits soupers*, for the chosen few of the *beau monde*, were now heard of no more.

Through the pious vigilance of an anxious daughter, Madame Geoffrin, then approaching her eightieth year, had in some degree been lured from that gay world of whose votaries she had long been so distinguished a leader, and induced to turn her thoughts towards that unknown one she ere long was to enter. Yet curiosity to see the far-famed "mother of the philosophers" often impelled foreign princes and ambassadors still to visit her. The survivors of the old philosophic band, and the younger men who had imbibed in her *salon* the principles that by and by were to revolutionise France, and in whose advancement or social merits she was interested, were yet constant in their devotion to her. The extreme watchfulness of her daughter — who was somewhat of a devotee — to hold these latter aloof, as disturbing by their presence her mother's serenity of mind, was sometimes resented by Madame Geoffrin herself, as depriving her of the solace she still found in the congenial society of her old friends. Yet her philosophical opinions had been to a great extent modified for a considerable time; and she had never forgiven Marmontel for publishing "Bélisaire" in 1766, though she did not withdraw from him the *entrée* to her *salons*.

Madame Geoffrin having left the world's stage in 1777, there remained of those famous *femmes célèbres* of the old *régime* only the still more aged Marquise du Deffand. In her youth cold, selfish, cynical, an atheist, and without a particle of feeling for any one but herself, she continued unchanged as a blind old woman of eighty. She was perhaps even something more venomous than in her earlier years. In the tiny rooms of her convent apartment, the scandal of the day was still brought to her by old gossips of both sexes. This — dressed up after the mood she was in at the time — she repeated for the benefit of Horace Walpole. How vigorously she clung to Walpole, notwithstanding his many rebuffs! Her correspondence with him furnished her with a secret outlet for spite and dissatisfaction; and it was with a sort of zest that enlivened her dreary existence that she reported as her opinions, and stated as facts, many things wholly at variance with facts and with her communications to others.

It was, however, with a mingled feeling of pity and curiosity that, during the last three or four years of her life, strangers in Paris occasionally saw this poor old blind woman — the once renowned *monstre d'esprit* — led in by the hand and placed in an arm-chair reserved for her in the philosophic *salon* of the learned Madame Necker. The marquise professed great esteem for M. Necker's character and abilities, and found her reward accordingly; for M. Necker was thought by his wife and young daughter to possess most of the attributes of divinity. She recognised also much merit and *esprit* in madame, but here the marquise would pause for awhile; it was so painful to her to utter a word that seemed like disparagement of her excellent friend, — a friend whose suppers were so much better than any she now partook of elsewhere, that they reminded her of the *petits soupers* of the days, or nights, of the olden time.

"Yes, Madame Necker had a sweet, insinuating voice, and, as the marquise was told, a charming face and fine figure. She possessed all the home virtues, and was one of the few really learned women of that day; but unfortunately her nature was unsympathetic, and much as she desired to make herself agreeable, poor thing, she had not the talent of making herself liked. With all the *esprit* and vivacity too, of her own conversation, she yet wanted that certain kind of facility possessed by some" — the marquise probably alluded to herself — " of imparting *esprit* to the person with whom she conversed, and which in fact formed," as she said, "the art of conversing." Poor Madame Necker!

Madame Necker's *salon* was known as the "*Salon Helvétique,*" a term applied to it by those who, impelled by jealousy or political feeling, chose to express superciliously that it was not to be classed with the *salons français.* Yet Madame Geoffrin's *salon* was the model on which it was founded, and Madame Necker aspired to take up that lady's falling sceptre and to assume her place in society. If, as yet, the visits of the *beau monde* to the *salons* of the wealthy Swiss banker's wife were but few and far between, on the other hand, learning and philosophy were not backward in showing their appreciation of the merits of the new establishment, — of the mental gifts of the lady who presided, and the superior talent of the banker's *chef de cuisine.*

The death of the sentimental Mdlle. de l'Espinasse, who reigned over D'Alembert's modest home, and presided at his encyclopædical *réunions,* had deprived many of the philosophers and encyclopædists of a social *salon* and a supper. The lady had lately departed this life, aged forty-four, the victim of unrequited love for an interesting young Spaniard, leaving poor D'Alembert inconsolable for her loss, and his friends lamenting their supper.

For, whatever the object of a *réunion,* — whether general conversation, music, cards, playing at proverbs, *bouts-rimés,* and forfeits, or the discussion of the graver subjects of literature and politics, — a light, lively supper of kickshaws and champagne, served up with plenty of laughter and repartee, was the invariably looked-for conclusion. All these, and the good things of life in general, the needy men of letters found amply supplied at M. and Madame Necker's *petits soupers.*

Diderot, indeed, declared that he was far more at his ease there than ever he had been at Madame Geoffrin's. For, singularly enough, Madame Necker, who aspired to be the "friend and protectress of the philosophers," and who was a strict Calvinist Protestant, was much less vigilant to restrain the profane conversation of such men as Diderot and the Abbé Raynal than was Madame Geoffrin, "the mother of the sect," and who was supposed to have no religion at all. But Madame Geoffrin had adopted the maxim of Saint Paul, that all things should be done decently and in order. So that, as she thought it due to her position to have her box at the Opéra and the Théâtre Français, she felt it equally incumbent on her to have her own specially reserved seats at St. Sulpice and St. Roch. A taste and excessive enthusiasm for literature enabled the classically educated Madame Necker to tolerate with complacency Diderot's threadbare coat and soiled linen; while Madame Geoffrin, with more regard for *les bienséances,* only tolerated them in her *salon* with a shudder. This may account for his feeling sometimes ill at ease there. It was only, then, as a purely literary *salon* that Madame Necker's could have rivalled Madame Geoffrin's. It was the accident of passing events that gave it pre-eminence afterwards.

But Madame Necker and her *salon* had not yet arrived at their destined zenith of glory, for M. Necker had not yet secured the great object of his ambition, — the control of the finances of France. He was only intriguing to secure it, or allowing another to intrigue for him, while he was diligently seeking popularity by issuing pamphlets, whose aim was to bring M. Turgot and his system into disrepute. His "*Éloge de Colbert*" — of which Voltaire said there was in it "as much exaggeration as truth, and as many obscure phrases as clear ones" — was written less as a tribute of respect for the enlightened judgment and far-seeing views of a great statesman, than as affording an opportunity of pointing disparagingly, though indirectly, to the means adopted for the removing of abuses, and the abolishing of unjust imposts, by the minister who stood between him and the post he so ardently coveted.

Neither in person nor manners did M. Necker possess the qualities that usually inspire popularity. He appears to have been a tall, very stout man, with a countenance of so singular a type that writers of the time who were acquainted with him

Necker.

Photo-etching from an Old Print.

Mr. NECKER.
Ancien Directeur Général des Finances.

can find no other words to describe it than "very strange," "most extraordinary," "resembling no other," "quite unique." But Madame Necker, who wrote her husband's "*Éloge*" — which was published, with his sanction, during his lifetime — says that his countenance was "celestial;" that it was impossible to look on it without admiration and even becoming deeply affected; while there was a something so indefinably heavenly in its expression "that no painters had ever dared to attempt to depict it, except in the faces of angels."

M. Necker, as we learn from other authorities, was in the habit of carrying this wonderful head of his very erect. Its features were large and prominent, and his manner of wearing his hair, brushed up in a lofty toupet on his forehead, and rolled in a thick sort of curl sitting close to his face on each side, added not a little to the singularity of the whole. There was much gravity in his manners, and a certain air of importance, denoting that M. Necker was thoroughly convinced of his own transcendent merits, and of the accuracy of his wife's judgment, when she daily proclaimed him a god. "Yet," says a French historian (Amadée Renée), "there was nothing in Necker that pleases, dazzles, or subjugates men. He had not the attribute of seductiveness. Firmness was the dominant quality of his mind, but it was firmness that rather alienated than subdued."

M. Necker, first a clerk, then a partner, in the

Swiss banking-house of Thellusson and Co., had realised a splendid fortune at a comparatively early age. (He was forty-four at the period referred to, 1776.) His ambition grew with his fortunes, and the Swiss Cantons having lately appointed him their resident, — an office that invested him with some diplomatic functions, — he bought an elegant hôtel, and, with a wife devoted to the furthering of his interests to do the honours, threw open his *salons*. There a welcome awaited as many of the philosophic brotherhood, the literary world, and the *beau monde*, as chose to visit him and partake of his hospitality. And the circle soon became numerous. It was, however, speedily discovered that Madame Necker, so unwearyingly occupied with endeavouring to make her dinners, her evening receptions, and suppers, pleasant to her guests, was by no means exerting herself for the sake of those guests, but entirely for the exaltation of her husband.

She desired that those around her table should recognise in M. Necker the sublime being she saw in him herself; that their hearts and minds should be drawn towards him; that they should sound his praises in other *salons*; and, in fact, that his name should be echoed far and wide by the trumpet of literary fame. The host himself meanwhile sat a silent, frigid spectator of all that wifely devotion was striving to accomplish, as well for his amusement as in his honour.

"With the exception of a few subtle words thrown into the conversation at long intervals, Necker was habitually dumb," says Marmontel, who with the academician, M. Thomas, was one of Madame Necker's first literary guests. He received the company civilly, but without cordiality, and left the task of entertaining them entirely to his wife. Her extreme anxiety to keep up conversation unflaggingly, and to a certain point of brilliancy, to prevent any awkward pauses, or to reply herself to any flash of wit that met with no immediate rejoinder from others, was one of the causes of that painfully nervous malady from which later on she suffered so terribly.

It was, however, not very complimentary, thought many of the guests, to be invited to dinner merely to admire the superb M. Necker, and to amuse him, as with a sort of *spectacle*. For Necker, with his head thrown back, his eyes glancing upwards, and his thoughts apparently in the seventh heaven, deigned only occasionally to come down from the lofty heights — to which in imagination he had doubtless been soaring — to cast a benignant, approving smile on the philosophy and learning which his genius and virtues, as he fancied and as his wife told him, had gathered around him. If, as happened at times, a feeling of languor, sympathetically, as it were, overspread the whole company, Madame Necker, in the agitated state of her mind, would naïvely complain to her friend Marmontel. "Why complain, madame," he would reply. "The wittiest cannot always be witty; and the most amiable are not always in an amiable mood. Observe M. Necker; even he is not always amusing." This must have sounded strangely in madame's ears. Was it not a condescension on the part of the sublime Necker to allow himself to be amused?

But if M. Necker's novel mode of playing the host imposed restraint on his own guests, it inspired much mirth among the company at other *réunions*, and especially in the *salon* of the beautiful Madame de Condorcet. There D'Alembert, Suard, Marmontel, and Grimm often spent the evening, and took supper. One or other of them had probably on the same day sat at M. Necker's convivial board. Full details would then be eagerly sought, and often were given, it may be conjectured with much exaggeration, of the manner in which the lofty financier had borne himself. The anxious madame's flashes of wit, described, unfairly perhaps, as being usually flashes in the pan, were duly repeated, and of course imparted more zest to the supper than they had originally given to the dinner. Even the sayings and doings of the odd little girl, Anne-Germaine, who was present at all the Necker *réunions*, and often made very droll and amusing remarks, were garnered up by Necker's treacherous guests, to make mirth for the *Salon* Condorcet.

Before the Revolution, the society that met in the *salons* of the wife of the celebrated philosophical writer, the Marquis de Condorcet, was chiefly composed of distinguished savants, men of eminent scientific attainments, and women of rank, but more especially remarkable for their culture and *esprit*. The gentlemen usually discussed serious and abstruse questions. But lighter themes were not disdained. Music formed a more prominent feature in the evening entertainment than was usual at that period, — attracting even the then famous amateur, the Abbé Morellet, — and there was plenty of lively conversation. But Madame de Condorcet — a very lovely and accomplished woman, much younger than her husband — was deeply interested in the progress of the new doctrines that were to regenerate human nature, as understood and advocated by the marquis. This sympathy with his views — developed in his "*Esquisse du progrès de l'Esprit humain*"— gave her an immense influence over him, which, by urging him on to extremes from which at the period in question both would have recoiled, led eventually to his miserable end.

The ministers MM. Turgot and Malesherbes, also the Marquis de Mirabeau, the economist, and father of the orator, were frequenters of the *Salon* Condorcet. Hence the eagerness of the ladies to hear of all that occurred in the "*Salon Helvêtique.*" The grave savants and learned philosophers affected to turn a deaf ear to the gossiping reports of the less serious of the brotherhood. They were, however, by no means averse to the marquise and her fair friends being amused by this showing up of the grand airs of the upstart Protestant Swiss banker and his admiring pedantic wife.

M. Necker's vehement attacks on M. Turgot had been read by his friends and partisans with the deepest indignation.

"He is aiming at a revival of the 'Système Law,' exclaimed Condorcet."

"He is preparing ills for France," rejoined Turgot, "that will take her many years to recover from."

Yet M. Turgot, leaning on that broken reed, the king's approbation of his measures, thought himself secure in his post, notwithstanding his enemy's persistent open attacks and secret intrigues. His theories pleased the king; he pronounced them excellent,— for the minister and the monarch alike desired only the public good. The Marquis de Mirabeau said that his friend Turgot sought, as he himself did, to make humanity perfect. At all events, these excellent theories needed time for their full development. And had the king possessed firmness enough to support M. Turgot, and to enable him to maintain himself in the ministerial post he held, he would have accomplished by his ordinances all that it needed the revolution subsequently to effect, — the emancipation of the people from the oppression of the privileged classes, and the compelling the latter to contribute their due quota to the revenue of the state. At least, so the historian, M. Mignet, seems to have thought.

But the downfall of M. Turgot and his theories was at hand. He had been nearly two years in the ministry; his projects had offended the *noblesse*, and were ill understood by those whom they were intended to benefit. Some attempts — futile indeed, though favoured by the king — to check the extravagance of the court had excited there a resentful feeling towards him. A more recent effort to restrain the profuse expenditure, so burdensome to the state, in the households of the royal princes, had made Monsieur and the Comte d'Artois his enemies. The queen then joined the cabal against the economist minister, from whom she had lately received a reproof that her vindictive spirit could not brook. She had formed for the young widowed Princesse de Lamballe one of those sudden and violent attachments she was so prone to. In order that the princess might be more constantly in her society, and as a pretext for lavishing favours upon her, and placing a suite of apartments at her disposal at Versailles, it occurred to the queen to revive the abolished sinecure post of *surintendante* of her household. The king, much annoyed, but, as usual, not having the courage to refuse, gave a frigid consent to the proposal.

Eighty thousand *francs* the queen thought was the smallest salary that could be offered to, or be accepted by, a wealthy princess. And the payment of this sum annually she requested the contrôleur-général to ratify. To her immense surprise and indignation, he objected to this waste of the public money. "His conscience would not allow him to burden the bankrupt state with new charges, whilst long arrears of salary remained unpaid to its most hard-worked and useful employés." Secretly, the king was glad to sanction this. But the growing favour of M. Turgot with his royal master alarmed the veteran First Minister. Becoming more infirm, though without losing his gaiety, he was now, with his imperious old countess, almost constantly domiciled at Versailles, in an apartment in near communication with the king's. There he proposed to remain to the end of his days; and as the contrôleur seemed likely to become his rival, he began to look around him for an able and popular man to replace him. His office, however, was difficult to fill.

Another — and perhaps the most potent — of M. Turgot's enemies had appeared on the scene but a short time before. This was the Church, represented by Christophe de Beaumont, Archbishop of Paris, and other of its highest dignitaries. M. de Beaumont was a stern, unyielding priest, a fanatic in his zeal for maintaining the power of the hierarchy. But among those associated with him were men deeply imbued with the philosophism of the age — atheistic in their opinions, and of dissolute lives; as, for instance, the Archbishop of Toulouse, M. Loménie de Brienne, afterwards minister. Possessing large revenues, they had become alarmed at some proposed innovations that threatened, at least, greatly to diminish them. A conclave of the higher clergy was therefore held at the archbishop's residence.

"Ah, my Saviour!" exclaimed the pious M. de Beaumont, raising his eyes towards heaven, "that two atheists should be the ministers most in favour! That my request for an immediate reprint of the works of Saint Augustin and Saint Thomas should be refused by an infidel — M. de Malesherbes! And why?" — the archbishop's face assumed an expression of horror — "the royal printing-presses were engaged in issuing a work on astronomy, by a person named Lalande, — a work imbued, I am told, with the most fatal doctrines!"

A general groan ran through this pious conclave, — MM. de Dillon, de Boyer, and others of the Loménie school, no doubt, laughing in their sleeves at the same time.

"The king is good," said the pious M. de Pompignon; "he cannot desire the ruin of his kingdom."

He advised, therefore, that an address should be presented to his majesty. Forthwith it was prepared, — M. de Pompignon and M. de Loménie being deputed to carry it to Versailles and to lay the statement of their grievances before the king. They were accompanied by a young *abbé*, who, though but just twenty-one, held a lucrative clerical office, and for some years had openly led a life of such extreme depravity that it had furnished a theme for more than one of the meretricious novels of that day. His name was Charles Maurice de Talleyrand-Périgord.

The object of the address was very fully explained to the king by M. de Loménie. He especially directed his majesty's attention to the presumption of the Protestants, who, emboldened by his leniency, dared to perform the rite of baptism and to administer the sacrament. The king's reply, transmitted by M. de Malesherbes to M. de Loménie, was extremely laconic. "He relied," he said, "on the bishops and archbishops to continue, by their wisdom and their example, to contribute towards the success of his measures for the public good." This was thought so little to the purpose, and was so unsatisfactory to M. de Beaumont and his colleagues, that fresh remonstrances were forwarded to the king. Heresy, he was told, was advancing with rapid strides, and under favour of the royal printing-press. This really alarmed the king. He promised his clergy that he would not fail to put a stop to it, and assured them that the report of protection being afforded by him to the Protestants was wholly unfounded. Louis therefore lost no time in issuing a decree forbidding the publication of all books against religion, and also prohibiting their authors from residing in the kingdom. For a time this was strictly carried out. But the country even then was not in a mood to tolerate long any arbitrary interdict.

It cost the poor king a pang to give up a minister who was "the only man," he said, "beside himself, who really was interested and desired the welfare of the people." But the cabal was strong against M. Turgot. "He has raised the hopes of the nation," cried his enemies, "only bitterly to disappoint them." And, besides, a certain intriguing *soi-disant* marquis, De Pesay, a great ally of M. Necker, had contrived to enter into a secret correspondence with the king, to obtain private interviews with him, and to bring his banker friend's plans under his notice. M. Necker is said to have often waited, concealed in a coach-house, and in disguise, to learn from his friend that their scheme was successfully progressing; while madame was on the tenter-hooks at home, longing to hear from her divine husband that the desired result was attained.

Louis XVI. was fond of acquiring information by indirect means; and as M. le Marquis was a plausible person, and succeeded in gaining his favour, he one day introduced him to M. de Maurepas. The old minister was much amazed to find that this artful young gentleman was his godson. He had but a poor opinion of his abilities, and was even inclined to feel some resentment at the mysterious proceedings of the king and M. de Pezay. But the finances were at their lowest ebb, and money pressingly called for on all sides; while the proposals M. Necker laid before him for replenishing the treasury looked too enticing to be, from mere pique, rejected.

M. Turgot, wholly unaware of this plot, was engaged with the business of his department, when a message, in his sovereign's name, required him to deliver up his *portefeuille*. It was received by the king with a sigh of regret. The dismissal of M. Turgot involved the resignation of M. de Malesherbes, and the friends "retired together from public life, without disgrace, shame, or remorse." But M. Necker did not immediately succeed to the office of his fallen foe. M. Clugny de Nuis was named to the *contrôle-général*, and M. Necker to the direction of the treasury, with the charge of negotiating the loans of the Bank of France. A few months elapsed; M. Clugny died, and M. and Madame Necker then reigned in his stead. But it was as *directeur-général des finances*, not *contrôleur*,— that designation giving the right to a seat in the council, which could not be permitted to a Protestant.

The clergy clamoured loudly at the nomination of a Calvinist minister, and heaped reproaches on M. de Maurepas for consenting to it. But Necker had begun to pour forth his millions, — his system, though better considered and far less reckless, being in some measure based on the "Système Law." Maurepas, dazzled by this sudden influx of gold into the coffers of the state, replied to the deputation that came to remonstrate with him, "The state is in need of money. Supply it to us as abundantly as M. Necker is doing, and the bishops themselves shall nominate whom they will to the controllership of the finances."

CHAPTER IX.

A Severe Winter. — Sledges and Polonaises. — Sledging on the Boulevards. — Rival Favourites. — The King's Sledges. — The Queen and the *Danseuse*. — The Dignity of the Crown. — The Kingly Halo of Divinity. — The *Maison Militaire*. — The Two "Forty-eights." — The King in His Belvedere. — The Queen's Sanctum Sanctorum. — Cæsar's Wife. — A Private Interview. — The Queen's *Gardes Malades*. — Thoughtfulness for the King. — Ethics and Sentimentality. — Strait-laced People. — The Comte de Périgord. — A Mystification. — The *Petits Appartements*. — Absolution for the Queen. — The *Vox Populi*. — Alas! Poor Queen.

THE winter of 1776–7 was one of great severity in France. Misery and suffering prevailed, both in the provincial towns and the rural districts of the kingdom. Wood was scarce; bread was dear in Versailles and Paris; and cold and hunger were the cause of murmuring that was scarcely at all suppressed by the distribution among the poor, by order of the king, of rations of bread and numerous cartloads of fagots.

Nevertheless, the Carnival was this year exceedingly gay. The queen introduced sledging, and the court and the *beau monde*, wearing masks, *coiffures de circonstance*, and enveloped in furs, skimmed over the frozen lakes of the park of Versailles and Bois de Boulogne, and along the firm, deep, snowy roads of the Champs Élysées, even to the boulevards of Paris.

As a compliment to Marie Leczinska soon after she became Queen of France, there had been an attempt to naturalise, together with the Polish costume, which for a time was the rage in court circles, the winter amusement of sledging. But this favourite recreation of more northern climes met with little success in France; while the queen, being a strict devotee and fond of retirement, shrank from taking the lead in the pleasures and diversions of the court; so that after her first winter at Versailles the sledges and the polonaises were heard of no more. Fifty years had elapsed. The sledges during that period had been relegated to the sheds assigned to vehicles out of date or out of favour. They are now again brought forth — these being professedly economical times — for examination as to their possibly serviceable condition. A glance, however, suffices to show that fifty years of disuse and neglect have put them completely *hors de service*.

New ones of more modern and convenient construction, as well as more elegant form, must forthwith therefore be ordered for the queen and her ladies. Monsieur and the Comte d'Artois, and generally the grand seigneurs of the queen's *cercle intime*, also prepare sledges of great magnificence, — with abundance of painting and gilding, trappings of embroidered crimson leather and velvet, and innumerable tinkling bells of gold or silver. The queen's little fiery coursers are distinguished by plumes of white feathers. The queen herself is therefore easily recognised, notwithstanding her mask. And the people frown disapprovingly on her when, without any retinue, she enters Paris, and gliding swiftly along makes the tour of the boulevards, returning to the Champs Élysées with wonderful rapidity. On one of those occasions, the masked grandee who conducted her sledge was thrown from his seat by a sudden jerk; when the queen, with great nerve and presence of mind, caught the reins and effectually restrained the impetuous affrighted steeds until assistance came to her.

Those sledging parties doubtless formed pretty and exciting scenes; while the exhilaration of feeling the keen pure air inspired in those who took part in them in some degree animated also those who were merely spectators. But beyond the court circle they were regarded with extreme displeasure. The "Autrichienne," it was said, "had made the rigour of the season, which caused such widespread misery and want in France, an occasion for introducing her Austrian pastimes and lavishly wasting the public money."

The groups of people assembled in the Bois or in the Champs Élysées would point out to each other, and often with much indignation, the ostentatiously displayed wealth of the queen's new favourites, the Polignac family, so recently in straitened circumstances. Then there glided by the elaborately carved and gilded sledge of the Princesse de Lamballe, *surintendante* of the queen's household. A coldness had lately arisen between this princess and the queen. The newly sworn eternal friendship of her royal mistress for the Comtesse Jules had excited the princess's jealousy. For both those ladies had a host of needy, grasping, or favoured friends, for whom pensions, places, titles, or estates were through their influence obtained; and the lion's or lioness's share of those good things was at that time falling into the lap of the countess. Monsieur "Tartuffe" kept the public well informed on these subjects. Epigrams, libels, satirical *chansonnettes*, all flowed rapidly from his scandalous pen, and, unfortunately, the conduct of poor Marie Antoinette was but too well calculated to give an air of credibility to this arch-enemy's every artful innuendo.

The king never joined those gay winter parties. Once, pressed to do so, he pointed to a train of wagons which then chanced to be passing by, laden with wood for the poor of Versailles. "Those are my sledges," he said; "I care naught for the rest."

After seven weeks of frost, a thaw suddenly set in, when the sledges, with their fanciful trappings, were carefully put away, to reappear no more for a considerable time, — the queen not venturing again that winter to brave the people's marked disapprobation, as she supposed, of her pastime. But their disapprobation appears to have been in some sort misconstrued. Had Marie Antoinette, with her retinue, been content, like Marie Leczinska, to restrict her sledging to the frost-bound lakes of the park of Versailles, no objection could reasonably have been taken to her enjoyment of exercise so healthy and animating. But when in carnival costume, and in her shell-shaped sledge, her horses covered with jingling bells, and their heads decked, like her own, with flying plumes, she dashed recklessly into Paris and along the boulevards, causing a commotion similar to that occasioned by the famous *danseuse*, Mdlle. Guimard; when, in her painted and gilded carriage, and covered with jewels, she appeared at Longchamps or other public resorts, — it was indeed very generally considered that Marie Antoinette's heedlessness compromised her dignity as queen.

A stately mien and pompous surroundings had ever been associated with royalty in France; and the people, however desirous of reforms tending to ameliorate their condition, were, at that early period of the young monarch's reign, far from the thought of dragging him and his consort from their throne to place them, as M. and Mme. Capet, on a level with themselves. The first steps in that terrible descent were doubtless taken voluntarily by both the king and the queen. With totally opposite characters, and widely differing motives, both were alike anxious to cast off and escape from the *rôle* of sovereign, — the king from inertness, mental and bodily, and sheer incapacity to carry out his decidedly expressed intention of governing alone; the queen from unwillingness to submit to the restraints it imposed on the selection of her circle of intimates and choice of amusements.

The pious and humane disposition of Louis XVI., together with his natural weakness of character, led him, from the very beginning of his reign, to yield a too ready consent to innovations compromising the dignity of the crown; though he probably regarded them as mere personal sacrifices with which he himself was mainly concerned. Certainly he was not prevailed on to forego being crowned at Rheims by the Minister Turgot's representations of the enormous cost it would entail on the impoverished state, as well as distress on a large number of the peasantry by the exaction of unpaid labour. This arose from a superstitious feeling in his mind of the nullity of the rite if performed elsewhere. But he committed a fatal mistake in allowing the eccentric military theorist, the Comte de Saint-Germain, to signalise his entry on his short career as Minister of War by the disorganisation of the royal Maison Militaire or household troops.*

The imaginary halo of divinity supposed to hedge a king has for the eyes of the multitude an outward and visible sign in the *éclat* and magnificence of his *entourage*. It was especially so at that period. And a dazzlingly brilliant show were those household troops, in their rich and varied uniforms of blue and scarlet and gold; the

---

* After the death of M. de Muy, the king announced that when his successor was appointed it would be a great surprise to every one. So much was this the case that on hearing his name many inquired: "Who is this M. de Saint-Germain? and what has he done to supplant in the favour of his sovereign the men who have merits which he certainly has not, — namely, friends at court?" The Comte de Saint-Germain was then verging on his seventieth year. He had served in his youth under the great Maréchal Saxe, and later on in his career his able generalship had covered the retreat and saved the armies of less distinguished commanders, — Richelieu, Clermont, and the two De Broglies. The two latter, however, chose to throw upon him the blame of their disastrous campaign. Saint-Germain immediately sent his resignation to the king, together with his grand cordon of the Order of St. Louis; left France, and took service, with the consent of Louis XV., under the King of Denmark. On retiring from the army some years after, he placed with a Hamburg banker 300,000 *francs* (£12,000), being nearly the whole of the capital from which his modest income was derived. The banker failed, and the old general was reduced to poverty. He was then living at his native place, Cernay, in Alsace. The officers of the regiment, called the Royal Alsace, on learning the misfortune that had fallen on him, proposed to subscribe among themselves a yearly sum for the relief of their countryman, and, of some of them, former commander. But M. de Muy reprimanded them. "He would not sanction an act of

dashing mousquetaires, the troop of light horse, the *Cent Suisses*, the *gens-d'armes*, and others, composing the habitual royal *cortège* and escort of the sovereigns of France. The Comte de Saint-Germain abolished all this — with the king's consent of course. He disbanded the ancient corps of mousquetaires, and drafted the light-horse into a cavalry regiment, with the exception

generosity that involved a reproach to the king." A pension of 10,000 *francs* was then conferred on M. de Saint-Germain. Soon after M. de Muy died, when, Louis XVI. considering that a man whose former comrades were so ready to help him in his trouble must be honest and worthy — and M. de Maurepas not objecting — it was announced to M. de Saint-Germain, to his very great amazement, that he was named to fill the vacant post of Minister of War. "Ah! ah!" he exclaimed, "wonderful indeed, that I should still be remembered at court." This appointment gave general dissatisfaction, except to the king. The old count's enthusiasm for Prussian drill, and his attempts to reorganise the army on the system of the great Frederick, brought him into more disfavour than even his elevation as an unknown man to ministerial power. He was also unsuccessful in his economical schemes, — having refused to receive the sum usually granted to ministers on entering office, to set up their establishments, saying "it was far too much, and that he would send in the accounts." These, when delivered, were found to amount to nearly as much again as the sum allowed. He also declined to accept his pension, but afterwards changed his mind and applied for it. His almost entire abolition of the royal guard — though from mistaken motives of economy it was sanctioned by the king — has been since attributed to treasonable designs in which he was believed to be concerned. Others have thought that his unexpected elevation to high office turned his head. His career as minister, however, was short, being terminated by his death early in 1778.

of forty-eight of their number. These, with forty-eight of the *gens-d'armes*, were alone reserved for military duty at Versailles, and "to attend the king when, on any public occasion, a *Te Deum* was sung," as Saint-Germain himself told the queen, when she inquired "if the 'forty-eights' were reserved as an escort for his majesty when he held a Bed of Justice."

Her inquiry was prompted by no dissatisfaction with the count's proceedings. She was well pleased with the dismissal of the guards. For if royalty lost something of its prestige when shorn of its outward state, there was, in her view of the matter, a counterbalancing gain in the removal of much troublesome restraint; and she expressed a hope that "even the 'two forty-eights' might ere long be also withdrawn, and no redcoat again be seen lounging in the galleries of Versailles." *
And in one sense the reduction of the guard in the galleries and anterooms of the state apartments of the château was a gain to Marie Antoinette. For few of those loungers failed to recognise the queen when — flitting like a shadow along some dimly lighted corridor, or emerging from the entrance of a private staircase of the *petits appartements*, dressed like some little Parisian *bourgeoise*, or masked, and enveloped in a domino, and accompanied only by some favourite

---

* Some few years later the king gratified her majesty in this respect.

lady of honour — she was bent on an adventurous ramble amongst strangers in the park, or on a visit to some place of public resort in Paris.

The Château of Versailles abounded in turnings and windings and mysterious staircases, which for many a year past had facilitated the intrigues of its monarchs. Had Louis XVI. shown a disposition to follow the example of his predecessors, he might have availed himself of the obscure inlets and outlets of his palace with far less remark than when he ascended to his workrooms, to clean and arrange with his own royal hands the implements used in his manual occupations; or when mounting still higher, to the belvedere on the roof of the château, he amused a leisure hour by surveying through a telescope all that was passing in the courtyard and gardens, and discerned from afar what travellers were approaching Versailles by the Avenue de Paris. But as soon as watchful eyes detected that private doors and staircases were of more service to the queen than the king, instantly the curious fact was blazoned abroad, and became the theme of numberless low jests. Secrecy, if her majesty desired it, was no longer possible; and it was this — apparently, at all events — undeniable foundation for many of the scandalous tales then afloat respecting her, both in Paris and Versailles — in fact, all over the country — that secured for a host of libellous and obscene scribblers exemption from the punishment their audacity seemed to merit.

Yet even amongst those whom the queen called her friends — courtiers of the favoured " Société de Trianon," and frequenters of her *réunions*, held in the Comtesse de Polignac's *salons* — she was very freely blamed. It was considered not only imprudent, but daring, privately to reserve, in a remote part of the château, a suite of small, mean rooms as a sort of sanctum sanctorum of royal ease and freedom; where, after the manner of Louis XV., she could (to use her own words) "retire with a few chosen friends, and, in their society, throwing off the restraints of royalty, forget for a while that she was queen." Both her friends and her foes assigned other reasons for this whim. " Had not she Trianon," they said, " sacred to dairymaids and shepherdesses, and whence royalty at her bidding was excluded? — a theatre, too, where she could assume the part of a *soubrette ?*" The gaiety and heedlessness of youth could not always be accepted as sufficiently excusing the fanciful freaks of even a royal lady, — an Austrian archduchess who disdained to be Queen of France.

But there were limits which her flattering circle of intimates could not, without some trepidation, see her venture to pass. Certainly this feeling was due much less to respect for the queen, or any anxiety on her account, than to a sort of involuntary homage paid to a principle, tacitly established, but long fully recognised by the French court, that, however lax the moral conduct of the sovereign, his courtiers, his *maîtresses-en-titre*, or the ladies of the household, on his queen, as on Cæsar's wife, not even the taint of suspicion must rest. She must be pure, though all around should be corrupt, — the one white lamb amidst a flock of black sheep.

It was under such an impression that the Baron de Besenval wrote that brief remark in his memoirs implying so much that seems damaging to the reputation of Marie Antoinette. With the view of communicating with him on the subject of the duel between the Prince de Bourbon and the Comte d'Artois — Besenval being one of the seconds — the queen sent a message to the baron, naming an hour for an interview. What, then, was his surprise when, on arriving at the château, he was conducted up narrow passages and staircases to its topmost story, where, in a small, meanly furnished apartment, the Queen of France waited to receive him! The baron was one of the most favoured members of her intimate circle, but he apparently was unaware of the existence of this mysterious cabinet. At any rate, it was his first introduction to what seemed to him a revelation of the queen's habits of secret intrigue. He knew that an unsullied reputation was the exception rather than the rule as regarded the ladies of the court. Being therefore familiar with vice, he was "not surprised," he says, "that the queen herself should wish for the facilities he saw, but he was astonished that she had *dared* to procure them."

Madame Campan relates this incident differently. A vague remembrance of what the queen had told her respecting it was brought to her mind when, many years after, the Besenval memoirs were published. In her version, the baron, who at the time was a middle-aged man, is represented as falling on his knees and in an impassioned manner making a declaration of love to the queen; while she, highly incensed, bids him "rise, and instantly leave her presence." This, of course, should have excluded the presumptuous elderly swain from being again received at Trianon, and have made a gap in the *cercle intime*. But pardon must have promptly followed the asserted offence, as no change appears to have occurred in their very familiar relations. For when, soon after, the queen had the measles, Besenval was one of the four devoted friends (the Ducs de Coigny and de Guines and Prince Esterhazy being the other three) who were permitted to pass the day at her bedside, *en gardes malades*, and to amuse her majesty with sprightly talk.

"'T is true," says Mercy-Argenteau when writing of this strange occurrence to the Empress Maria Theresa (who was much grieved, even alarmed, on being informed of this extreme instance of her daughter's want of both delicacy and discretion), "that the king gave his consent to it; only, however, because the queen requested him to do so, and that, unfortunately, he never knows how to refuse." The king himself was excluded from her apartment lest he should take the complaint, "*pauvre homme!*" But the four friends, courageously braving the possibility of any such danger to themselves, "remained in close attendance on her majesty from seven in the morning until eleven at night, retiring only for a short time to dine." They even proposed, in their extreme devotedness to the royal invalid, to spend the night also in watching by her couch. But this was so resolutely opposed by Mercy-Argenteau that they were compelled to withdraw, — resuming, however, their post in the morning, and continuing their attendance during the queen's convalescence. It was not a protracted illness, and, as may well be imagined, it was at no time severe. While it lasted, the Comtesse d'Artois would sometimes join the nursing party; but so did the count. And as the former detested the queen, she spared her not on an occasion so open to ill-natured comment. Generally, however, the court was more amused than shocked at these proceedings, which gave rise to numerous jokes; and it was asked: "In the case of the king being also indisposed, would the proposal of four ladies to attend upon and amuse him — of course to the exclusion of the queen — be accepted?"

The long and profligate career of both Louis XIV. and Louis XV., together with the licentiousness of the Regent d'Orléans and family, had greatly tended to blunt the susceptibilities of the French on the score of morality. The ethical code of the day in "*la bonne compagnie*" included little beyond stately politeness, with amiability of manner, agreeable conversational powers, a due observance of social conventionalities, a fair reputation as a wit, or *bel esprit*, with that of an atheist, or *esprit fort*. Then sentimentality was greatly in vogue, — sentimentality *à la Rousseau*. Tender-hearted, loving Julias abounded in the queen's household, — Julias who, with husbands and *chers amis*, lived in great domestic harmony; forming families as united and happy as were the very amiable model trio of the "*Nouvelle Héloïse*."

As an instance, though she was by no means a solitary one, the Comtesse de Polignac may be named. She was the bosom friend of Marie Antoinette, and completely dominated her. Her *liaison* with M. de Vaudreuil was not only openly avowed and recognised, but had also the approving sanction of her husband. It is possible that this sanction was needed for the satisfaction of strait-laced, scrupulous people; and to impart, according to the stern moralists' view of such domestic arrangements at that day, a certain halo of respectability to the connection. But whether so or not, when Madame de Polignac was confined of a son at Gennevilliers, the country house of M. de Vaudreuil,* the queen, to be nearer her dearest friend at that interesting moment, went to La Muette, and was almost a nurse to the countess, with whom she remained until able to return with her to Versailles. This, with much more to the same or similar effect, which letters, memoirs, and MSS. of the time relate, helps to bear out the assertion of contemporary writers, that "under the early part of the reign of the pious and virtuous Louis XVI. the court and general society were actually more depraved than during the dissolute period of the regency."

Of course there were honourable exceptions. The Duchesse de Mailly, *dame d'atours*, or mistress of the robes, may be cited as one of them. Being of a retiring disposition, and disliking the intriguing, slanderous life of the court, she resigned her office, and no entreaties of the queen, who was disposed at the time to place the duchess on her list of favourites, could prevail on her to resume it. She was the daughter of the Comte de Périgord, uncle of M. de Talleyrand.

* It was this son who, as Duc de Polignac, was afterwards Minister of Foreign Affairs under Charles X., and signed the famous Ordinances that led to the downfall of the elder branch of the Bourbons in July, 1830.

The count had once the courage frankly to tell the queen the opinion which, outside the court circle, was generally held of her mode of life. His daughter's retirement from the court having necessitated an interview with the queen, he was informed by the Comtesse de Polignac that she requested he would wait the next day in the corridor in front of the chapel, and that, after mass, her majesty's confidential *valet de chambre* would be there to conduct him to her. The count was astonished at this new mode of granting an audience. He was an aged man, and had never been the Adonis that his famous nephew, the young Abbé de Périgord, was at that period, and for whom such a rendezvous seemed to be more appropriate than for himself. However, the count was punctual, and was limping along the corridor (he had that defect in one foot, occasioning a slight lameness, which in a more or less degree was hereditary in the Talleyrand-Périgord family), when Louis, the *valet de chambre* who, later on, displayed so much fidelity to the queen, made his appearance.

By a sign he indicated that the count should follow him. Leisurely leading the way, to suit the count's slow pace, the door of the *petits appartements* under the leads was reached at last. M. de Périgord had rested more than once on his upward journey, and more than once had said to Louis: "There is surely some mistake."

But the discreet *serviteur* merely shook his head. The greater mystery observed on this occasion than when M. de Besenval was conducted to those upper regions, was probably intended by the queen — silly mystifications being one of the amusements of the period — to heighten the old count's curiosity, which she expected to end in an amusing surprise. But he took an entirely different view of the matter. And when, after Louis's three knocks were answered by a corresponding signal from within, the door was opened, and the queen with a smiling face welcomed her visitor, the grave and pained expression of his countenance, and the scrutinising glance he cast around the apartment, both startled and offended her.

"I perceive you pity me," she said, in a haughty tone, "at finding me in a retreat where I strive to forget that I am Queen of France."

"Ah, Madame!" he replied, "I trust you neither do, nor ever will, regret that you are our queen; but, pardon me, I pray you, that I am unable wholly to repress my regret and astonishment at seeing you here."

"It is a retreat that pleases me," she said; "in what does it displease you? It is surely simple enough. And you see that, though accused of extravagance, I am not so extravagant as Madame de Balby, the favourite of Monsieur, who lately set fire to the rich furniture provided for her apartment because it was not, to her fancy, rich enough. I sometimes sup here," she continued, "with a few discreet friends whom I can trust not to talk of it. We meet to be gay, to play a game of billiards" (the queen was an expert player), "and to amuse ourselves like simple human beings. The king, too, has sometimes been here. If he has never supped with us it is because, as every one knows, nothing in the world would make him forego either the supper *en famille*, or the dinner in public." As this thought, which amused the queen, crossed her mind, the tone she had assumed towards the count became less severe. Throwing open the door of the adjoining apartment, which was her billiard-room, "M. le Comte," she said, "there are two other rooms beyond that. You have heard all; you may now see all; and I shall then ask you for absolution."

"And of the vicious intentions attributed to her, I fully absolved her," said the count (addressing Madame de Permon, to whom the above particulars were related); "of extremest imprudence, I could not. But she did me the favour of listening to me, and without displeasure, when I endeavoured to impress on her that in her position of Queen of France she had a higher duty to perform than the mere seeking of congenial amusements. Should she think otherwise, I ventured to observe, there was still a duty she owed to the nation, no less than to herself and the king,— that of not contemning, or appearing to be wholly oblivious of public opinion with regard to the nature of those amusements. She smiled her thanks, but could not comprehend of what 'the people' complained."

Though a *grand seigneur* of the old school, M. de Périgord had evidently begun to recognise the growing power of the *vox populi;* but Marie Antoinette did not yet know that public opinion was of any importance to her. She remained too thoroughly in character and feeling an Austrian to comprehend that the lower race of beings called "the people" could ever presume to dictate to, or meddle with the acts of, royalty. The slanderous tongues of Mesdames and the pious court of Bellevue; the envyings, backbitings, and jealousies of her own immediate circle; the infamous accusations brought against her by her sisters-in-law in the course of their frequent vituperative family quarrels; the insidious attacks of Monsieur, and the want of support she experienced in the apathy and reserve of the king,—all this she understood, resented and defied. It seemed almost a matter of course that thus it should be; but the right of "the people" to interfere with her amusements and to call in question their propriety was a mystery to her.

Alas! poor queen, the dreadful significancy of that expression, "THE PEOPLE," and the vengeful acts to which an infuriated people could be driven, were the two terrible lessons she had yet to learn.

CHAPTER X.

Eventful Years. — The American Colonists. — Beaumarchais's Secret Mission. — Aiding the Insurgents. — Easing the King's Conscience. — Jerusalem at Philadelphia. — The American Planter. — The "*Ragoût Philadelphique*" — Franklin Puzzled. — The *Salon Helvétique*. — "Never Too Old to Learn." — "*Ça Ira! Mes Amis, Ça Ira!*" — Superfluous Cash. — The King's Generosity. — Lansquenet. — The "*Jeu de la Reine*." The *Fête* of All Saints.

THE years 1777 and 1778 were eventful ones in France. In the course of them incidents occurred, seemingly calculated to divert the attention of the nation from its own domestic troubles and special public grievances, but which, in reality, became the means of inciting the people to greater impatience under them, and of hastening the downfall of the tottering French monarchy.

Marie Antoinette had recently written to the empress-queen: "The king thinks Beaumarchais mad," — referring to the ardent zeal and persistency of his romantic pursuit of a libellist, who, after being lavishly paid for the suppression of an infamous libel on the queen, fled to Nuremberg with a copy of it, intending to reprint and republish it there. But so far was Louis XVI. from thinking the energetic, active-minded author of the "Barber of Séville" mad that this peace-loving monarch was, at that very time — together with the sprightly, easy-going M. de Maurepas, and the Comte de Vergennes, "one of the most enlightened, firm, and prudent of French ministers" — induced to sanction a scheme, proposed by Beaumarchais, for supplying the insurgent American colonists with the military stores they needed for carrying on their struggle with the mother country, and enabling them to throw off her yoke. The immense secret influence of that remarkable man with the government of the day, and the great part he played in facilitating the triumph of the Americans in their contest with England, were but imperfectly known, even in France, until the publication of M. de Loménie's work, "*Beaumarchais et son Temps.*" *

While in London, arranging with that extraordinary personage, the Chevalier d'Éon, for the surrender of papers relating to the secret diplo-

* The principal papers relating to the furnishing of arms, ammunition, etc., from the royal arsenals, with the connivance of the government, as well as of the vast projects, carried out singly by Beaumarchais himself, are given *in extenso* in the above named work. The heirs of Beaumarchais considered it prejudicial to their interests to publish them before a final arrangement was come to respecting their heavy claims on the United States Government. This was not affected until 1835 — thirty-six years after Beaumarchais's death — when, again, many years elapsed before his papers, public and private, were confided for examination to M. de Loménie.

macy of Louis XV., and believed, erroneously, to be of great importance, he became acquainted with several influential Americans; from whom he learned much of the state of feeling in their country, and their probable needs in the case of a prolonged struggle with England. His secret mission brought him also into communication with two or three cabinet ministers; while his genial temper, reputed wealth, great musical talent, and many social qualities, secured him a welcome in general society. His keenness of insight, together with the authentic information he gathered from the two opposing parties on the leading question of the day, enabled him to assure the king of his full conviction that, "in spite of all the efforts of England, America would, sooner or later, slip from her grasp." And he succeeded in convincing him and his two confidential ministers, that it was to the interest of France to aid America, though not, at that moment, to risk a conflict with England by doing so openly.

Louis XVI. detested the English, but had no desire to provoke a war with them. Therefore, though willing that Beaumarchais should be allowed to buy military stores of the government at stipulated prices — named by the Comte de Saint-Germain — and no inquiry should be made as to their destination, yet both he and his ministers required that the Americans should not be made aware of the fact that the government favoured this enterprise. France, in fact, consented to be blind to Beaumarchais's proceedings, and England and America were to be persuaded that there was nothing unusual in them. But the American Congress affected to treat Beaumarchais merely as an agent, through whom the French government dispensed aid to them, in order to shield the real nature of the transaction from suspicion in England. The cargoes of clothing for their half-naked troops, the ample supplies of arms and ammunition, to which, being hitherto destitute of them, they mainly owed their successes in the future campaigns, they chose to receive as gifts.

To carry on this enterprise, Beaumarchais had risked millions in establishing in Paris a great commercial house, trading under the name of Roderigue Hortalez et Compagnie. Naturally, therefore, he was much disappointed when his forty vessels came back to Nantes and Bordeaux without the return cargoes expected, — such as indigo, Maryland tobacco, and salt fish. The terms of his agreement with the government precluded him from requiring payment in money,— Congress having as little of that commodity as of other material of war. He was to be indemnified by facilities afforded him for evading the duties and satisfactorily disposing of his goods. These underhand doings were arranged to set at ease the weakly whispering conscience of "the virtuous Louis XVI.," who, swayed by this inward monitor, constantly feared to do wrong, but unhappily was never impelled by it to dare to do right.

Though his own interests seemed likely to suffer from the unpromising aspect his scheme had assumed, yet Beaumarchais would not abandon it. Trusting to the result of the struggle, and to explanations that took place between him and the accredited American agents, he not only continued to furnish supplies, but used his influence to engage sympathy for the American cause amongst young men of family. It was his vivid, if overdrawn, descriptions of the "struggles of a brave people to cast off the yoke of the oppressor," that inspired the youthful Marquis de La Fayette, and others of that enthusiastic band, with a burning desire to leave their country to break a lance in the cause of freedom. To some of them he furnished the funds they needed while absent from France. La Fayette, writing to excuse his having requested M. Francy (Beaumarchais's agent) to supply his pecuniary wants, remarks that "in seeking such accommodation from American bankers he had found Jerusalem at Philadelphia."

In February, 1777, Benjamin Franklin arrived in Paris, commissioned by Congress to press the French government to furnish further aid to his countrymen, and especially to recognise the independence of the United States and to enter into an alliance with them. The "*Mercure de France*" announced the thrilling news to the Parisians that "the great man who had snatched the lightning from the gods of Olympus, and torn the sceptre from the hands of tyrants, the gods of the earth," was among them. All were equally anxious to get a glimpse of this wonderful individual. The court graciously welcomed him. Ladies of the *grand monde* vied with each other in their efforts to secure the honour of his presence in their *salons*, which his unpolished manners, his homely suit of brown cloth, with gloveless hands to match — as Madame de Créquy says — dark gray stockings, stout-soled shoes, red striped cravat, and leather skull-cap, which he constantly wore, could hardly be said to have graced. This costume was supposed to be the ordinary one of an American planter. Perhaps it was. At any rate, it must have contrasted oddly enough with the embroidered coats, lace ruffles and jabots, silk stockings, diamond buckles, swords, and powder of the beaux of the period who frequented the *salons*. But Franklin had a fine open countenance, to which his flowing white locks gave a venerable air.

Sensitive ladies, however, were shocked to see him cut a melon with a knife, but reject both knife and fork for teeth and fingers when asparagus was served to him. And it was with shuddering emotion they watched him prepare for himself that terrible mess, still in favour with his countrymen, of eggs mixed up in a glass with salt, pepper, and mustard; and then, with evident relish, sip it up in small spoonfuls. They named it the "*ragoût philadelphique*," but the compliment never extended to placing it on any French *menu*. On the other hand, to Franklin the manners and customs of fashionable and courtly circles were often no less amazing than were his own uncouth habits to the fastidious taste of Parisian society.

The once imposing grandeur and stately magnificence of the ceremonial of the court of Versailles — as planned by the great Colbert to inspire deep reverence for the sovereign, and to place before the nation, in the person of the *Grand Monarque*, a king of kings, a ruler before whom every knee must bow — had almost entirely dwindled away. Poor Louis XVI. was now distinguished in his court chiefly by the indifference and disrespect his courtiers, with few exceptions, affected towards him. Yet some outward forms of court etiquette, still retained or overlooked, were the more conspicuously ridiculous from the total absence of other signs of respectful homage to the king. For instance, none ever dreamt of passing through the throne-room without bowing almost to prostration before the vacant throne; while the monarch himself may have been passed *sans cérémonie* immediately before, and without any recognition of his presence.

In the room adjoining that where the king dined, when his meal was not eaten in public, was a large polished and gilded casket or chest. Before this chest, as Franklin, on one of his visits to Versailles, remarked with surprise, all who entered the apartment profoundly bowed. Amongst others who attended on that occasion was the Cardinal de Rochefoucauld. Perceiving that his eminence also bent the knee on passing the mysterious piece of furniture, Franklin, unable any longer to repress his curiosity, took an opportunity of asking the cardinal whether the chest contained relics. Thus only could he account for the veneration in which it apparently was held. Imagine, then, this unsophisticated republican's surprise when the cardinal, with a smile, but in a confidentially low tone, informed him that the chest contained the silver knives and forks, with other plate, used for his majesty's private dinner. "Pro-dig-ious!" he exclaimed. "Pro-dig-ious! indeed!" He could scarcely overcome his amazement. The cause of it, when known, excited great merriment among all present, and the anecdote was told amidst much laughter and glee in the *salons*.

Of Parisian *réunions*, none were so attractive to the distinguished and much-fêted American as those of Madame Necker. Republican sympathies, probably, and admiration of the money-making powers of the superb god of those *réunions*. There, too, the guests were freely admitted, though, perchance, they might not be in full evening costume; and whether arriving in *voitures de place* or their own private carriages, were equally privileged to drive up to, and alight at, the grand vestibule of the hôtel. He may also have been in some degree reminded of New England manners in the staidness or stiffness of the lady who presided in the *Salon Helvêtique,* as well as have found greater facility in making himself understood in her professedly learned and philosophical circle. The philosophic band, indeed, claimed him as their own, though they scarcely comprehended his principles and opinions. For the difference of language was as perpetual an obstacle to the flow of conversation in the *salons* as to confidential communication with the government. Silas Deane, Arthur Hill, and other delegates of Congress, were unable to express themselves in French. And at that period not many Frenchmen could give utterance to more than a few disjointed sentences in English.

But there was a great and general desire to hear the "Philadelphian Oracle" hold forth; and to gather up words of republican wisdom that were expected to fall from his lips. Franklin, who had picked up odds and ends of knowledge of various kinds, had certainly an advantage which other delegates possessed not, in a moderate acquaintance with French. He could read a French book, and, until he found himself in Paris, probably thought he could speak the language. But, with his strange pronunciation and Yankee twang, he was scarcely less unintelligible to French ears than when he spoke American-English. He quickly perceived this; also that the objects of his secret mission were in some degree likely to be frustrated by it.

Franklin, as every one knows, was a man of many maxims. " Never too late to mend, and never too old to learn," was one of his adopted favourites. Therefore, lending an observant ear to the conversation around him, he set himself the task of improving his accent — making for a time fewer attempts to speak. His silence was not unnoticed; but it was attributed to moody dissatisfaction at the tardiness of the king and his ministers in acknowledging American independence. Truly, the United States had proclaimed their independence, though it was not quite clear to others that they had yet fully secured it. The French government, even the poor king himself, though longing to be revenged on England for the Treaty of 1763 and its stipulations concerning the port of Dunquerque, prudently preferred, before entering openly into alliance with the new republic, to wait yet awhile the course of events, and in the meantime to reorganise the navy. This certainly did not quite satisfy Franklin; who was accustomed, when, on the arrival of news from "the States," sympathisers eagerly inquired of the progress of "the cause of liberty," to reply in a joyous tone: " Ça ira mes amis, ça ira !" The phrase found favour; was often repeated; and thus the familiar exclamation of the American revolutionary agent became in after years almost the watchword of Revolutionary France.

Secretly, however, at this time many millions of *francs* were passing out of the public treasury into Franklin's hands, for the use of his insurgent countrymen. For the coffers of France had filled fast of late. "M. Necker," as the old Comte de Maurepas said, "had found the philosopher's stone," — the philosopher's stone that had effected so much for the bankrupt state being M. Necker's great credit as a financier. Mainly on the strength of it the Genevese banker had raised immense loans, which should have relieved France from her burden of debt, and have enabled " Louis, *le désiré*," to carry out his long promised reforms. But things had a tendency to slip back into old grooves. Abuses it was once proposed to abolish, when practicable, had dropped quite out of mind since the reforming minister, Turgot, had given place to the money-producing minister, Necker.

The king, possessing for the first time in his life an abundance of superfluous cash, was under the pleasing delusion that the country was actually prospering. Louis was not content, therefore, merely to lavish these borrowed millions on "patriotism and republican virtues," then so much in vogue, and personified in Paris by the "Apostle of Liberty," and idol, *pro tem.*, of the *salons*, where rank, fashion and beauty, learning and philosophy, congregated to worship him. But the king thought it a favourable moment for assisting his brother of Provence — notwithstanding the very large revenues that wily youth possessed — to add an adjoining domain to the park and grounds of Brunoy. At the same time, as a mark of his favour, he presented the libertine Comte d'Artois with a sum of two millions, to relieve him from a portion of his overwhelming debts.

Nor was this all. A sprinkling of the golden shower must also fall on the queen. Her pin-money had been largely increased, and other liberal pecuniary arrangements made, on the reappointment of her household. But she had been scarcely more than two years on the throne when her debts amounted to twenty thousand pounds. The king, on hearing this, immediately, as a first instalment, handed her majesty two thousand *louis d'or*, proposing to pay the rest at stated intervals, and from his own private purse, as he said. But neither the queen nor the count thought it necessary to apply the funds furnished by the king's generosity to the payment of their debts. The Comte d'Artois preferred to spend, or waste, his two millions in lavishly decorating the little bijou villa of "Bagatelle," where he held his orgies, after the Palais Royal fashion. The queen carried her rouleaux of *louis d'or* to her lansquenet table, and lost them there.

The queen's gambling propensities proved a rankling thorn in the flesh to Maria Theresa. The Prince de Ligne has endeavoured to exculpate Marie Antoinette from the charge of being a confirmed gambler. He asserts that he never saw her risk more than from five hundred to a thousand *louis d'or* in one evening; which establishes, rather than refutes, the charge. It would make the cost of her evening's amusement, at the present rate of money, from two to four thousand pounds. For it was by a very rare chance that she won; and although the king, generally with the display of a good deal of silent ill-humour, paid her gambling debts from his private purse, that purse was of course replenished from the public one. The king rarely played, and never for money. The same rule prevailed at the tables of Mesdames at Bellevue. It was a rule established at the queen's tables, and those of the dauphin, when Marie Leczinska reigned at Versailles. Card playing was otherwise deemed an abomination in those pious circles. The honour of defeating one's adversary by superior skill in the game was the sole gratification sought. Rouleaux of fifties, and hundreds, and thousands, never changed hands there. Consequently the "*système Louis Seize*" was not favoured by the young queen's circle. The "*Jeu du roi,*" in fact, which had been so grand an affair in former reigns, and at which many an obsequious courtier had ruined himself, was a thing of the past — supplanted by the "*Jeu de la reine.*"

Love of the excitement of play must have been very strong in Marie Antoinette. She spent not only whole evenings, but often whole nights, at the gambling-table. A very mixed circle was frequently admitted to them, and strange familiarities of manners and speech were tolerated. On one occasion, at Compiègne, the queen requested the king to send her professional players to take charge of her tables. Louis faintly remonstrated, and urged that it would be setting a bad example, since he had recently forbidden gambling in Paris. But the queen persisting, he consented, as she required them, she said, for one night only.

The bankers arrived, and play, which began early in the evening, was continued until five the next morning, when the company separated to take a few hours' rest. In the afternoon of the following day, the 31st of October, the queen reassembled her card-party; but the solemn Roman Catholic *fête* of All Saints had for some hours begun before those devotees of the gambling-table finally laid down their cards. This flagrant disregard of the *bienséances* gave considerable offence, and was regarded as a great court scandal. Pious folk lifted their eyes and hands in horror. The queen jestingly excused herself to the king, who was certainly more blamable than even his thoughtless consort. The *abbé* of course absolved her. But Mercy-Argenteau did not conceal the incident from her "sacred majesty" the empress, or spare her the reports it had given rise to. Both as a strict devotee and a sovereign, Maria Theresa was deeply pained. She declared that the queen was running headlong to destruction, and she had even a word of reproof for the "excellent *abbé*."

Not long after, and while the court, the *beau monde*, and indeed all classes in Paris, were fêting the revolutionary "Apostle of Liberty," the Emperor Joseph II. obtained the consent of the empress-queen to travel, and to pay the long-looked-for visit to his sister at Versailles.

CHAPTER XI.

An Imperial Visitor. — Joseph II. — The King on His Guard. — A Diplomatic Letter. — The Emperor's Quarters. — *Mauvais Sujets* and *Polissons*. — Visiting Marly *en Polisson*. — The Queen's *Cercle Intime*. — Joseph's Opinion of Louis XVI. — A Taste for Perfection. — Pedlars' Stalls in the Palace. — Exploring Paris. — Lecturing the King. — A Changed Man. — The Archduke Charles. — An Imperial Traveller. — Mozart. — The Emperor at the Opera. — The "*Coiffure Iphigénie.*" — Speakingly Evident. — The Emperor's Sayings and Doings. — The Philosopher's Stone. — A Successful Alchemist. — A Conference with M. Necker. — The Apostle of Liberty. — A Memento of Franklin. — Bewildering Politics. — The King Taken to Task.

MARIA THERESA'S consent to her son's departure had, on various pretexts, long been delayed. For Joseph's object in leaving his country was not merely to pay a visit to his sister at Versailles. "He desired," he said, "to free himself from old prejudices," and proposed, as Count von Falkenstein, to travel *incognito* through France; also to see other countries, to inform himself of their system of government; and at one time he had an idea, after visiting Spain and Portugal, of extending his travels to England. It was this part of his project the empress objected to. Generally, she disliked his roaming habits, and although he began to exhibit some impatience of the restraints laid upon him, yet before he set out she exacted a promise that he would not be persuaded to accept any invitation or yield to other inducement to cross the Channel.

Joseph was then thirty-six years of age, and for the second time a widower. He had visited Parma and other Italian courts, and was no stranger to the dissipations that prevailed, though discountenanced by the empress, in the higher circles of Viennese society. He was also so much under the influence of the French school of philosophy, and so deeply imbued with the liberal ideas then fast gaining ground throughout Europe, that he was regarded as the head of the "party of progress," then established in Austria, in spite of clerical remonstrances, and the empress-queen's efforts to suppress it. Knowing this, she still feared, or affected to do so, that intercourse with the English nation would contaminate the emperor's moral principles, and shake his belief in everything held sacred among Roman Catholics, — "the English," as she said, "being nearly all deists, atheists, and freethinkers."* In Paris, however, his visit to the French court was generally ascribed to secret political motives, veiled by the ostensible one of a desire to see his sister.

The king, therefore, was put on his guard by M. de Maurepas against too freely communicating

* Wraxall's "Courts of Vienna, Berlin," etc.

on subjects of state importance with this apt pupil of the old wily diplomatist, Kaunitz, and ardent disciple of the great Frederick, who, however, denounced the designs on Bavaria entertained by the ambitious son of a no less ambitious sovereign. In the philosophical *salons* also, where the "advanced ideas" the emperor was credited with should have ensured him, one would have supposed, as a congenial spirit, a very warm welcome, he was looked on with some suspicion, — as an Austrian, in fact, for the French disliked the Austrians, and especially the family of "the Autrichienne." Even the Duc de Choiseul, on whom Maria Theresa once so confidently relied to promote her daughter's influence and to further Austrian interests in France, retired to Chanteloup, where he remained self-banished during Joseph's stay in Paris. None, indeed, but poor Marie Antoinette, looked forward to his arrival with any feeling of pleasure.

His departure from Vienna was announced by the empress to the queen, in a letter treating of the dissensions between the Turks and the Russians, and the Spaniards and Portuguese; also of the progress of the American revolt, and of the state of Polish affairs. These matters, the empress thought, "might be satisfactorily settled for the benefit of their respective kingdoms, and even of the whole of Europe, by mutual confidence between Joseph and Louis XVI. — both so young," she said, "but on whose good hearts and great qualities she founded her hopes." The queen, with her habitual impatient shrug of the shoulders, handed this epistle to Comte de Mercy-Argenteau, whom it seemed most to concern, and informed the king of her brother's expected arrival.

Prince Louis de Rohan was immediately despatched to the frontier to receive the royal guest. An apartment was arranged for him and his suite at Versailles, and the hôtel of the Austrian minister was placed at his disposal in Paris. But disregarding the preparations made to welcome him in a manner befitting his rank, the Count von Falkenstein, in strict *incognito* and accompanied only by Counts Cobenzel and Colloredo and two or three servants, entered Paris without beat of drum, and installed himself in an inn or *hôtel garni* of modest pretensions, l'Hôtel de Tréville, in the Rue Tournon, in the Luxembourg neighbourhood. On the morrow he visited the queen at Versailles; but no solicitations could prevail on him to change his quarters. "It was his custom," he said, "when travelling, to lodge in a '*cabaret*,' and his valet having already arranged his bed and other camp furniture in the rooms he had taken, he should not remove thence until he left Paris."

The queen, during those years that had elapsed since she left Vienna, had so constantly vaunted her brother's great abilities and acquirements, and many agreeable personal qualities, that in her own immediate circle curiosity was much excited respecting him. But Joseph was destined to disappoint both the queen and her partisans, as well as many others composing the French court. His very unreserved and sarcastic comments on all that came under his notice were not always perhaps in excellent taste. Frequently they were excessively mortifying to the queen and her favourites, while they gratified those members of the royal family between whom and herself a strong mutual ill feeling existed. It was, however, impossible that one so observant should long be blind to the real character of the women who were the queen's chosen and most intimate friends, or to her own excessive levity and frivolity,

He spared neither the Princesse de Lamballe and her Palais Royal circle, the Princesse de Gueménée and her gambling-tables, the effrontery of the Duchesse de Grammont, nor the immorality and grasping propensities of the disreputable Polignacs. "The court," he said, "could only be compared to a '*tripot*,' or ordinary gambling-house; a scandal which, if not timely put an end to, must lead to terrible results," — Versailles being full of *mauvais sujets*, and too many *polissons* sheltered there. Such were the epithets he applied to the mixed male society that frequented Madame de Polignac's *salon*, or more correctly the *salon* of Marie Antoinette, where the queen did not enter. "*C'est moi!*" she would exclaim, exultingly, as she came in; "*La reine n'entre pas ici.*" But the term *polisson*, though employed by the emperor as one of extreme disparagement, was not then used as such in the sense of the present day. It rather implied a *parvenu*, or one who could not produce proofs of nobility of an earlier date than 1400. Only those *grands seigneurs* who were able to do so were privileged to expect an invitation to accompany the court, when the periodical state visits were made to Compiègne, Fontainebleau, and especially to Marly; for which there were prescribed costumes, "*habits de cour, de Marly.*" The unfortunate individuals who could trace their noble descent to no remoter period than three centuries back, were, however, graciously permitted to pay their court to their sovereign in a sort of flying visit. They must take their leave on the day of their arrival. Marly offered to such no shelter for the night. This was called going to Marly *en polisson*. But the *polissons* to whom the emperor referred, and who were received on so familiar a footing at Versailles, were, in most instances, nobles of far more recent date, and some were not nobles at all.

Grimm, for instance, the famous purveyor of piquant criticism and Parisian scandal to the minor German courts, had been transformed into Baron von Grimm of the holy Roman Empire, by the favour of one of his princely patrons. But the position he obtained in the courtly, but corrupt and demoralised, society of which his writings afford many a vivid sketch, was chiefly due to his wit, talent, and musical skill. Yet his folly in painting his face, which was far from handsome, and was not improved by the artistic labour he bestowed on it, exposed him to sarcastic retorts; often as keenly cutting as the malice that flowed so freely from his own satirical tongue and pen. Then there was the *spirituel littérateur*, Rivarol, a confessed plebeian. He was a great opponent of Beaumarchais, and made several virulent attacks on him. But the latter, with a torrent of playful wit, contrived always to submerge his venomous adversary. Rivarol, Grimm, the Chevalier de Parny, and others of similar pretensions — light, lively, talented, and agreeable, indiscreet, and rather dissipated — enlivened the private social gatherings at Versailles, and found favour in the queen's *cercle intime*.

The king and his royal brothers were also but lightly esteemed by the imperial cynic. He seemed to discern the treachery and dissimulation in the character of the Comte de Provence, and instinctively to dislike and avoid his sister's subtle foe. For that sister's doubtful friend, the arrogant and libertine Comte d'Artois, his contempt was scarcely less marked; while, with reference to the king, he wrote to the empress, who had hoped for such beneficial political results to Europe from the confidential relations of the brothers-in-law: "The man is surely very weak, but he is not the imbecile some pretend. He has certain notions of justice; but he is apathetic, excessively so, both in mind and body. He can converse sensibly enough; but he has no curiosity, no desire for information. In a word, he is a chaotic mass as yet, without form, and void."

It was expected that Joseph would be greatly dazzled by the splendour of the royal apartments at Versailles. And there were still very evident traces of the excessive sumptuousness with which Louis XIV. had furnished and decorated his vast but comfortless palace, in that portion then inhabited by the king and queen. The changes and modifications of the Louis Quinze period — chiefly made in conformity with the artistic tastes of Madame de Pompadour and the expensive and luxurious ones of Madame du Barry — had given the relief of brilliance and variety, where before the sameness of a sort of lugubrious pomp had prevailed. But as the emperor, though he had chosen to make his abode for a time in a "*cabaret*," was no stranger to princely palaces and marble halls, he was much less struck, it appears, by the splendour of the château than by the general want of order pervading it. His thirty-six years giving him the privilege, as he conceived, to assume the part of mentor to a king of twenty-three, who was his brother-in-law, he took upon himself the thankless office of reproving and advising both king and queen,— though, of course, his words and acts were narrowly watched by ministers.

In the Château of Versailles, no less than in the magnificent châteaux and splendid Parisian hôtels of the wealthy *noblesse*, much that was really grand and imposing was marred by the meanness and misery in proximity to it. Joseph had a taste for perfection, which involves the miserable gift of seeing at a glance all that tends to produce imperfection. It tried his temper to see the itinerant vendors of eatables; the sellers of cocoa, coffee, and " *le plaisir des dames*," otherwise gingerbread; the knife-grinders, lantern merchants, and many others of the numerous traders who pursued their calling in the streets, — establish themselves in small shops, or set up their baskets, tables, or stools against the walls of the royal château, and, unmolested, carry on a brisk business there. All the idlers of the neighbourhood would usually be attracted to the spot; and if, as was often the case, the wandering scraper of an old fiddle, or Provençal with drum and fife, should join the throng, then a dance would ensue, and the noisy mirth of this improvised fair be continued for hours together. Joseph was fastidious. He thought such proceedings directly under the windows, and at the very gates of a royal residence, derogatory and unseemly.

But, most of all, his sense of the fitness of

things was offended, and his philosophy failed him, when he saw the very entrances and vestibules of Versailles filled with pedlars' stalls; and each of the elegant and spacious landings of the grand marble staircase — whose fine proportions and exquisite workmanship he would fain have examined and admired — similarly occupied. Trumpery wares of all kinds were there exposed for sale. And under the pretext of disposing of such things, trash of a more objectionable kind — forbidden and even infamous books — were surreptitiously introduced into the palace. No less just than severe were the emperor's expostulations with the king, on his toleration of a nuisance that might so easily be the means — as indeed he knew it had been — of poisoning the minds of the queen and her ladies, by bringing under their notice literature of a most meretricious kind.

Conversing with the king on an interesting visit of inspection he had made in the course of the day to the École Militaire and the Hôtel des Invalides, what was his amazement on learning that the king and queen had seen neither of these important establishments, and were listless and indifferent concerning them. It was the same with the Jardin des Plantes; where Joseph had been and had sought to make the *amende honorable* to Buffon, for Maximilian's gross mistake. "He had come," he told that *grand seigneur*, "to take away the books his brother had forgotten." Royalty, in fact, knew little of the capital, and nothing at all of the provinces; which, as Joseph told the king, he ought to have made a point of visiting. (He himself had travelled over every part of Bohemia, Hungary, and Transylvania.) Of the special needs of the people, or what were actually the changes they clamoured for, Louis XVI. scarcely knew more than that when famine and frost afflicted the land, they raised a cry for bread to appease their hunger, and for fuel to warm themselves. And with bread and fuel, enough and to spare, he would have gladly provided them; for doubtless he had the will, the barren will, to do good, without energy to find out the way.

There were many fine pictures and priceless treasures of art shut up in the dusty *garde-meubles* of the crown, or put away and forgotten in the *gréniers* of the château. Joseph, well-informed on most subjects, and curious and interested in all that concerned art, passed some time in examining them. Dining afterwards with the king and queen and royal family, and, as usual, talking incessantly, and with utter disregard of the attentively listening ears of the numerous officers of the household in attendance around him, he began to dilate on the merits of the various works he had seen; to express regret that they were so unworthily placed, so little appreciated by their owner; and finally, in no measured terms, to rate both king and queen for their indifference towards art in general. Artists, he told them, of even known merit, experienced discouragement, not only from lack of patronage, but of that interest in their labours which hitherto they had been accustomed to look for, and to receive, from royalty.

The king listened to these admonitions with a smiling, resigned air. Usually he made no reply; though he would sometimes acknowledge that the reproofs were deserved. The queen, however, showed signs of extreme indignation; and the feast of reason, or reasoning, supplied by the guest, seemed likely to be followed by a flow of soul, on the part of the hostess, little in harmony with the stateliness of a royal dinner-party. Scarcely, indeed, could poor Marie Antoinette recognise in this cynical, hypercritical, middle-aged Count von Falkenstein the loved brother she remembered at Vienna, — the brilliant young man who had always smiled fondly upon her, and so often had found excuses for the many wilful and wayward acts of his youngest and favourite sister.

Yes, a change — a very great change — had come over Joseph, both in mind and in person. Tall, slight, and elegant, with an abundance of light brown hair, falling in curls over his shoulders, an expressive, animated countenance, an aquiline nose, and a fine set of teeth, he looked, we are told by one who had seen him in the pride of young manhood, and habited in the rich old Spanish dress it was then customary to wear at the Austrian court on state occasions, a majestic and striking figure. But these flowing locks had thinned so rapidly that he was now nearly bald, and wore a toupee with a thin pigtail. From boyhood he had been checked and thwarted in the best instincts of his nature; treated with severity by both parents, whose affection was lavished on their second son, the Archduke Charles, to whom, had it been permitted, they would gladly have transferred the birthright of the elder. Between Joseph and this marvellous youth — regarded as a sort of "Admirable Crichton" — little amity naturally existed. Charles, however, died in his sixteenth year, — a happy event, as some thought, from the violent temper and arrogant manners he had already begun to exhibit.

Both Joseph's wives died of smallpox. To the first, the Infanta Elizabeth of Parma, he was devotedly attached; he cherished her memory, and wore her portrait on his heart till his death. To the second, a Bavarian princess, he was married, contrary to his own wish, at the command of the emperor and empress. Her death in 1767 was soon followed by that of his only child, the daughter of his first wife. Joseph was then emperor, — his father, Francis I., having been carried off suddenly by apoplexy in 1765. Though but twenty-six years of age, no suggestions or persuasions of Maria Theresa could now prevail on him to contract a third marriage; and as she withheld from him as much as possible any active share in the government of the empire, he took to travelling, and leisurely making himself acquainted with every part of the territory he at some future day was, independently, to rule over. Many reforms were planned by him, if not possible then, to be carried out hereafter. He visited the great Frederick at Neiss. The visit was returned at Neustadt, where the partition of Poland was settled.

A passion for a wandering life led him to Italy, where his love for the fine arts, hitherto dormant, was strongly developed. His father had been a very lavish patron of sculptors, painters, and musicians. Joseph possessed a more accurate taste than Francis I., a more appreciative judgment, but was, it appears, less open-handed; while the empress, with little discrimination as regarded their worthy employment, gave away large sums in charity, and for the needs of the Church. This once led the emperor to remark, on hearing that his pecuniary awards to artists were considered parsimonious, compared with hers for ecclesiastical purposes: " If I were to give away as much as my mother throws away, we should soon have nothing to give." He was fond of music, played the harpsichord and violin remarkably well, and sang with more satisfaction to musical ears than did Marie Antoinette. Gluck was especially patronised by him, as was the younger and greater musician, Mozart. The latter, at seven years of age, had created an immense sensation in Paris, as a musical prodigy. But when he returned in 1778, a finished master of his art, his wonderful talent failed to meet with its due recognition, and the great virtuoso, neglected, disappointed, discouraged, soon quitted the scene of his infantine triumphs.

The emperor, on accompanying the queen to the opera when Gluck's "*Iphigénie en Aulide*" was given, was evidently pleased at the reception he personally met with. But much more was he gratified by the enthusiasm of the audience, and the spirit and verve of the singers, when the famous chorus, "*Chantons, célébrons notre reine*" was sung, and, being again demanded, resung, — all eyes, as apparently all thoughts, resting on the queen. In that ardent and spontaneous burst of loyalty, though mainly inspired by the vigour and animation of the music, Joseph perceived, as he thought, that the feeling of the Parisians towards the queen was not one of such great and growing alienation as he had been led to expect. More circumspect conduct on her part might yet retrieve, he fancied, the hold she was supposed to have lost on their respect and affection by her folly and indiscretion, and the calamities he had feared were impending for the future thus be averted. His countenance beamed with the satisfaction he felt; and Marie Antoinette, perceiving it, may have condoned the offence he had given her that day, before leaving Versailles for the opera.

He had openly remarked on the quantity of *rouge* which, to his taste, disfigured her face. "Why not put on a little more?" he said, satirically, glancing around at the highly rouged ladies then present, as if seeking their approval. "Under the eyes; *rouge en furie;* it is very becoming — is not it, Mesdames?" And Mesdames, in reply, smiled a strange smile, and for a moment averted their hard, bold eyes. Through the thick coating of red and white that covered their faces, it would have been difficult to detect a blush, even had they been in the habit of blushing. But if her ladies seemed amused, the queen was unmistakably angry, and requested her brother to refrain from similar jests in future.

Perhaps he would have obeyed, had it not happened that, although the opera of "Iphigénie" was not quite a novelty to him, the "*coiffure Iphigénie*" decidedly was. Being in a jesting, caustic mood, he affected surprise at the singular unanimity of taste the ladies displayed that evening in selecting a head-dress. Now this head-dress was one of the many *chefs-d'œuvre* of the great Léonard. That sublime *artiste*, after the second or third representation of Gluck's opera, perceiving it was likely to be often reproduced, conceived it to be incumbent on him to invent for such occasions an appropriate, emblematical, mythological, and classical *coiffure.*

On submitting to her majesty the artistic result of long and anxious cogitations and many experiments, he was rewarded for his skilfulness, taste, and zeal by her entire approval, — "*C'est ravissant, Léonard!*" she exclaimed, with delight. And Léonard bowed himself to the earth, prostrate almost under the weight of his veneration and gratitude. The next evening the queen attended the performance of "Iphigénie," wearing a full wreath of black flowers surmounted by the crescent of Diana, in diamonds.* A veil flowed down from the back of her head, and on the top was a nodding plume. This classical creation of the distinguished court *coiffure* achieved immense success. The appropriateness of the emblems was so speakingly evident, that their meaning was instantly seized. It should, however, be mentioned that the feathers were a concession to Marie Antoinette's well-known weakness for a lofty plume. Besides, the eyes of the great *coiffeur* himself, as well as those of the *belles* of the *grand monde*, had become too much accustomed to head-dresses of immoderate height, suddenly to tolerate a lower elevation. But change is the life and soul, and the very essence of fashion; which tolerates not a long, or at all

* Métra.

events, an uninterrupted reign, even to the whims of a queen. A change, then, was at hand; and as ladies could hardly carry their heads any higher, a descent was imminent. The observant Métra had already announced that they were beginning to shed their plumes, and that a caprice of the moment was an arrangement in the form of a pigeon. "Of course," he says, "they expect the compliment of some allusion to the attendant doves of Venus."

But except to laugh at, and to mortify the queen and her favourites when at Versailles, fashion, with its extravagances and frivolities, occupied very little of the emperor's attention. He was far too intent on exploring Paris, and seeking information on every subject of interest. "He has been everywhere," writes the aged Madame du Deffand to Walpole. "He has inquired into the past, the present, and the future; but no one has yet discovered which epoch he prefers." In the memoirs and letters of that period, there are numerous remarks on his sayings and doings. They appear to have attracted considerable notice, and, together with the desire to learn his opinions, and to ascertain the precise objects of his journey to France, were the constant theme of speculation and comment, both in the *salons* and with the Parisian public.

Some credited him with matrimonial intentions, as he had been observed to show an interest in

Versailles.
Photogravure from a Painting.

little plump, rosy-faced Madame Elisabeth, — then in her thirteenth year, and supposed to be the destined bride of a prince of Portugal, whose pretensions might be made to yield to those of an imperial bridegroom. But nothing could have been further from Joseph's thoughts.

His visit to the economist ex-minister, M. Turgot, and his friend, M. de Malesherbes, was viewed with much disfavour by the court. But if, on the one hand, he sought lessons of political economy from the man who, as Louis XVI. said, was the only one in France, beside himself, that had the welfare of the people at heart; he, on the other, did not fail to hold long private conversations on the subject of finance with M. Turgot's rival and successor, the money-making minister, M. Necker.

He may, indeed, have expected to learn from him something of the nature of the philosopher's stone that had enabled him so rapidly to fill with gold the empty treasury of France, and which it was affirmed that Necker had found. For diligent efforts were then making in Vienna in many private laboratories for the discovery of that desirable possession, and with the full sanction of the wise and pious Maria Theresa. The Austrian government actually provided the apparatus and chemicals deemed necessary for experimental alchemy, and a large reward was ensured to any competitor whose labours should be crowned with success. But it was a punishable offence to endeavour to discover the valuable secret for private personal benefit. There was a tradition, which had obtained general acceptance as a fact, that the discovery had actually been made by an ancestor of the Lichtenstein family, and that it was the origin of their great wealth and immense landed possessions. This selfish transmuter of base metals into purest gold left the world with his secret undivulged. He lived in great splendour, though inheriting but a small patrimony. He built princely palaces, and had a passion, it appears, for buying land, — adding estate to estate with such astonishing rapidity that it became necessary to put a stop to his acquisitions, lest the whole of Bohemia and Moravia should become his, and he, as was supposed to be his aim, their sovereign. It was natural, then, that the state should regard with jealous eyes a pursuit so fraught, in the event of success, with probable danger to itself, and should put difficulties in its way, other than those specially incidental to it.

So thought that great and enlightened sovereign, Maria Theresa. The Emperor Francis had held similar views, and had even expended very large sums in the encouragement of futile attempts to make gold. But Joseph was believed to think but slightingly of such labours, and to wait but the opportunity to banish, at least from the royal residence, all the crucibles, pots, and phials, the charcoal stoves, and other apparatus of alchemy. Whether in his conferences with Necker, a more practical method of putting money in his purse was pointed out to him, none could tell. For though, as Madame du Deffand — to whom he had requested M. Necker to present him — assures us that he was most courteous, affable, and fond of lively conversation, he yet had his share of the Austrian reserve, and when he chose was impenetrable.

However, his conference with the great financier being ended, Count von Falkenstein would remain for an hour or two conversing with the ladies and philosophers of the *Salon Helvêtique*. There he, of course, met the rival lion of the day, the "Apostle of Liberty," but appears to have refrained from evincing any sympathy or interest in him or the cause he came to plead. When Marie Antoinette sought to elicit his opinion of Franklin and American Independence, he replied in the same words as, when reproached, as a philosopher of the French school, for his singular indifference towards Voltaire, — its leader, the great genius of the age, and the friend of humanity, — "*C'est mon métier d'être souverain.*" Born to reign, it was his duty to govern and to be a leader of mankind; in fact, not to be led, even by those at whose feet he might sit as a disciple. Yet, to the great alarm of Maria Theresa, Joseph was then sufficiently interested in the events taking place in the New World to propose making a voyage to America.

The enthusiasm inspired in monarchical France by the revolt of England's American colonies was then at its height. A very brisk business was done, even on the grand staircase of Versailles, by those traders who had added to their wares the medallion portrait of Franklin. It was in Sèvres porcelain, with the famous Latin inscription to the effect that he had snatched the lightning from heaven and the sceptre from earthly tyrants. The ladies of the court were all anxious to possess so precious a memento of their hero, overlooking its insult to their own sovereign. A rather coarse anecdote is told by Madame Campan, of the king's manner of tacitly expressing his contempt both for Franklin and this last mania of his worshippers. A very singular present was manufactured by his order at Sèvres and forwarded to the Comtesse Diane de Polignac, who was one of Franklin's most earnest partisans. Doubtless, had he dared, he would have made it more publicly known that he was no sharer in the general enthusiasm. But he was looking forward to be avenged on England for her retention of Dunquerque, and, advised by MM. de Maurepas and de Vergennes, had rejected the line of policy which the emperor and empress-queen were desirous that France, at that crisis, should adopt.

Adhering strictly to his *incognito*, the Count

von Falkenstein entered into no direct political discussion with the king and his ministers. But Comte de Mercy-Argenteau, the Austrian ambassador, informed the king and private council that the cabinet of Vienna strongly urged him, in the best interests of France, to refrain from the dangerous course of taking part against England in the rupture that had occurred between her and her insurgent American colonies. A far wiser policy, it was suggested, was to show a firmer front to the Prussian king, to obstruct the encroachments of Russia, — who had just taken possession of the Crimea, — and to aid in strengthening the hands of Austria. Otherwise the cabinet of Vienna must change its system, and ally itself more closely with that of St. Petersburg; which would naturally lead to the loss of French influence in Germany.

Long and frequent were the letters from the empress, explaining to the bewildered Marie Antoinette the political and financial position of Austria and the military projects of Frederick. "For the sake of her country and family," the mother implored her daughter "to use every persuasion, and to employ her utmost influence to bring the king over to their views." And, probably prompted by Comte de Mercy, she did her best to carry out the empress's injunctions. But, although, with fatal facility, she obtained from the king — who grudged while he granted —

places and pensions for her favourites and their *protégés*, she was too narrowly watched by both M. de Maurepas and M. de Vergennes to secure any real influence in state affairs.

The queen's replies to Maria Theresa — suggested in most cases by her private clerical secretary, Vermond — would seem to insinuate that she sharply rebuked the ministers for recommending to the king a different policy from that she had laid before him in the interests of Austria, which, as the empress told her, were identical with those of France. While the king, — as stated by the queen, — being also severely taken to task by her for listening to his ministerial advisers, was fain to acknowledge that he "was so much in the wrong for doing so that he had not a word of excuse to offer her." "She believed," she wrote, "that she had made some impression on him, and that she would probably next day send for M. de Maurepas and M. de Vergennes, and speak to them seriously in the king's presence."

If Maria Theresa founded any hopes of assistance from France on such assertions as these, those hopes were destined speedily to vanish. For nothing was conceded to Austria, to relieve the empress-queen's anxiety or to further Joseph's pretentions to annex Bavaria.

CHAPTER XII.

The Théâtre Français. — The *Élite* of Society. — The Duc de Cossé-Brissac. — Alone, in his *Loge Grillée*. — The *Début* of Mdlle. Contat. — One of Nature's *Grandes Dames*. — The Lady of Luviciennes. — An Imperial Guest. — A Presentiment of Evil. — An Amiable Nation. — The Temple of Love. — Mademoiselle Guimard. — "The Incorruptible Chérin." — Terpsichorean Divinities. — Delicate Hints. — "Royally Bad." — The Fire of Love. — *Les Adieux*. — A Brother's Counsels. It Is Time — Ah! More than Time. — Poor Marie Antoinette!

BRILLIANT audience filled the *salle* of the Théâtre Français. The queen was present, with the Count von Falkenstein, the lackadaisical Princesse de Lamballe, the vivacious Comtesse Jules de Polignac, the courtly and handsome though middle-aged Baron de Besenval, and the Comte de Vaudreuil. The reputation of the latter stood high in court circles as *un homme d'esprit* and a man of gallantry. In his manner of saluting ladies, the Comtesse Jules declared that he was unsurpassed. "She had seen but one man who could at all compare with him in that air of respect and deference with which he approached *le beau sexe*, while becomingly retaining his own manly dignity."

The man thus exceptionally endowed was Le Kain, the tragedian.

In the box adjoining the queen's, and with much more parade and appearance of royal state, sat Monsieur and Madame de Provence and the Comtesse d'Artois — Madame de Balby, in attendance on Monsieur, and quite a retinue of *dames d'honneur*, and gentlemen-in-waiting on the ladies. Then entered the Duc and Duchesse de Chartres, — she, as usual, resplendent with diamonds and jewels, magnificent attire, and original and exclusive head-dress. At her side was her bosom friend, — some said with significant smile, "more particularly the duke's bosom friend," — the pretty, fascinating, and talented Madame de Genlis. Slander was always striving to blur the fair fame of this literary celebrity of the eighteenth century, and chiefly because the age had no respect for the moral principles which — if with a little fanfare at times — she certainly aimed to inculcate in her writings for the young. But not only the *élite* of Parisian society were assembled at "Le Français" that evening, but apparently all the critics and play-going public of the capital.

Some of the courtly throng fancied they recognised the Comtesse du Barry in a glimpse they caught of a very elegant woman, simply dressed and closely veiled, passing along the corridor on the arm of the Duc de Cossé-Brissac, — that *preux* chevalier who, replying to the ill-timed jesting of Louis XV., when that monarch bade him "take courage and not grieve for so small a disaster as his wife's infidelity," said: "Sire, I trust that I have courage to bear resignedly any disaster, though none to support dishonour." Watchful eyes afterwards discovered, in spite of her veil, the thick silk curtains of her box, and her evident wish to remain unknown, that it really was Madame du Barry — interested also, it would appear, in the event of the evening, for she was then rarely seen beyond her own lovely domain of Luviciennes.

But where was that constant frequenter of the theatres, the Comte d'Artois? His countess would probably have been more surprised had he been present than she was at his absence; for, according to the not over-refined jest then current amongst his companions, he generally preferred *du thé* * in Paris to *gâteau de savoie* at Versailles. He had the privilege of the *entrée* to the *foyer*, or greenroom, of every theatre in Paris. But just then the count was actually among the audience, in the Théâtre Français — alone, and in a *loge grillée*, well out of the way of royal eyes, and caring that none, royal or otherwise, should intrude on his privacy that evening. The caprice for

---

* The extravagant, rather than great, actress, Mdlle. Duthé, who for a brief space held the French Don Juan captive in her chains, to the mortification of his Savoyard princess, though she had her own sentimental flirtations.

Duthé was past; for this poor libertine youth was in love — really in love — and, as he fancied, for the very first time. And it may have been so; for he was barely twenty-one, though married nearly six years.

But the curtain is about to rise. The entry of the queen is the signal for it. No state visit has attracted this large and brilliant audience. No new play has brought together the band of critics, but simply a very young actress on her trial before the public — otherwise, making her *débuts* — this being her third appearance. So successful were the two previous ones, and so warmly is she welcomed now, that there can be little doubt but that general approval will be the verdict heartily awarded on this third and final *coup d'essai*. She is a lovely and graceful girl, just entering her seventeenth year, — as intelligent and amiable as she is beautiful, and destined, when experience shall have matured her talent, to win for herself the appellation of the " Thalia of the French stage."

Interest in her is heightened by the fact of her being the pupil of Madame Préville, wife of the inimitable actor of that name, and herself celebrated in the *rôles* of *grandes coquettes*. She had been for many years on the stage, and her attractions being now rather on the wane for the line of parts she had hitherto played, she was desirous, on yielding them to another, in order to assume more elderly ones, that that other should be a young aspirant of her own training. She believed she had found a worthy successor in a pupil she could present to the public with pride. And the public voice confirmed Madame Préville's choice, and hailed in the first appearance of the youthful and charming Louise Contat, the rising of a brilliant star on the theatrical horizon.

Envy assigned this distinguished actress a very humble origin. One of the several versions of her history is that she was the daughter of a laundress, and that Madame Préville, struck by the intelligence and beauty of her countenance and the singular grace of her movements, adopted the little Louise when about ten years of age, and brought her up for the stage. If this even be true, it is no less certain that the ease and distinction of her manners, her perfect diction, her sweetly modulated voice, the exquisite grace and charm of her smile, her amiable yet dignified air, her gestures, and the pervading tone of refinement that invariably characterised her, denoted one of nature's most finished *grandes dames*. There is no exaggeration in this. Rapturous admiration welcomed her at her *début*, and remained with her unto the end; and many lovers beside her royal one, the Comte d'Artois, sought the smiles of the accomplished, witty, and beautiful Mademoiselle Contat, — in the aurora of life so lovely; in her declining years, as the Comtesse de Parny, so charming.

It was noticed that Madame du Barry left the theatre some time before the conclusion of the play, — perceiving, probably, that she had not escaped recognition by the royal party. And she may have been aware that the queen had the habit when, by chance, any allusion was made to Madame du Barry, to speak of her as "that creature." Even Maria Theresa was shocked on meeting with the expression in her letters. It was not a judicious one. The retired life of "the creature" at Luviciennes naturally provoked comparison with that of "the creatures" of Versailles, and was not always in favor of the latter. With the Parisian public the favourite of the late king was far less unpopular than the new favourites of the queen; while at and around Luviciennes she was greatly revered and beloved for her kindness of heart, the interest she took in the poor, and her extreme benevolence. She could not on this occasion have heard the queen's petulant exclamation, or the whispered rebuke of the *incognito* emperor.

On the morrow, however, she was informed that the Counts von Falkenstein and Cobenzel begged permission to pay their respects to the lady of Luviciennes, and to be allowed to walk through the picturesque grounds surrounding the château. Madame du Barry took much pride in her park and grounds. She was accustomed to walk in them daily, often for hours together. They were charmingly laid out, in the English style; and the fine range of greenhouses was filled with the choicest and most beautiful flowers, — a luxury then attainable only by the wealthy and great. The pavilion was a perfect museum of objects of art. Joseph and his friend seem to have been greatly interested in them, and generally well pleased with all they saw, — not omitting the fair châtelaine herself.

She was then in her thirty-second year, and still retained, without any tendency to *embonpoint*, the youthful grace of her tall, slight, elegant figure. Powder dimmed not the golden tinge of her wavy light brown hair, and no rouge disfigured her face. A strange contrast this must have presented to eyes accustomed to the painted faces of Versailles. She now dressed with great simplicity, but always in excellent taste. Leaning on the arm of her imperial guest, she conducted him through those fine avenues of lofty forest trees for which her domain was famous, and to those sites whence the finest prospects were obtained. And when, after spending with her the greater part of the day in admiring the beauties of nature and art, in both of which Luviciennes was so rich, Joseph took his leave, he replied to her "thanks for the honor of his visit to a poor recluse:" "Madame, beauty is everywhere a queen; and it is I who am honoured by your receiving my visit."

Cynical as he was, and sometimes even offensive, yet the Emperor Joseph, when he pleased, could make very gallant speeches and pay very flattering compliments. Madame de Genlis — towards whom, singularly enough, the queen had conceived so intense a dislike that she had ordered her name to be erased from the list of ladies received at Versailles — mentions two or three instances of it, and of his being generally lively and agreeable. Nowhere does he seem to have shown to so much disadvantage as at Versailles. For all he beheld there was out of harmony with his ideas of what ought to be. He had a strong presentiment of evil looming in the future for France, and that the gloomy horizon was fraught with danger both to her inert sovereign and his thoughtless queen.

Though not suspecting it at the time, he was under the strictest surveillance of M. Lenoir, the lieutenant of police. Through his reports, the king, who detested Joseph, became aware that he had on several occasions, in disguise, mixed with the people with the view of ascertaining the real reason of their wide-spread discontent, as well as their opinion of their rulers. "The French," he was reported to have said, "were an amiable nation, and nothing more." However, but a part of the nation was included in this dictum; for he excepted from the disparaging "nothing more" the working classes, and the political economists of whose principles and opinions M. Turgot was the representative.

But Count von Falkenstein's visit is drawing to a close. He is going to Switzerland; and at the urgent request of Maria Theresa — which he obeys, as it falls in with his own inclination — he proposes to pass by Ferney, thus declining to do homage to the father of the philosophers. Yet he would willingly have paid that tribute of honour to their "nursing mother" (Madame Geoffrin), as he did to Madame du Deffand, had she not chanced to die at the time of his arrival in Paris, — her death following closely on that of her friend, the youngest of that influential band of female philosophers of the Louis Quinze period, the love-sick Mademoiselle de l'Espinasse.

Although her brother's proceedings have not given Marie Antoinette entire satisfaction, and the pleasure derived from his visit has not been so great as she had expected, yet she purposes, before his departure, giving a brilliant *fête* in his honour at Trianon. Her theatre, which has been for some time in course of erection, is now complete, scenery and accessories perfect; and the opening piece is to be Rousseau's operetta, "*Le Devin du Village*" — the queen in her favourite part of Colette. But the event of the evening is the illumination of the gardens, on a perfectly novel plan. Especially the Temple of Love, also recently finished, is to be conspicuous in the midst of a halo of light, representing the flames of love, or the ardour of the tender passion as emitted from hearts supposed to be enshrined within that allegorical edifice. On its summit sits a smiling, but malicious-looking, dimpled, little Cupid; bow in hand and arrow well poised, as if about to aim. He seems to say, "*Gare à vous!*" for his wings are spread, and should he pierce your heart he will, after the pitiless fashion of young Lochinvar, fly, if he cannot ride, away.

The morning of that famous *fête* was a remarkably busy one. The queen exerted herself as though she had been a hard-worked member of some inferior operatic troupe. Mademoiselle Bertin prepared the costumes; Mademoiselle Guimard was also summoned to a consultation with the queen; for she rivalled even the great Léonard in the invention of startlingly novel headdresses. It was as a dancer she won her celebrity, and astonished the Parisian public by the lavish extravagance of her equipages and generally reckless mode of living. Her arrogance and insolence towards the director of the opera, and her companion nymphs of Terpsichore, sometimes passed all bounds; and a visit to Fort l'Evêque would be the consequence. But Mademoiselle had but to write a line and despatch it by her *femme de chambre* to the queen, with a hint that a bright idea had dropped into her head of a new decoration for the outside of it, and forthwith a messenger would be sent off with an order for her release, and a conveyance to bring her to Versailles.

She was an immense favourite there, and although the number of her lovers was legion, it was thought well to close the eyes to that fact; because she was so useful, and made herself so agreeable to the queen. And surely there were ladies of the court, not a few, who could keep poor Guimard in countenance. But it was with a difference, truly. Their peccadilloes were overshadowed by their numerous coats, or quarterings; but Guimard, as she knew to her cost, had no justification of this kind to offer for lapsing into error. Had not that great man, the king's *juge d'armes*, the "incorruptible Chérin," strict to the minutest punctilio in all that concerned genealogy, cruelly convinced her of this? He had compelled her — as he had compelled many other similar offenders — to descend from her carriage into the muddy Paris streets; because she had decorated that wondrously carved and painted vehicle, the work of the first artists of the day, with armorial ensigns chosen from the escutcheons of her friends, and deftly arranged into a very pretty emblazonment. Her splendid carriage was confiscated, and a fine inflicted, with a menace of Fort l'Evêque for a twelvemonth, should she repeat the heinous offence.

Mademoiselle Guimard bore the humiliation bravely; but considered that she was more sinned against than sinning. She confessed that "if she herself was a *parvenue*, yet her *amis intimes* were not *polissons*," but noble chevaliers of the twelfth and thirteenth centuries, and that a faint gleam from the glory of their antique shields mysteriously fell on her. Poor Guimard! she had great redeeming qualities, which the writer of these pages has referred to elsewhere.*

A mythological ballet was to follow the operetta, and Mademoiselle Guimard was to divide the Terpsichorean honours with the immortal *dieu de la danse*, — if that divinity, Vestris *père*, could believe such a division possible where he and that other divinity, Vestris *fils*, were concerned. Of the latter his proud parent said, "he scarce deigned to touch the earth when performing a *pas seul*, and only did so in pity to his companion in the dance when taking part in a *pas de deux*." These great *artistes*, and a host of minor ones, had diligently rehearsed their parts, and Sacchini, the queen's singing-master, had done his best to train the tuneless voice of his royal pupil to go through the part of Colette without too great a shock to the nerves of those listeners with musical feeling, or musical ears, who might perchance be among the too obsequious audience. Great applause always followed her efforts as a would-be *cantatrice*, and the less deserved the more vociferous were the acclamations.

* In "The Old Régime."

The rule, in former reigns, when the "king's comedians" (the troupe of the Théâtre Français) played before the court at Versailles, Marly, Fontainebleau, etc., was that no noisy demonstration, either of approval or otherwise, should be made while the king was present. But when royalty itself began to sing and perform in operas and plays, the rule, it appears, ceased to be in force, and the queen, like any other public actress, bowed her thanks to her audience after having elicited their applause. Seated in a box with Comte de Mercy-Argenteau, the hero of this *fête* leans towards his ambassador, and expresses much dissatisfaction at the scene before him. As delicately as possible, that confidential correspondent of the empress-queen had, at her request, frequently endeavoured to impress on Marie Antoinette that it was more conformable with the dignity of the Queen of France to patronise and protect singers and musicians of merit, than to perform in public herself. And the more so, that the natural gifts of voice and ear, the first requirements for a singer, — which, could she have believed so monstrous a thing, she might indirectly have learned from him that she had not, — needed longer and more diligent cultivation, before they could delight a musical audience, than, with the many duties of her high position on her hands, time permitted her to give to them.

But poor Marie Antoinette knew not then that

she had any duties beyond devising amusement for the passing hour. Besides, her circle of self-seeking flatterers told her a different tale from Comte de Mercy's; and in this, as in more serious follies, "fooled her to the top of her bent." Every word, every false note, was hailed as charming, ravishing, before her face; but no sooner were the enraptured auditors relieved of her presence than they changed their tone, and, with a sneer pronounced her performance, spoken or sung, "royally bad." But no applause did she receive on the occasion of this *fête d'adieu*, either from her brother Joseph or from the king, who was in the same box. He, indeed, dozed off into a comfortable nap, as he was wont to do when required to hear an opera — whether the *prima donna* chanced to be Madame Marie Antoinette or the celebrated Madame Saint-Huberti. The *ballet*, which with dancers of such repute could hardly fail to please, being ended, the closely packed audience gladly escaped from the little stuffy, though elegant theatre, to breathe, as they hoped, the purer air of the gardens.

The Temple, sacred to Venus's mischievous son, is now revealed to the company's admiring gaze in a blaze of golden light, typifying the consuming fire of love. All around there is light, not as of noonday, as was promised, but a sort of weird glare; now flashing up brightly, then dying away in a red and murky gleam. But whence comes this light? What is its origin? If, as the company pass and repass in their promenade, it lends an occasional sparkle and glow to the jewels and dresses of the ladies, yet it seems to impregnate the air with a very strange odour, — an odour unlike the sweet breath of flowers, or the perfume of new-mown hay. Dimmer and dimmer grow the flames of love, and more dusky the shadows in the remoter parts of the grounds; when it is discovered that the smoke and the odour which have greatly marred the success of this much-talked-of *fête* are caused by the dying embers of fagots and the unconsumed dregs of pitch-pots. Thousands of them, ranged behind a temporary screen, have kept up the aureola of light around the Temple. While earthen pots, filled with pitch and tallow, and placed in trenches concealed by plants imitated in wood and painted green, have produced the flickering lurid gleams, and, as their contents burned out, filled the air with an offensively smelling smoke.*

* This *fête*, in honour of the emperor, served the malignant Comte de Provence and his wife — as great an intriguer as himself — with a fresh subject for their libellous songs and epigrams. The minds of the people were still further incensed against the queen, and a bitter outcry was raised at the disregard she had shown of the needs of the distressed peasantry and the poor of Paris. "Fuel, so scarce and dear, had been consumed at that *fête* in enormous quantities, and what would have afforded warmth to shivering, starving thousands, had been wantonly wasted on a thoughtless woman's puerile fancies." As the theatres and some of the streets of Paris were still lighted with

It was a lovely summer night. Lookers-on, assembled outside the gardens, were as numerous as the company within. As the latter dispersed, how gladdening, how refreshing it must have been to both heart and eyes to gaze on the calm grandeur of the deep blue sky, and the pure brilliant light of the stars, after witnessing the scene of folly and frippery in the illuminated garden *fête* of Trianon.

Some few days after, the imperial traveller pursued his journey southward. Though he and his sister had so long been separated, and were in habits and feelings so dissimilar, yet the parting was one of affectionate emotion on both sides, — so strong and abiding is the family tie in German hearts. Full justice was not done to the Emperor Joseph II. either by the French royal family or by the French people. He who saw so much to lament and condemn in France and her government was said to be jealous of her prosperity. Yet at that time her peasantry were starving, the manufacturing towns and artisans in distress, and the government living on the credit of M. Necker. It was also asserted that he coveted Lorraine.

On the whole, his visit was unfavourable to Marie Antoinette. Yet it might well have been otherwise, for doubtless he desired her welfare;

tallow candles, it was probably by an oversight that the waste of tallow was not also pathetically deplored.

and had she but laid his counsels to heart, it is more than probable that much future misery might have been spared her. He promised to visit her again; but the course of events ordained otherwise. They met no more. He left with her, for her guidance, a letter or paper he had prepared, entitled "*Reflexions données à la reine de France.*"* It is a MS. of several sheets. As if aware of the difficulty of fixing the attention of so volatile a person as the queen on any serious subject, however important to her own well-being, he again and again, in slightly varied form, repeats his exhortations, and solemnly calls on her to observe them. He had formed a very mean opinion of the king, both in his private life and as a ruler. Yet he imagined that a high-minded, well-principled woman might rouse him from his apathy; excite his *amour propre*, and impart to him something of her own strength of character. But such a task Marie Antoinette was unequal to, and Joseph's counsels, therefore, were useless.

More to the purpose is his earnest recommendation that she will endeavour to moderate rather than encourage lavish expenditure, and that taste for reckless gambling then fast ruining many of the most noble and wealthy families in France. Further, he implores her carefully to avoid even the appearance of levity, and, by the example of rectitude in her own conduct, to purge her court

* A copy of it still exists in the archives of Vienna.

of the disorder and immorality that too generally prevailed there. "You were formed," he writes, "to be virtuous and happy. And it is now time — ah! more than time — to begin to reflect, and to lay down for yourself a line of conduct, and steadily to pursue it. Years advance, and you have no longer the excuse of girlhood. What will you become if you delay any longer? What but an unhappy woman, and a still more unhappy princess? Thus you will pierce the heart, which, in this world, has the most affection for you; for how can I bear to know that you are unhappy? Seek, then, I implore you, to gain the reputation of which your virtues, your attractions, and your real character are worthy."

Poor Marie Antoinette! Did she ever read her brother's counsels, or reflect for a moment on his pleadings with her to save herself from the evil he too clearly saw must otherwise overtake her? If she ever from curiosity bestowed a glance on them, remorse must have increased the anguish of her mind, when, in the day of her deep distress, she reproached herself for having laid them so little to heart.

CHAPTER XIII.

An Equivocal Personage. — La Chevalière d'Éon. — A Ladylike Gentleman. — A Secret of State. — The Empress Elizabeth's Reader. — The Modern Jeanne d'Arc. — Jeanne d'Arc at the Opera. — M. Campan in Doubt. — "*Ça Ira! Ça Ira!*" — La Fayette's *Preux Chevaliers*. — American Independence. — The Rebukes of the Empress. — The Farce of the 12,000,000 — Birth of the Duc de Berry.

THE court and Parisian society soon ceased to think of the visit of the Emperor Joseph. Other sensational events occupied the public mind. Not the least of them was the return to France of a man whose rank and fame differed materially from those of the parting guest. But the singularity of the circumstances attending his return both excited curiosity and afforded much general amusement. This gentleman (the epithet has since been conceded to him, but at that time he was regarded as a very equivocal personage) had won on the battlefield his spurs, his fame, and the cross of St. Louis. He had acquired some reputation as a diplomatist, or rather perhaps as a wily, secret political agent; and he had been secretary of embassy under Comte de Guerchy in London, unsuited though his habits would seem to have been for the office.

There was the swagger of the camp in his bearing, and the oath of the trooper too frequently on his tongue. Report also said "he would drink like a fish," only that, unlike the fish, he preferred a beverage stronger than water. He was at the period referred to about forty-seven years of age, tall and muscular, swarthy, sunburnt, weather-beaten, scarred, — having been wounded in several engagements since, as a youth of fifteen, he began his career at Fontenoy. For many a year this bold colonel of dragoons had been known as the Chevalier Éon de Beaumont. What then is the astonishment of all acquainted with him when he returns from England announcing himself as Mademoiselle, or "la Chevalière" d'Éon, and wearing the vestments of a woman — having, otherwise, by no means the appearance of being of the gentler sex.

D'Éon's *trousseau* was provided by the king to the extent of 2,000 *francs;* and with his long-trained dress, tucked up behind, not for graceful effect but for the convenience of striding along at a quick march pace; his triple row of ruffles, *mantelet à la reine*, and *bonnet à la baigneuse*, surmounting a row of grizzly gray curls, he looks a very odd figure of fun. From under the shade of his thick shaggy eyebrows gleam a pair of bright, bold-looking eyes. They have an odd expression,

— a little defiant, yet as if inwardly laughing at himself. And he most certainly allows none besides to laugh at him. Few, indeed, would thus venture to wound the womanly dignity of this ladylike gentleman. For he is notoriously a dead shot, and more skilled in the use of the broadsword than almost any other man of the day.

The cross of St. Louis, of an enlarged size, hangs dangling outside his gown or mantle. An officer of higher military rank, and a chevalier of the same order, once remarked, in the presence of D'Éon, on the impropriety, as he considered, of a woman wearing the order in that fashion. Throwing up his legs and displaying the military boots which he always wore, D'Éon began to gesticulate violently, and at last roared out — beginning with one of his most emphatic oaths — "I would have you know, sir, that this cross was won by me when such things were won and bestowed on the field, not as they usually are now, at the chimney-corner."

A secret of state was connected with this singularly ridiculous travesty, and the mystery has never been satisfactorily cleared up. Very inadequate motives were privately assigned for so strange a metamorphosis being exacted by the king and French government, and acceded to by so intrepid a personage as the Chevalier d'Éon. When in London, it appears, he had most grossly insulted M. de Guerchy, for which offence a *lettre de cachet*, that would have sent him to a French fortress, probably for a considerable time, awaited his return to France. But, strange to say, a letter written by Louis XV., and secretly sent to him by that monarch, put D'Éon on his guard against being entrapped in France or arrested in England. But when, after the death of the king, M. de Guerchy also died, and the chevalier began to insult the memory of his former chief, and to bring infamous charges against him, M. de Guerchy, the ambassador's son, felt it to be his duty to call the slanderer to account, and a challenge was the only means then open to him.

A whisper of warning, however, reaches the ear of M. de Guerchy, and puts an end to his project. "This pretended chevalier is a woman!" Was this to spare M. de Guerchy? For what would have been his fate in a duel with D'Éon, there can scarcely be a doubt. He may not have wished to take the life of the son, though he had not scrupled to insult and malign the father. Beaumarchais was at that time arranging terms with him for the surrender of the Louis Quinze correspondence, and either believed, or pretended to believe the report. Some slight colour was certainly given to it from the fact that Louis XV. had sent this chevalier, when a youth, to Russia, where, disguised as a woman, he became reader to the Empress Elizabeth. This was to get at political secrets, D'Éon being one of the agents employed by the king in his famous secret diplomacy. But Beaumarchais now writes that "he, or she, drinks and smokes and swears like a Walloon."

The key to this enigma was probably discovered in the letters destroyed by order of Louis XVI., who, to spare his ignoble predecessor's memory from further contumely, as well as to soothe the aggrieved feelings of the De Guerchy family, agreed with the sprightly M. de Maurepas — to whom the whole affair was a pleasant jest — and with the more serious M. de Vergennes, to hush up the matter, to continue to D'Éon the pension granted by Louis XV., and allow him, as he requested, to return to France. The conditions were that he should publicly avow himself a woman, and invariably wear the dress of one. To France then he came, showed himself in public, and, partly from curiosity, was received in society. His barrack-room manners are said to have greatly diverted some persons. Others, it would seem, were disgusted by them, and a few, apparently, much edified. These latter addressed odes and sonnets to the "Chevalière," extolling her as Minerva, and the modern Jeanne d'Arc. Several of the best Parisian houses, however, were closed to him, and only in private was he received by the king and his ministers. Yet Madame Larochejaquelein remembered to have seen "the hideous creature," as she says, at Versailles, in the apartments of her grandmother, the Duchesse de Civrac, who was *dame d'honneur* to Madame Victoire.

It was a perilous matter to offend the charming Mademoiselle d'Éon. She once was concerned in a terrible squabble with a party of young officers at the opera. It was found necessary to call in the guard to remove the fair lady by force. A sojourn in the castle of Dijon was the consequence; but the imprisonment did not last long. Some occult influence always screened D'Éon from the penalties he incurred by his recklessness and audacity. Released from durance, he returned to England, and, at Bath and other fashionable resorts of that day, gave public exhibitions of his wonderful skill as a swordsman. He had probably left France ill-provided with cash; but he made a good deal of money by his *séances d'armes*, which were well attended. The price of admission to them was a half-crown each person. Thenceforth, he remained in England; the pecuniary supplies from France arrived less frequently and in smaller amounts, and with the Revolution came entirely to an end. As years advanced, and money was less plentiful, his character became more subdued. Hoping, however, that quieter times in France might possibly restore to him a part, at least, of his pension, he did not entirely renounce the feminine garb, but wore a kind of compound dress; in which, combined with the petticoat, there was in the upper part much that resembled the *costume militaire*. D'Éon was eighty-two or eighty-three, when he died at Islington, in straitened pecuniary circumstances, in May, 1810.*

When this famous chevalier arrived in France as Mademoiselle d'Éon, Marie Antoinette, like many other ladies of the court, was anxious to see *her*. She even desired M. Campan, at whose house D'Éon was staying, to bring the strange lady into her presence. M. Campan felt some hesitation as to the propriety of obeying the command of his royal mistress, and determined first to inform M. de Vergennes of her wishes. The minister immediately requested to speak with her privately, and in a very brief interview seems to have convinced her of the inexpediency of gratifying her curiosity. With what reasons he satisfied

---

* Of the many guesses as to the real motive for the chevalier's assumption of female attire, and his retention of it, in hybrid form, after he ceased to live in France, none is more ridiculous than that of a M. Gaillardet, who, in a work called "*Mémoires du Chevalier d'Éon*," suggests that D'Éon was Queen Charlotte's lover. The king is supposed to have surprised the chevalier on his knees before the queen, kissing her hand. To save the honour of this royal lady, who had always been regarded as of spotless fame, the favoured lover declared himself a woman, though it was not until four or five years after that he assumed the garb of one, and that at the command of the French government. This story is too ridiculous. George the Third is said to have had his doubts on the subject of the chevalier's sex, and that the mental aberration that sometimes afflicted him was due to that circumstance!

her so completely is not stated; but it may be safely affirmed that he was far too prudent to reveal a secret to the queen which the king and his ministers had determined should be closely kept.

Whilst this and other nine day wonders amused the Parisian public, the struggle between England and the revolted American states was still going on. Thanks to the surreptitious aid afforded by France, the fortune of war inclined towards the insurgents. Franklin's cry of "*Ça ira! ça ira!*" grew daily more confident; his appeal to the king to recognise American independence, more urgent; and "Freedom and the downfall of tyranny" began to be echoed with enthusiasm throughout France.

The young Marquis de La Fayette was very graciously received by the queen at Versailles, on returning from his first voyage to America. An ardent band of youthful volunteers also eagerly desired to unsheathe their swords in the cause of liberty; to recross the Atlantic with the young general; and under his leadership "help the oppressed to crush the oppressor." Amongst many others who sought permission to join this *corps d'élite* was the young Comte de Mirabeau, temporarily escaped from the tyranny of his inexorable father. But the evil reputation he had acquired under the persecution of his philanthropical parent precluded his enrolment among

Marquis de La Fayette.
Photo-etching from Engraving by Hopwood.

La Fayette's *preux chevaliers*. Fate destined him to figure in scenes of still greater tumult. Meanwhile, one of those numerous *lettres de cachet* the merciless old marquis so readily procured consigned poor erring Mirabeau, for the next three years and a half, to the lonely fortress of Portalier, in the Jura mountains.

But while Louis XVI. still hesitated whether openly to enter into alliance with the Americans, or to continue secretly to supply them with the means of fighting out their own battle, the English cruisers neglected no opportunity of searching suspected French merchantmen; often confiscating the vessels and cargoes despatched by the enterprising M. de Beaumarchais. At length, pressed on all sides, the king, in February, 1778, secretly concluded a treaty of alliance with the United States (offensive and defensive, in case of a rupture between France and England), and on the 13th of March it was notified to the English government that France had recognised American independence. This was received as a declaration war. The ambassador was recalled, and the two nations prepared for a naval contest.

It was perhaps in consequence of the further report that an army, 40,000 strong, was also about to embark, with the view of making a descent on England, that a demand from Austria for 24,000 men, or an equivalent of twelve millions in money, was made almost simultaneously with the announcement of the signing of the treaty between France and the American states. Maximilian of Bavaria having recently died, the Emperor Joseph had immediately passed a body of troops into the electorate to enforce his pretended claims on it. Frederick of Prussia, unwilling to allow Austria to increase her territory, at once despatched a large force to threaten Bohemia, and another to oppose the emperor's pretensions to possess himself of the greater part of Bavaria. Very pressing at this time were the letters of Maria Theresa to Marie Antoinette, and most urgent her injunctions to Comte de Mercy. Her demand for aid was founded on the treaty of 1756 between the empress and Madame de Pompadour, when the marquise and M. de Choiseul ruled France.

It was one of its stipulations that, to the extent named above, France should assist the empress to oppose the encroachments of her inveterate enemy Frederick. The ministers of 1778 took a different view of the matter, and declined to assist Joseph to encroach on Bavaria; relying on the king's Austrian prejudices to keep him obstinately firm in that decision. And in his resolve not to weaken the strength of his proposed invading army, for the sake of serving Joseph's ambition, he did remain firm. But the queen, piqued at being bitterly rebuked by her mother for the extreme prodigality with which she heaped favours on *la Polignac, et ses intimes,* while she displayed so lukewarm an interest in the concerns of her country, her family, and the troubles that beset her *bonne vieille maman,* proceeded in her turn haughtily to reproach the ministers — Maurepas and Vergennes — for a breach of faith in respect to the treaty. Failing to bring them over to her views, she sought the king.

He, who in his mind's eye already saw Plymouth invaded, the insolent Britannia, who claimed to rule the waves, beggared by the loss of her American colonies, and George of England on his knees before Louis of France, would not hear of the 40,000 being reduced by a single regiment. But she found him more tractable when she named the twelve millions; for, like herself, he had no idea of the value of money, fond as he was of petty economies. Just then, too, Necker's financial ability in negotiating loans kept the treasury well filled. The twelve millions were therefore promised.

But scarcely are they secretly sent off by a courier to Vienna when, in eager haste, M. de Vergennes seeks the king. Rapidly he lays the whole matter before him, and sets the consequences of this subsidy to Austria in a very different light from that they had been placed in by the queen, or even protested against by M. Necker. A farce then ensues, similar to that which gave M. de Maurepas instead of M. de Machault the post of First Minister. At about seven leagues from Paris the second courier, after riding as if for his life, comes up with the first; and the twelve millions are brought back. By refusing Joseph the means of pursuing his designs on Bavaria, the peace of Teschen, in the following year, was doubtless facilitated, and Bohemia, probably, saved from the grasp of Prussia. Thus a service was done to Austria against her will. The non-arrival of the promised twelve millions at Vienna was of course known to the queen; but that she was aware to what cause it was attributable is doubtful.

It was, however, a period of great excitement. Not only had war and war's alarms for some months past agitated the king and his ministers, been discussed in court circles and the *salons*, and by the public generally, but events in the musical and theatrical world had unusually interested all classes of Parisian society. Envy and jealousy had sometimes been excited; at others general enthusiasm; while such incidents as a royal duel, and the birth of a royal infant, had received their due share of notice. The latter auspicious event — the birth of the Duc de Berry, second son of the Comte d'Artois — had indeed been made an occasion for casting so much obloquy on the queen for failing to present France with an heir to the throne that she may be pardoned if, in the midst of so many distractions and vexations, she failed also to inquire into the singular fact that the twelve millions, once despatched, never reached their destination.

CHAPTER XIV.

Gluck's Return. — Madame Saint-Huberti. — Gluck and Piccini. — An Iconoclast of Eighteenth Century Shams. — Misgivings. — Voltaire's Arrival in Paris. — The Patriarch's Lever. — The Benediction. — The Philosopher's Wig. — First Performance of Irène. — *La Grande Citoyenne.* — Apotheosis of Voltaire. — Glory and Literary Renown. — The Old Duc de Richelieu. — Voltaire and Jean - Jacques. — In Death United.

THE return of Gluck from Germany with the finished score of "Armida" — "a most superb opera," as he assured the queen — seemed at one time to threaten to revive, in all its bitterness, the feud between his and Piccini's partisans.

As asserted by the Princesse de Lamballe, the subject of the opera was chosen by the composer to afford him an opportunity of paying extravagant compliments to Marie Antoinette. But if his royal patroness was indeed the enchantress whose perfections he vaunted under the name of Armida, he was certainly not sparing of the undisguised compliments he paid to himself. His new work, he said, was his finest composition, and he would have wished with that *chef-d'œuvre* to end his musical career. It was dedicated to the queen; and probably it was in acknowledgment of that honour that she submitted patiently to the slavery of the composer's caprices, while preparing it for representation. Each part was rehearsed before her three or four times, — Gluck, in his fear of his great talent not being duly appreciated, allowing no striking beauty in the music to pass without calling her attention to it.

The part of the enchantress, Armida, who, he said, must be beautiful, he assigned to Madame Saint-Huberti, an elegant woman and charming singer, who even succeeded in eliciting approval from this most fastidious composer, of her manner of singing his music. Sophie Arnould, his Iphigénie, could take no new part, being about to retire from the operatic stage. Her once full, clear voice had become, at the age of thirty-four, a mere raven's croak. That "Armida" might be in all respects perfect, the splendid dresses worn by Madame Saint-Huberti, and made by the court *couturière*, Mdlle. Bertin, were a present from the queen.* Yet this opera obtained but a *succès d'estime* when first brought out, though afterwards it became a favourite. Piccini, since the

---

* Madame Saint-Huberti, who afterwards married the Comte d'Entraigues, was, with her husband, in 1812, mysteriously assassinated on leaving her house at Barnes, near London, to take a drive. The count in 1797 had been concerned with Général Pichegru in the royalist plots. Arrested in Italy, he was liberated on *parole* by General Bonaparte. He then escaped to Switzerland.

production of "Roland," during the absence of the German composer, having advanced greatly in public favour, even with the Gluckites, a renewal of the musical cabal, on Gluck's return, seemed imminent. It was, however, prevented by Piccini, who generously declared himself one of Gluck's most enthusiastic admirers, though his own merits were still unrecognised by his rival.

But the respective claims to preëminence put forth by the partisans of the Italian and German composers were suddenly thrown into the shade by temporary enthusiasm for the French poetic drama, — on the return of Voltaire to France, and his apotheosis at the Théâtre Français. The name of Voltaire was then a power in France; and a thrill of emotion ran through every heart when it became known to the people of Paris that, after an absence of twenty-seven years, the great dramatic poet of the day, the philosopher, the friend of humanity, and "iconoclast of eighteenth-century shams," was again coming among them.

It had for a time seemed doubtful at Versailles to what conclusion the vacillating mind of Louis XVI. would finally be urged respecting Voltaire's visit. There were men of infamous lives among the dignitaries of the Church; but appealed to by the austere Christophe de Beaumont, Archbishop of Paris, they united with him in representing to the king the necessity of placing an authoritative check on the spread of that philosophism of which

Voltaire was the representative. On the other hand, all Paris was expecting the aged philosopher; and from the moment when it was whispered that the visit was contemplated, the only doubt that he would undertake it was suggested by the extreme inclemency of the weather, his great age, and his many bodily infirmities. But though his body was weak, the spirit of Voltaire was strong and willing, and recoiled not before the discomforts of a journey then, and especially in winter, a long and arduous one. The king, therefore, yielded to the opinion of other advisers, who saw more danger in opposing the general wish to do honour to one of the most distinguished of French *littérateurs*, than in readily falling in with it.

Still there were some who had misgivings as to the wisdom of this decision; who would have preferred that his predecessor's reply to Madame de Pompadour, " Let him stay where he is," should have been repeated by Louis XVI. For they looked forward to the return of Voltaire to France with considerable alarm, as likely to excite the "masses" and lead to commotion in the capital not easy to repress.

It was one of those cruelly severe winters, so constantly recurring in France at that period. Paris, at such times, was a scene of misery and desolation. For miles round, the starving population flocked into the capital, for the chance of obtaining there a morsel of black bread at its daily public distribution, and for the fires that gave a pleasant glow to the streets, if but little warmth was derived from them. Most of the large hotels kept fires burning through the day, and, when the necessary fuel could be obtained, through the night also. In weather such as this, the roads hardened by a three weeks' frost, Voltaire, towards the end of January, set out on his journey, accompanied by his niece. He travelled in a large old coach, of the early Louis Quinze date, painted a light blue and dotted over with stars. But for the keen glancing of the small fiery black eyes that lighted up his thin wizened face, the little decrepit old man, as he lay extended on the cushions, might have been taken for a mummy. He was enveloped in a crimson velvet pelisse, lined with rich furs (the gift of the great Catherine), and a large fur cap covered his head.

Messengers were stationed outside the barriers to give notice of his approach. When it was announced, a number of old friends and recent *protégés* rode out to meet and welcome him; and on his arrival in Paris, he was received by the people with frenzied acclamations and almost delirious joy. Momentarily he appeared overcome by it, but quickly rallied. And as it was no passing burst of enthusiasm that hailed him, but the beginning of a continuous ovation, it acted for awhile on his feeble frame as a pulse-stirring, life-giving elixir. All Paris flocked to his *lever* the next morning. Rank, fashion, and beauty, science, letters, and *les beaux arts*, hastened to lay their tribute of homage at the feet of the *grand poète* and "patriarch of the philosophers."

The indifference shown by the court towards the distinguished visitor contrasting so pointedly with the honours lavished upon him in general society, it was suggested as politic that the queen should receive him at Versailles, and address a few words of compliment to him on his "Henriade" and tragedy of "Zaire." But this was to take place in the *grands appartements* only, — a distinction, it appears, that conferred less honour than a formal presentation. But the idea was not carried out, anxious as the queen was to see him. The clergy — and especially the vain and arrogant Vermond, himself an atheist — strongly opposed Voltaire's reception at court. Yet several of the philosophical bishops saw him privately and gave the chief of the sect no frigid welcome.

The "rosewater *abbé*," young Talleyrand-Périgord, was an ardent disciple of Voltaire. He had long desired to become personally acquainted with his master, and did not allow so favourable an opportunity of doing so to pass away unimproved. At one of the brilliant receptions of the young Marquise de Villette (Voltaire's *protégée*, "*Belle et bonne*"), the *abbé* sought the blessing of the "Patriarch," who, in the presence of this numerous company, amongst whom were several distinguished persons of the court, spread his hands over the head of the kneeling priest, and, with much mock solemnity, gave him his benediction. Less open to scandal was Doctor Benjamin Franklin's solicitation of the philosopher's blessing on his grandson. "Kneel, my son," he said, "kneel before the great man." The youth obeyed, and Voltaire laying his hand on his head, said in English, "God and liberty."

The journals of the time turned Voltaire's visit to good account, — entering into the minutest details on even the most insignificant circumstances attending it. In the *cafés*, on the public promenades, at the theatres, the one subject of conversation was Voltaire. The smallest piece of news concerning him was welcome. All that he said was duly recorded, as well as much that he did not say. Bachaumont's daily manuscript sheet is full of details of what he did, how he looked, and especially he concerns himself with the great man's *toilette*. It was certainly a remarkable one, whether he appeared in his morning wrapper and ample nightcap, or in all the glory of full dress, — velvet coat, antique in cut, and lined with ermine, and a Louis Quatorze wig, without powder. That he should have chosen to wear this enormous and unpowdered wig is singular. Its vogue disappeared with the *Grand Monarque;* and Voltaire's days of fashionable young manhood were those of the regency and early

Louis Quinze period, when wigs of far less magnificent proportions came into favour, and powder, that had been sternly rejected by the sublime Louis, was generally adopted. For the rest of his dress, it was unique, belonging to no special period, and it may fairly be termed *à la fantasie de Voltaire*.

The ostensible object of Voltaire's visit to Paris was to drill the actors who were to play his new tragedy of "Irène." He was difficult to please, and liked that they should hear the chief speeches declaimed by himself. Any favourite point of his missed, threw him into a terrible rage. Le Kain, whom he considered the greatest of French actors, and whose early patron he had been, was ill when Voltaire arrived, and indeed died, to the great grief of the poet, in less than a month after. When "Irène" was announced the theatre was densely crowded in every part, in expectation of seeing the author. But the fast failing powers of the feeble frame were unequal to the strain put upon them by the vivacious spirit, and compelled Voltaire to keep his bed.

The queen and the Comtesse Jules were present, and the Comte d'Artois. The duel between him and the Duc de Bourbon had taken place that same day. D'Artois had insulted the duchess at a masquerade. She had complained to the king, and demanded that justice should be done her, and an apology made. "She exacted it," she said, "not in her quality of duchess, but as a woman and a citizen." On entering her box, she was therefore received by the audience with loud acclamations. To assume the appellation of *cito-yen*, or *citoyenne*, was to ensure public favour. The *grand citoyen français*, Beaumarchais, and the great American citizen, "Franklin, the founder of liberty," had given it immense popularity. The duchess undoubtedly was the first of her class proclaimed *grand citoyenne*.

The king forbade the duel, — but it took place notwithstanding, — and commanded the offender to apologise. This he at first haughtily refused to do, at the king's command. M. de Maurepas, who conveyed the message to him, informed him that the result of a refusal would be the heavy displeasure of the king. The young count sneeringly replied :

"His displeasure! What can the king in his displeasure do to me?"

"He can, in the exercise of his royal prerogative, bestow a pardon on you, M. le Comte, for braving his displeasure," replied the old minister.

Both the Comte d'Artois and the queen, whose great intimacy with him precluded her from taking part with the duchess in this affair, received very scant notice on the occasion in question, from the assembled throng. "It was remarked," says Bachaumont's paper, "that her majesty seemed to be in a very bad temper all the evening." Eventually the count apologised to the duchess.

To return to Voltaire and his tragedy: the success of "Irène" was less real than complimentary. Exaggerated accounts of the enthusiasm it created were carried to him at the end of each act. At its sixth representation he was able to be present himself; and if all Paris was not there to welcome him, the fault was in the size of the theatre. The scene that ensued has been rightly termed his apotheosis. His bust was placed in the centre of the stage; a poetic address was spoken by Madame Vestris, in the character of "Irène," which she had played, and Brizard, who had performed Memnos, placed a laurel crown, in the name of the nation, on the brow of the aged poet. "It is France that awards it," was the cry of the excited audience, — a cry taken up by the dense crowd outside the theatre, and echoed, one may say, through every street in Paris. Voltaire, who had been nerved for this scene by a stimulative potion, its effects being passed, was carried almost senseless to his carriage. The frantic crowd would have drawn the vehicle themselves, but his friends prayed them to forbear. Arrived at the hôtel of the Marquis de Villette, he was sufficiently roused from his partial fainting fit to express a few words of gratitude to the people around him.

Tottering, as he knew, on the brink of the grave, he yet in the ardour of the moment resolved to buy a house in Paris, — henceforth, he said, to be his home. On the following day, April 2d, as generally stated, an honour, greater, if less noisily demonstrative than that of the previous evening, awaited him in the brilliant reception the learned academicians gave their distinguished *confrère*. In his restless eagerness for occupation he proposed that the forty should undertake, conjointly, to prepare a new dictionary on an enlarged plan. To gratify him, probably, the twenty-two academicians present consented; and Voltaire, as proposer of the scheme, took charge of the letter A. On returning to his home and his bed, he immediately required writing materials, at once to begin his lexicographical labours. A drowsiness coming over him, he raved for strong coffee. It served but to increase his malady, to rack him with pain, and to banish sleep when he most needed it. Marmontel being present, counselled him to lay aside his task. "Had he not yet enough of glory and literary renown?"

"Ah, my friend," he said, "you talk to me of glory, and I am in agony — dying in frightful torment."

The sleep he had banished he sought to woo back, but in vain, when his old friend, the Maréchal Duc de Richelieu called to see him. He was but two years younger than Voltaire, and, in spite of the very free life he had led, was hale and hearty, and seriously thinking of taking a third wife.* But sometimes he, too, could not get to sleep so soon as he wished without the aid of certain narcotic pills. These he recommended to Voltaire, and sent him that morning a supply of them. Disregarding the directions, he took a double dose, and as its effects were not immediate, repeated it; but in still larger quantity. Drowsiness soon followed, then lethargy; from which he was two or three times partly aroused to be questioned by the Abbé Gauthier concerning his religious faith. His answers were, of course, incoherent and unsatisfactory.

His last words were spoken when made to comprehend that the imputations on the character of M. de Lally-Tolendal — so cruelly and unjustly condemned to death in the preceding reign — were acknowledged to have been unfounded. Voltaire had greatly contributed towards the removal of this blot from the family escutcheon. "The king, I perceive, is just," he exclaimed, "I die content." His body was

* The old duke soon after married the widow of an Irish officer who had died in the French service. This third Duchesse de Richelieu was a very charming woman of forty. The duke survived the marriage nine years; his death at the age of ninety-one was occasioned by a neglected cold. He comforted himself on his death-bed with the reflection that he had done less evil in the course of his long libertine life, than he might have done, had he chosen. It was a great consolation to him, he said. Yet he desired that Sainte Geneviève might be appealed to on his behalf.

conveyed with all haste to the Abbey of Sellières. Twelve years later it was transferred to the Pantheon with extraordinary pomp.

In July following — scarcely three months after the death of Voltaire — Jean Jacques Rousseau suddenly died. Whether it was a suicide, or a natural death, is still an open question. But in either case, it occurred like that of Voltaire, under circumstances that seemingly were best suited to his habits and usual state of feeling. In a quiet, secluded spot, almost alone with nature, the morbid, querulous spirit of Jean Jacques breathed its last sigh; while the active-minded, sprightly, petulant Voltaire — his death-bed surrounded by ardent admirers of his genius — passed away in the midst of triumph, and a chorus of applause. In life their mutual jealousy engendered mutual hate. Yet they were destined in death to be united, to lie side by side in the temple of fame; and their names and their works, inseparably connected, were to pass down to posterity together.

CHAPTER XV.

The First Hostile Shot. — The *Belle Poule* and *Arethusa*. — The *Coiffure Belle Poule*. — A British Heroine. — The English and French Fleets. — The Fleets in a Gale. — A Victory Lost. — *Lâcheté*, or Indiscipline? — Immortalised at the Opera. — Disappointed Hopes. — A Blow to the Empress-queen. — An Unsympathetic Virgin. — Better Success Next Time. — Starlight Revels. — Madame Campan. — Christening of Madame Royale. — Thirst for Military Glory. — A Swedish Hero of Romance. — Count Fersen's Departure. — American Independence. — American Gratitude.

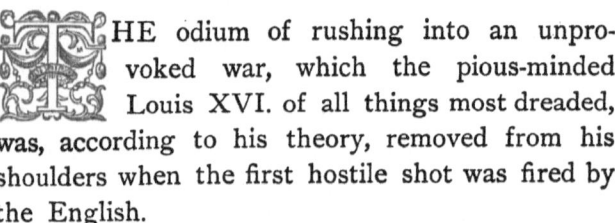HE odium of rushing into an unprovoked war, which the pious-minded Louis XVI. of all things most dreaded, was, according to his theory, removed from his shoulders when the first hostile shot was fired by the English.

It was on the 18th of June, 1778, when a part of Admiral Keppel's fleet encountered the French frigates *Licorne* and *Belle Poule*, and after a two hours' chase the *Licorne*, finding herself between the fire of two English ships, struck her flag and surrendered to the *Hector*. The conflict between the *Arethusa* and *Belle Poule* was more favourable to the French, — the English vessel, after a desperate fight, being so completely crippled by the powerful broadsides poured into her, that the cry "*À l'abordage!*" was raised by the *Belle Poule*. But just as her commander, M. de la Clochetterie, and his frantically eager crew were preparing to secure the prize, the *Monarch* and *Valiant*, perceiving the *Arethusa's* distress, bore down on the French frigate. The probability of becoming a prize instead of taking one soon appeared evident to La Clochetterie. He therefore thought it prudent to retire, and firing a few parting shots, returned to Brest. Fifty-four of the French crew were killed, and twenty or thirty wounded; among them four or five officers.

The English fleet, with its prize *La Licorne*, and a French lugger, afterwards captured, returned to Plymouth. In England some dissatisfaction, it appears, was expressed at the escape of the *Belle Poule*. The French, however, more grateful than the English for small mercies, though they had lost a frigate, proclaimed a great naval victory, which was celebrated with enthusiasm throughout the length and breadth of the land. De la Clochetterie and his officers were promoted, and pensions were liberally granted, though probably never paid, — government payments at that time being more than ever the exception than the rule, unless the pensioner were a court favourite, or a court favourite's *protégé!*

The queen and the ladies of the court and of

the *beau monde*, being desirous of expressing their sympathy with the proud feeling of the nation, in the abasement by France of the maritime power of England, gracefully wore on their heads at the *fêtes*, models, as large as was practicable, of the *Belle Poule* under full sail, ploughing the waves of a stormy sea of green gauze, and in hot pursuit of the *Arethusa*. This was the "*coiffure Belle Poule*," and so popular was it, until new creations suggested by new victories took its place, that all other *coiffures* may be said to have struck their flags, or their pendants, to it.

The wife of an English naval officer chanced to be in Paris at that time. Considering the "*coiffure Belle Poule*" an open affront to the British navy, she courageously resolved as openly to resent it. On the next festive occasion connected with the revived naval glory of France, this spirited Englishwoman triumphantly appeared carrying on her head five English line-of-battle ships, a French frigate and a lugger. At the back was an artistic arrangement of silk and gauze covering stiff net, and representing Plymouth harbour, into which the English ships with their prizes were entering. That there might be no misinterpretation of this symbolical head-dress, a streamer bearing the vessel's name was attached to each, and on the edifice at the back was placed the word Plymouth in glittering beads. The audacity of this British heroine is said to have "struck every one dumb."

Well for her, perhaps, that it did not raise a general outcry. Well, too, that "good Louis Seize" was slow to take offence, and slow to resent when offended, or surely, instead of being invited by the lieutenant of police, M. Lenoir, to take an early opportunity of crossing the frontier, a *lettre de cachet* would have consigned her to some strong French fortress, there to hide her diminished head or head-dress.

The second naval combat between the English and French fleets in the following month (July 27th) was an affair of greater importance. It is more especially referred to in these pages — where, generally, such events can, of course, be but glanced at — because of the conduct of the Duc de Chartres in that engagement, in which he commanded an eighty-gun vessel, the *Saint Esprit*, and its eventual evil influence on the fate of Marie Antoinette and the king.

On the morning of the 23d a squadron of thirty ships, under Admiral Keppel and Vice-Admiral Palliser, fell in, off Ushant, with thirty-six French sail of the line, commanded by Admiral Comte d'Orvilliers. The weather was extremely tempestuous, and obscured by thick mists, that occasionally clearing off, now revealed, now concealed with tantalising effect the movements of the hostile squadrons. For three days they endeavoured in vain to begin the attack, the French admiral, with that object, manœuvring with great skill. On the morning of the 27th the wind fell, and veering about, gave the advantage to the French. At ten, a brisk cannonading began and continued till three, with much damaging results to both squadrons. Sudden squalls then came on, making it difficult for the ships to maintain the position assigned them in the order of battle. In a dilemma of this kind, on the part of the English fleet, Admiral d'Orvilliers saw his opportunity of gaining a victory. The manœuvre he contemplated was signalled to the *Saint Esprit* and on her prompt execution of it success depended. But vainly the signals floated at the mast-head of the admiral's ship, *La Brétagne;* no notice was taken of them, and no responsive movement made by the Duc de Chartres. Keppel meanwhile rescued his ships from the danger that threatened them, and disappointed D'Orvilliers of his expected victory. The weather continuing stormy, and several of the ships being *hors de combat* from the violence of the gales and the enemy's fire, the English squadron returned to port. The French fleet followed the example. The damage sustained was pretty nearly equal — advantage to either side there was none.

This undecisive engagement — for which Admirals Keppel and Palliser were called to account — the French rejoiced over as a victory. "The English fleet had been beaten off, and her ships so much damaged that, to escape capture, they had fled to the shelter of their ports." With the officers deputed to bear those glad tidings to the capital, there landed at the same time the Duc de Chartres. As the Parisians naturally supposed he had taken a prominent part in putting the arrogant mistress of the seas to flight, his entry into Paris was a triumph. He hastened on thence to Versailles, whither the glorious news had preceded him, and the people of that place received him with open arms. At the palace itself, so eager were all to offer congratulations that scarcely could he make his way up the grand staircase for the pressure of the throng.

But a more frigid reception awaits him. The king and queen display none of the enthusiasm that has thus far welcomed him throughout his journey, and which, probably, he had become persuaded he deserved. The French admiral, in a private despatch to the king, has claimed no victory, but deplores the loss of one. "In worse plight than his own ships, the English squadron withdrew from the field of action, refusing to renew the combat; a signal victory was in his hands, but a 'failure in discipline on board the *Saint Esprit* deprived the French navy of that glory.'" Naturally, the duke's stay at Versailles is short; he must away to further triumphs at Paris.

Since the Archduke Maximilian's visit to France there has been a growing aversion, that may now be called mutual hate, between the queen and the duke. From this time it becomes a very active principle in both their minds, but by far the more dangerous one in his — because of his naturally Satanic disposition, and his greater power to injure.

The walls of the Palace of Versailles must surely have had ears, and as Sheridan Knowles says: "Where are walls without them that have chinks?" The queen, too, was not always able to restrain the vehement expression of her feelings. "*Lâcheté! lâcheté!*" she had exclaimed, when the king read the admiral's letter, attributing want of discipline to the Duc de Chartres; and this correction of D'Orvillier's phrase came to her enemy's knowledge before leaving the palace. On his return to Paris, the crowd collected in and around the Palais Royal and Gardens, and compelled him and his duchess to appear in the balcony to receive their felicitations. A further ovation, on the same evening, awaited him at the Opéra. The crowded audience rose when he entered and greeted him with loud acclamations, again and again renewed. Branches of laurel were presented to him; and at the same time verses, hastily composed for the occasion, and beginning, "Young, brave, and brilliant warrior, to whom the victory is due," were recited in his honour.

On the morrow, however, the real state of the case was generally known; also the queen's remark. Paris now found amusement in laughing at its own mistake, and celebrating in songs, jests, and epigrams the "hero who, having seen the smoke of the enemy's guns, had been immortalised at the Opéra." The crew of the *Saint Esprit* petitioned the king to remove their commander, and, yielding to their wish, he conferred on the duke the appointment of General of Hussars. This pretended mark of the king's favour was received as an insult from the queen. In vain his second in command, Admiral La Motte Piquet, vaunted the gallantry the duke had displayed in action, and confirmed his own statement that smoke and mist had prevented D'Orvillier's signals being seen by the *Saint Esprit*. Whether deserved or not, the stigma of cowardice remained with him. "*Mauvaise française! Mauvaise reine!*" he is said to have exclaimed. "True as it is that I did not disgrace my race at Ushant, so true is it that *her* son shall never by me be acknowledged as king!" This was meant to cast back greater dishonour on the queen than she had cast on him.

The queen's confinement was then shortly expected; and as a dauphin was desired, a dauphin was generally looked for. It is singular that this long-anticipated event should have raised up new enemies for the queen in the Comte d'Artois's partisans, occasioned a coolness between her and the count himself, — hitherto, apparently, on such intimate terms of friendship, — and so deeply aggrieved the Comte de Provence. The latter, but for this *contretemps*, seems to have considered his speedy succession to the crown as certain; as though he were waiting for the vacant throne of a grandfather, instead of that of a brother but one year his senior. This is plain from the tenor of his letters to Gustavus III. "I will not conceal," he writes, "that this reverse"—or unfavourable turn of affairs (*revers*)—"sensibly affects me; but reason, perhaps a little philosophy, and *confidence in God*, have aided me to support it, and to accept the position valorously (*en grand capitaine*). The first shock to my feelings I speedily subdued, and have since resumed my usual manner—expressing no joy, which would certainly be suspected as false; and false it would be—for frankly, as you will readily believe, I have felt none."

On the 20th of December the queen gave birth to a daughter, amidst a scene of indescribable horror. Her life was for a time in danger, from the impure, heated atmosphere of the room, which, with the corridors leading to it, was filled with a crowd of people of the lowest grade. Pressing into the apartment, they climbed on the chairs and tables; and in the scuffle to surround the bed, prevented for a while the physician's needful attentions being paid her. Thenceforth the abominable custom of allowing all who could force their way into the private apartments to be present at a royal birth was abolished.

The intelligence of the sex of the child was a disappointment to the nation, and a very sad blow to Maria Theresa. She regarded it in the light both of a domestic and political misfortune. "While France was without a dauphin, the Austrian and Bourbon families were still not firmly united; their long hereditary animosity was not extinguished; their union incomplete." And surely she had done her part to obtain a happier result. She had worried heaven with ceaseless prayers; had prostrated herself for hours together before the images and shrines of virgins and saints; bestowed on them costly gifts, and caused masses innumerable to be said and sung. Week after week, month after month, had she earnestly supplicated the famous image of the *Vierge grosse* to lend a favourable ear to her prayers. But this dull, unsympathetic, or inattentive virgin vouchsafed a fine girl only to the urgent appeals for a fine boy. "The inauspicious event increased her gloom. She became even stricter in her devotions than before, and was often in tears. All public rejoicings were suppressed; even the usual carnival revels were prohibited. For besides her disappointed hope of the birth of an heir to the French throne, the pressure of the war, originating in her own and her son's ambition, and which then was unsettled, threatened disaster to the empire and trouble for the evening of her days." *

* Wraxall's "Court of Vienna."

The Parisians were disposed to take but little note of the occurrence, though preparations had been extensively made for public rejoicings and festivities. But in doing so they had tacitly bargained for a dauphin, and cared not to celebrate with much enthusiasm the advent of a Madame Royale. Their programme was therefore very partially carried out. "*Ce qui est différé n'est pas perdu,*" says the French proverb, with which they consoled themselves, — hoping for better success next time. The theatres were, however, opened to the public gratis; marriage portions were given to a hundred young girls of the poorer class, who were married at Notre-Dame. The queen was also well received at the opera, after the public ceremony of her *relevailles,* — *anglice,* churching. The birth of this infant necessitated the appointment of a "*Gouvernante des enfants de France.*" The Princesse de Guéménée was chosen for the office. She was the *chère amie* of the Duc de Coigny. Her *salon* was much frequented by the queen; but both she and her society were of such dissipated habits that even the Abbé Vermond remonstrated with his royal mistress on the little regard she paid to the character of the company she mixed with.

Poor Marie Antoinette! Her contempt for the *bienséances* had been very remarkable during the preceding summer and autumn. How many insults she had exposed herself to, and had received, in the course of those night promenades on the terraces of Versailles and Trianon! There, easily recognised by those who had once seen her, and eagerly pointed out to those who had not, — often named too by disrespectful epithets, — she strolled about for hours with one or two of her ladies. Or they would sit on the benches with the rest of the company, and be highly amused at a chance rencontre, or equivocal conversation with, perhaps, a soldier of the royal guard, or intrusive young man of the *bourgeois* class, or others of lower grade; for the gardens and terraces were thronged by people of all sorts from eleven at night until two or three in the morning. When these "saturnalia" (the queen's starlight revels were thus named at the time) began, the king was retiring for the night — punctually as the hand of the clock pointed to eleven — and as regardless that the queen's honour was at stake, as when, his crown being afterwards in the same predicament, he thought that great calamity less important to him than punctuality at the morning meet at Meudon.

Music enlivened these *al fresco* summer night promenades. They were no doubt pleasant enough when the weather was sultry, though the hours were rather unseasonable. This was one of the chief objections made to them. But the queen could not see or would not acknowledge that it was an objection; but imprudently thought only of the diversion she enjoyed when so entirely freed from the restraints of her high position. Even Madame Campan felt authorised by the familiarity to which the queen had admitted her, and by the attachment one can readily believe she felt for her royal mistress, to warn her of her danger. Yet she invents excuses for conduct in the highest degree reprehensible, and, like Weber, often denies truthfulness to the statements of other writers fully as trustworthy as herself. Her own life had been passed in a corrupt, demoralised court, so that it is not surprising that a film should have grown over her moral vision, making it difficult to perceive that a king or queen could do wrong.

Her memoirs were written many years after the events she records took place. Of most of them her memory had retained but faded impressions; for at the time of their occurrence they were to her but the every-day events of court life. It is but natural also, that, writing after poor Marie Antoinette's terrible expiation of those years of folly and extravagance, her attached and faithful attendant, with feelings softened by tender pity, should endeavour to throw a veil over her many faults and failings. Yet while excusing so much, and without for a moment admitting that she was what the world calls guilty, enough remains on undoubted authority to show that the career of this unfortunate Queen of France was one of unexampled levity, folly, and imprudence.

The christening of Madame Royale, who was named after the empress-queen — Marie Thérèse — had taken place. The Comte de Provence on that occasion represented the King of Spain as sponsor. It is asserted that the Grand Almoner who performed the baptismal ceremony having omitted as superfluous the question whether the child presented for baptism was the legitimate offspring of the king and queen, the Comte de Provence reminded him of it. When it was put to him, he replied "Yes;" but with a peculiar smile and motion of the head, intended to attract, as it did, general notice, and, as he knew, was understood as he wished. If this really be true, one can hardly imagine anything more infamous. It is, however, quite consistent with his character as previously and afterwards developed, and with the conduct he had steadily pursued towards the king and queen from the day of their accession.

At the beginning of February, 1779, the queen reappeared in the *salon* of Madame de Polignac, and again gathered her *cercle intime* around her. Some of its most favoured members were smitten with a thirst for military glory, and were preparing for the invasion of England, or to take part in its humiliation in America or India. De La Fayette and his volunteers had left France; but regular troops were equipping for the expedition at Havre, — the Comte de Vaux commanding. His aide-de-camp was a young Swedish noble, who had for two or three years been sojourning in England, but had returned to France in the preceding summer with a view of joining a volunteer corps. For some unexplained reason, his aversion to La Fayette prevented him from serving the cause of freedom under him; and as the English kept so vigilant a watch on the proceedings at Havre, it was found impossible to despatch a force thence.

Meanwhile, the impatience of the young Swede to take part in the War of Independence greatly subsided. Well received at Versailles, and included in the *cercle intime* of Trianon, he appears to have become content to play the courtier, — quietly, unobtrusively, but with a devotedness that evidently had its source in some strong feeling towards the queen of the revels. However he might struggle to overcome, or strive to conceal it, the avidity and lynx-eyed jealousy of a number of self-seeking favourites quickly surprised his secret — Count Fersen was in love. And his love, it was affirmed, and it can scarcely be doubted, was not unreciprocated.

Count Fersen was a man of noble character. At the period in question he was but twenty-four, — with the difference of a few months, the same age as the queen. He was tall, and of a fine figure; his face handsome and features regular. The

Duc de Lévis, describing him, says: "He displayed more judgment than *esprit;* being circumspect with men in his replies to questions put to him, as well as reserved with women. He conversed with but little animation, but was serious without being sad. His face and his bearing generally were well suited to a hero of romance — but not of a French romance, for which he had too little assurance and too much self-control." He was not a Frenchman, in fact. But happily for the queen he was an honourable man, and better able than she was to impose restraint on feelings he dared not indulge. The queen, indeed, did not scruple to sing with a languishing air, and with her eyes fixed on the young count, Dido's address to Æneas in Piccini's opera of "Didon,"

> "Ah! que je fus bien inspirée
> Quand je vous reçus dans ma cour!"

while neglected favourites listened with sneering smiles and jests.

Général Comte de Rochambeau was then about to embark at Brest with a detachment of troops for America. Fersen resolved to accompany him, and the Swedish ambassador, Count Creutz, approving his resolution, asked and obtained for him the appointment of aide-de-camp. In April, 1779, he left Paris to join the expedition. On the 10th of that month the count writes to the King of Sweden (Gustavus III.):

"Young Count Fersen was so well received by the queen that it gave offence to many people of the court. That she had a great regard for him I cannot, I confess, but believe. Indeed I have seen too many marked indications of it to leave any doubt on my mind.

"The modesty and reserve of the young man have been admirable. His determination to go to America is especially to be commended. He has thus liberated himself from danger; but it evidently needed firmness almost beyond his strength to resist the seduction that tacitly bade him stay. The queen's tearful eyes were fixed on him constantly during the last days he spent here.

"I entreat your majesty to regard this as confidential, both for the queen's sake and the senator's (Fersen's father). When his approaching departure became known, there was general delight amongst the court favourites. 'What! M. le Comte,' said the Duchesse de Fitzjames, 'do you abandon your conquest so soon?' 'If I had made a conquest,' he replied, 'I would not abandon it. But I leave quite free, and, unfortunately, without being regretted.'

"Your majesty will allow that this answer was wise and prudent beyond what one would expect from so young a man. The queen now conducts herself with more prudence and restraint than before; and the king is not only subjected to her will, but inclined also to share her tastes and pleasures." *

Marie Antoinette at this time was certainly much indebted to Fersen's discretion for silencing the tongue of slander; but it would have been well, perhaps, both for her and the king, had they seen him no more. He, however, returned to France with the French troops in 1783. His

---

* Geoffrey's "*Vie de Gustave III.*"

knowledge of English led to his being engaged in the negotiation that resulted in England's recognition of American independence and the signing of a general peace at Versailles, in September, 1783. This service procured Fersen a pension of 28,000 *francs*. Five years later it was reduced to 13,000, and ceased altogether in 1791.

American gratitude decreed that a statue of Louis XVI. should adorn the newly planned square of Philadelphia. "Strange event! singular contrast!" exclaims a French writer. "The establishing of the American republic placed a statue of our king on a pedestal, while the establishing of a republic in France sent the king himself to the scaffold."

CHAPTER XVI.

Changes in France. — M. Necker's "*Comptes Rendus.*" — M. de Maurepas's Successor. — Death of Maria Theresa. — The Secret Correspondence. — The Emperor Francis I. — "We Will Die for Our King." — Unto France a Child Is Born. — "*Mon Dieu! que Je Suis Heureuse!*" — An Overflowing Cup of Bliss. — Privileged People. — Sobering Down. — Mocking Tongues.

IN the course of the four years that had elapsed between the departure of Count Fersen for America and the signing at Versailles of a European peace, many changes had occurred in France, — as well in the government as in the domestic relations of the royal family. M. Necker, who for five years past had replenished with so much facility the empty coffers of the state, was no longer director of the finances. He had ventured to suggest more economy in expenditure, which, being vehemently opposed by the court, resulted in the appearance of his famous "*Comptes rendus,*" from which the nation obtained its first insight into the financial affairs of the kingdom.

To enable him to carry out his projected reforms, and to reply to those who were inimical to them face to face, M. Necker requested the king to name him Contrôleur des Finances — Minister of State in fact; Directeur having been substituted for Contrôleur because of his Protestantism, by which he was prohibited from taking his seat in the council. In reply, he was invited to abjure Calvinism. He, of course, declined, and soon after sent his resignation to the king in a very informal manner — for it was hastily written on a mere scrap of paper, and rather cavalierly expressed. It had been insinuated in the council that he desired to assimilate the position of a King of France with the nullity of that of a King of England. Thus ended M. Necker's first term of office. A French writer has called it "the initiation of the great Revolution; the second term, its consummation."

A few months later in the same year (1781) M. de Maurepas paid the debt of nature — gay to the last, and expiring with a *bon mot* hovering on his lips. The king and Mesdames deeply regretted the old courtier. "Ah!" said the king, in a tearful voice, and with almost childlike naïveté, "ah, my dear friend! I shall never again hear him walking about in his room above mine."

It devolved on M. de Vergennes, a man of more serious character, and who was probably more sincerely attached to the king, to continue his predecessor's work of sustaining the weak monarch on his throne, and, as far as possible, by concealing his deficiencies, to "throw, as it were, a cloak of respectability over his utter inaptitude as a ruler." Until then M. de Vergennes, as Minister of Foreign Affairs, had but acted in concert with his colleague, to whose office of First Minister, or President of the Council, he was now to succeed, but not to the title. In abolishing that designation the king fancied he freed himself from all undue influence,— "he reigned alone," — while he had, in fact, only surrendered himself to the far more dangerous influence and guidance of Marie Antoinette. The post of M. de Vergennes was, therefore, one of difficulty and danger, and the more so as the queen was bent on obtaining his dismissal. Probably she would have succeeded, but her aim was to reinstate M. de Choiseul. Again and again she returned to the subject. The minister was, of course, fully aware of it, and mutual espionage was the rule. He, however, continued to fortify the king in his resolution never to recall to power the friend of Austria and the suspected poisoner of his father.

"Let Madame de Polignac know that I mean to retain my place in the ministry until dismissed from it by death," said M. de Vergennes to one of that lady's intimate friends, and forthwith the message was conveyed to the queen. And she allowed him to keep his word. For though fond of domination, and when opposed vindictive, she was yet far too frivolous to offer any sustained resistance to a firmer will than her own.

But to return to 1780, the great event of that year as regarded the queen was the death of Maria Theresa. She died on the 29th of November, the news reaching Versailles only on the last day of the year. Though naturally at the time much affected by it, the queen's grief was but a transient emotion, the passing of a vapoury cloud over a bright summer sky, — the event scarcely interrupting the gay round of dissipation in which she now more than ever indulged. Years of separation, and at an age when the mind is more prone to receive new impressions than to retain the earlier ones, had also weakened the tie of home affections. In one sense the death of the empress-queen was a great relief to Marie Antoinette. She was exempted by it from an espionage that had been far more harmful than beneficial; and from those constant lecturings, whose chief, if not sole object, was to direct, through the young queen's influence, the policy of France, — to render it subservient to that of Austria, and to the furtherance of the emperor's and empress's own ambitious aims. For in no manner could her secret correspondence with De Mercy-Argenteau, and her private remonstrances to Marie Antoinette, founded on his reports, remedy the evil results — which, perhaps, she too late perceived — of her own shameful and utter neglect to give education and an early moral training to her young daughters, who were equally neglected by both parents.

Francis was a very handsome man, a graceful rider, and a good-tempered, extravagant libertine. But he could scarcely write his own name, or read that of another. It was customary when he attended the opera or theatre for some amiably disposed lady to read the programme to him, to spare him the shame — though probably she alone felt any — of not being able to make it out himself. With the politics and prayers of the empress, Francis never interfered; and as she was afraid he would be killed if he went to the wars (this was the subject of many a joke with her warlike foe, the great Frederick), he occupied himself with creating new distractions for the abundance of leisure that otherwise might have hung heavily on his hands. Thus, with a mother who was both an ambitious politician and a narrow-minded bigot, and a father wholly engrossed with amusements in which they could not share, the family of thirteen children, uncared for as the grass of the field, grew wild, after their own sweet will, during their early years.

Death must have been welcomed as a kindly visitor by Maria Theresa; for, though but sixty-three years of age, she was a mass of bodily ailments. In her youth her personal appearance was agreeable, though possessing none of the ideal beauty which, with singular servility, flatterers so often assign to women of royal or elevated rank, without evidence of any trace of the reality having existed to excuse it. It had been so with Maria Theresa. That scene of a weeping empress-queen of twenty-three — a vision of beauty with an infant cherub in her arms — surrounded by "haughty Magyars" in full picturesque costume; the sudden drawing forth of their "glittering swords;" the simultaneous exclamation, "We will die for our king, Maria Theresa" (it was only as king that they acknowledged her), is far more ideal than real. But having been worked up by imaginative writers to undue prominence, it has served to invest with romantic interest an able political schemer — one of the most unscrupulous of sovereigns when there occurred a chance of enlarging her own territory at the expense of her neighbors. The corruption in the carrying on of her government exceeded that of any other court in Europe; and her system of espionage was intolerable, — throwing that of Louis XIV. and Louis XV. quite into the shade. Many secret societies owed their origin to it, — men, and women too, of the higher classes being desirous, without at that time any treasonable objects, of securing a place of *réunion*, where, free from the surveillance of the empress's agents, they could unreservedly interchange thoughts and opinions.

Louis XVI. had always contrived to evade adopting the advice which the artful empress, *en bonne vieille maman*, would now and then endeavor to impress on the unsympathetic mind of her royal son-in-law. But his Austrian prejudices still grew and flourished; and Mesdames, who otherwise lived quietly at Bellevue in their own small circle — the last vestige of the old *régime* — made it a point of duty to aid their old friend Maurepas in keeping them in full vigour.

But the much distrusted empress is dead. M. de Maurepas has also quitted the world's stage, and a sad gap his departure has made in the little court of Bellevue. There yet remains, however, M. de Vergennes. He is as willing as Mesdames, and fully able, they imagine, to curb the now unaided pretensions of "the Autrichienne;" for Louis abhors the Abbé Vermond, and Comte de Mercy, though devoted to the queen, has been obtrusive only when thrust forward by the urgency of Maria Theresa.

Suddenly, however, "the Autrichienne" becomes a power in the state. At Versailles, on the 22d of October, 1781, a child is born. The king advances towards the couch on which the queen reposes. With a profound bow, and in a voice that falters with emotion, "Madame," he says, "you have fulfilled the dearest wishes of my heart and the anxious hopes of the nation; you are the mother of a dauphin." The auspicious event is proclaimed. There is joy, thrilling joy, throughout the kingdom, — save in the palaces of the Comtes de Provence and d'Artois, and in the Palais Royal. But Marie Antoinette can now clap her hands and repeat the exclamation of the little Comtesse d'Artois — six years ago so triumphant, now so cast down — "*Mon Dieu! que je suis heureuse!*" The Parisians, in extra and more brilliant *fêtes*, will more than make up for the curtailment of the rejoicings of 1778. But first they must regain a little composure, for it is recorded that their superabundant joy found expression in a sort of delirium, — people of all grades, and who had no previous acquaintance with each other, indulging in fraternal embraces in the street, with mutual congratulations on the birth of a son to France. Others, less demonstrative, were content with a hearty hand-shaking; while the more emotional fell into one another's arms and sobbed out their gratitude to *le bon Dieu*, who had vouchsafed to France this pledge of a prosperous future, — this earnest of peace, plenty, and public tranquillity.

It is remarkable that this singular manner of expressing their feelings on any occasion of great public interest was not infrequent with the Parisian public. With few exceptions, so large-hearted did each individual suddenly become, and so exuberant in his sentiments of good-will to all mankind, that nothing could satisfy him under this fervour and expansion of soul but a rush into the street to clutch, in a stifling embrace, the first person encountered. He may never have been met before, never be seen again; he may be beggar or noble, intimate friend or deadly foe, a congenial soul or frigid old curmudgeon; no matter, in short, what or who he may be, but he (and sometimes it was she) must then and there be pressed to his heart and share with him, though it be but for a moment, his overflowing cup of ineffable bliss.

Louis himself, on the occasion in question, went through a similar farcical display of excessive joy. He laughed, he wept, the tears streaming down his fat face. He ran in and out of the anteroom, presenting his hand, to kiss or to shake, or both if they pleased, to all and each indiscriminately, from the solemn grandees, who were there to attest the birth, to the humblest lackey in attendance. The royal infant, splendidly arrayed and with the grand cross of St. Louis on his breast, was placed in his satin and point-lace bassinette to receive the homage of the great officers of state. It is recorded that he replied in a most suitable manner to the many flattering speeches addressed to him; and this being the first opportunity he had had of exhibiting the power of his lungs, he availed himself of it freely.

Paris and Versailles, and the chief towns of France, were in festive array, and the people in festive mood for a month at least. The *dames de la halle*, and the *poissardes* — those important and picturesque personages in all public rejoicings in France — visited Versailles in full costume to compliment and congratulate the queen. Returning to Paris, they filled the royal boxes at the

Opéra and theatres, as by prescriptive right they were privileged on such great occasions to do. And a pretty show they made in their black silk dresses, antique laces, and old-fashioned gold and diamond ornaments — the most venerable among the aged, the handsomest of the younger portion, being usually chosen to represent the rest of the sisterhood. The same privileges were then claimed by the chimney-sweepers. Their claim was allowed, but precedence was of course accorded to the ladies. The honourable company of chimney-sweepers, therefore, selecting only the *élite* of their number as delegates of the guild, graced the royal boxes on following nights. An extra bath was taken to do honour to the occasion, it is satisfactory to learn. "They wore powder in their hair, and their broadcloth was of remarkable fineness."

The customary presents have been made to the queen, — diamonds of great magnificence. The churching and christening are past; very grand ceremonies they were, no expense being spared, M. Necker having left a full treasury, to make them as imposing as possible. Popular excitement is subsiding, and generally France is relapsing into a soberer mood. Cold weather is setting in. The poor are beginning to shiver, and prophets of evil have predicted a winter of extreme severity, an evil that usually brings many others in its train. The nation, however, has given ample proof, in the unfeigned satisfaction it has so unmistakably evinced at the birth of an heir to the throne, that it is loyal, and still attached to its sovereign. And this in spite of the slanderous reports that flow from the impure pen of the Comte de Provence, and the jeers and jests with which the mocking tongue of the Duc de Chartres amuses the frequenters of the Palais Royal orgies.

caprice of this favourite. Her nomination made, the queen of course approved, and the poor king was then summoned to sign and seal. Often he did so with trembling hand.

M. de Maurepas, who was regarded as a model courtier of the old school, entirely mistrusted those of the new, when it was a question of admitting them to responsible posts in the government. He would have only men who enjoyed some share of public favour. And though he did not always support them in their views to the fullest extent, and thus neutralised in a measure the benefits of his system, so far no real harm had been done. But a remarkable change for the worse was speedily evident when court favourites began to take the places of popular ones. The crisis it had been the endeavour of the latter to avert became inevitable by the faults of the former. Its approach was hastened, and its violence increased, by the abandonment of all attempted reforms, and a return to the abuses and disorders of the old system.*

But to any details of state affairs Marie Antoinette gave but a very small part of her attention. Maternity had not abated her eager pursuit of frivolous pleasures. If she had taken the reins of power from the feeble hands of the king, it was but to deliver them into the grasping ones of others. She was content with the conviction

* Mignet's "*Revolution Française.*"

that she had leavened the ministry with men who would look well to her interests (uphold her power by upholding their own), and who would discourage unreasonable hopes which enthusiasm for the American cause, and the worship of Franklin, had given rise to in the lower strata of society. She expected them also to prevent the recurrence of those unpleasant murmurings with which the king, when ill advised, had accompanied his consent to demands she had now and then made for herself and her friends on the public purse. For the rest, her second self, the Duchesse Jules, and the duke's sister, the Comtesse Diane, would not fail to remind her, she knew, of any châteaux or wide domains at the king's disposal which it might be desirable to bestow on them; while the *chers amis* and other less dear friends of these ladies could also be trusted to take care of themselves.

When from any cause the dear duchess and the queen were separated for a few days or hours, whether only by the short distance from Trianon to Versailles, or by a longer one, a horse was always kept saddled, day and night, with a courier at hand ready to mount on the instant, to bear letters or messages from the queen to her much loved friend. As perchance she might desire personally to reply to the queen's missive, the duchess's carriage was likewise always in waiting, with horses ready harnessed, and coachmen and lackeys in attendance, to bear their mistress with all speed to her anxiously expectant sovereign lady. Had this charming duchess been the king's instead of M. de Vaudreuil's *maîtresse-en-titre*, French gallantry, as a writer of that nation, "*galante, par excellence*," has observed, would have prevented any notice other than lenient being taken of presents made to that lady, within any reasonable limits.

They could then have understood why he should bestow a large marriage portion and a *parure* of diamonds on her daughter, — a child of twelve years, just married to the Comte de Grammont, whom the king created Duc de Guiche, and on the wedding day gave him the important appointment of captain of the king's guards, — several lucrative places on the noble Duc de Polignac, the reversion of others and, *en attendant* possession, an adequate pension, with three millions of *francs* to the duchess as compensation for her disappointment at finding the duchy she had coveted was a fief of the crown and could not be alienated; all this, with the further bagatelle of half a million of *francs* to enable the *spirituel* M. de Vaudreuil to tide over a temporary pecuniary difficulty. Had it been done for the *bon plaisir* of the king, well and good; such had long been the habit of French kings, and Louis XVI. might in this respect have continued to tread in the steps of his predecessors without let or hindrance. However, even the foul breath of slander never attributed to him predilections of this kind. But he should have been wary of transferring his privileges to the queen.

One of the most brilliant of Parisian *salons* closed its doors at this time, — that of the Princesse de Rohan-Guémenée. The prince became a bankrupt, having ruined himself and brought ruin on many others by excessive gambling. His debts were enormous, and he had made away with funds entrusted to him. The princess, compelled to give up her hôtel and leave Paris, retired to Brussels, to the great chagrin of the distinguished but very equivocal circle she was accustomed to entertain three evenings in the week. Her disappearance from the world of rank and fashion was as the sudden fall of a brilliant meteor while swiftly traversing the heavens, paling all lesser lights, dazzling all beholders, until the moment of its extinction.

This disastrous *contretemps*, the news of which was received with consternation by all Paris, seemed, however, to have occurred for the special benefit of the Duchesse Jules. It compelled the princess to resign her appointment of governess to the Enfants de France. Her favour with the queen had lately, for some unexplained reason, been rapidly on the wane. That of her rival had proportionately increased, and but for the strong feeling of jealousy, now very openly displayed amongst less favoured members of her majesty's intimate circle, the post of governess would have been transferred to the duchess. It was true, as the queen observed, that the placid, languid temperament of her friend unfitted her for such a charge, and that she would herself probably be unwilling to accept it; but she hoped to prevail on her to set aside all scruples and to give her this proof of her friendship.

The emoluments of the office, then of course a mere sinecure, were considerable. As a further inducement to the duchess to accept it, the queen was prepared to assist her in its duties, — in short, to pay a brief visit sometimes with her to the royal nursery, and afterwards to lunch *tête-à-tête* with her in the duchess's room. This, as she most considerately said, would entail some further expense on her friend; she proposed, therefore, and the king approved, an addition of 65,000 *francs* to the salary. It may be inferred that Madame de Polignac did not refuse to oblige her majesty. The duke, in fact, who was *grand-écuyer* to the queen, — an office abolished in the former reign, but revived in the present one especially for him, — would not have permitted her. He allowed great latitude in the choice of male friends, and, as was the rule in the *bonne compagnie* of that day, was not overscrupulous as to the more or less intimacy of the friendship existing between them.

For instance, he would not have infringed the

rules of good breeding and the laws of polite society so far as to complain even to her that invitations to Madame de Polignac invariably included M. de Vaudreuil, but never made mention of him; or, again, that she found M. de Vaudreuil's country house a pleasanter residence than his own. Vaudreuil never complained of his wife's absence, why should Polignac of his? He, however, thought it but reasonable to require in return that she should make the most of the great opportunity a kind Providence had thrown in her way in their hour of need, of enriching herself and him, with their family and friends, even to the fourth generation. And so well did the duchess respond to her husband's expectations, that she even succeeded in encroaching on the rights of the Abbé Vermond, — securing several rich benefices and bishoprics for the Polignacs and Grammonts which the *abbé* had promised elsewhere.

Great was his virtuous indignation, and severe his spiritual upbraidings. "Never," he said, "had favouritism been carried to such lengths. It was unexampled in the history of nations. The great empress-queen herself had had favourites; but were they not men who could fight her battles, men great in the camp, in the council of state, and of powerful influence in the Church? — not silly women, and foolish flatterers, devoted to the pomps and vanities, affectations and sentimentalities, of a frivolous generation!" It was a terrible thing to offend the queen's confessor. This he knew; for the queen was fond of proclaiming that she was so much accustomed to the *abbé* she could not possibly do without him — could never satisfactorily supply his place, should he ever really dream of resigning. But she would add in an undertone, for the consolation of her favourites, that, notwithstanding, he had not the power to estrange her from her friends.

On this occasion, however, he chose to retire to one of his abbeys. As he did not return for some days, and the queen desired to be confessed and absolved, she was obliged to send him a pressing and persistent missive. But Vermond was not disposed to surrender at discretion. He did not — from humility of course — seek for himself ecclesiastical dignities; but he liked to accumulate rich abbeys, of which he already had several, and derived large revenues from them. But it was only on the offer of two more, by which his income was increased by 80,000 *francs*, that he condescended to yield to the queen's entreaties and return. His murmurings had been louder and deeper than before; for he had the unusual support of other favourites, equally aggrieved as himself, and perhaps even more alarmed at the ever increasing ascendancy of the duchess.

Among them was the Princesse de Lamballe, who had expected to add the charge of *gouver-*

nante to that she already enjoyed of *surintendante*. Her griefs and complaints were carried to the *salon* of the Duchesse de Chartres, and the errors political and domestic of Versailles were discussed by the ladies of the Palais Royal circle with considerable freedom and some little acrimony. The duchess, a very charming and amiable woman, — employed, as were most of the ladies, in knitting, netting, or knotting, while they conversed, — would occasionally put in an apologetic word for the queen. The duke, as was customary with him, walked with measured step up and down the *salon*, listening with a sardonic smile on his countenance, or speaking only to make some mocking, jeering remark.

Of the ladies of the Duchesse de Chartres's circle, the most distinguished for *esprit*, talents, and accomplishments was Madame de Sillery-Genlis. Her reputation was then also great in the literary world. The queen, in her singular vindictiveness towards the Duc de Chartres, had latterly included Madame de Genlis, and had taken the opportunity of publicly showing it when the congratulatory visits were paid at Versailles on the birth of the dauphin. Madame de Genlis was the niece of Madame de Montesson, whom the Duc d'Orléans, the father of De Chartres (Philippe Égalité), had privately married, and thenceforth lived in retirement at St. Cloud, or other of his estates. In 1777 the Duchesse de Chartres, on the birth of twin daughters,* appointed Madame de Genlis, who for some years had been one of the ladies of her household, governess to her children. But when the eldest of the three princes — Louis Philippe, Duc de Valois — entered his ninth year, they, as well as Mademoiselle, were placed under her care, she exchanging the name of governess for governor, — "*Gouverneur des Princes.*"

Certain preceptors engaged for the young princes are said to have taken offence at this unusual usurpation of their rights, and a very brusque reply was given by the king when consulted by the duke on the subject. But this story, as Madame de Genlis denies its truth, owes its origin probably to the gossiping, scandal-loving *coterie* of Versailles. For it is certain that all who were well received at the Palais Royal came under the ban of the queen's displeasure, and shared more or less in that deep-rooted aversion she felt towards the Duc de Chartres. The Princesse de Lamballe was excepted, probably because of her relationship to the duchess. But although her favour was great, and she obtained a fair share of the good things

---

* One only survived — Adélaïde d'Orléans, afterwards so influential in determining the political acts of her brother, Louis Philippe, as to be compared to the nymph Egeria from whom Numa received inspiration. M. de Talleyrand called her "the only man in the family."

that were so liberally dispensed until the final breaking-up of the monarchy, she never acquired an ascendancy over the queen equalling that of Madame de Polignac.

It appears that Madame de Genlis was prevented by indisposition from accompanying the Duchesse de Chartres to Versailles to congratulate the queen. She, however, prayed her majesty to accept her felicitations from the lips of that royal lady, and for the reason given to excuse her unavoidable absence. The queen replied haughtily that "the Duchesse de Chartres, under such circumstances, might send her excuses; but that Madame de Genlis, though her celebrity would perhaps occasion her absence to be noticed, was not of rank high enough to entitle her to do so."

The duchess was abashed; the duke considered that "the Autrichienne" had insulted her, and the *amour-propre* of the Marquise de Sillery-Genlis was deeply wounded. She was Comtesse de Lancy in her own right, and as such, after due examination of her pedigree, was, at seven years of age, admitted Chanoinesse of the very noble order of Alix, established in the Abbey near Lyons, and founded by the queen of Louis VII. in the twelfth century. She was therefore of more ancient family than the Duchesse Jules; and although she was accused of being on the same intimate terms of friendship with the Duc de Chartres as Madame de Polignac with M. de Vaudreuil, it was but on the slightest foundation. The supposition that the high moral tone of her works was but a veil concealing sentiments and habits of life according little with those she strove to inculcate, could originate only in malignancy. But there may have been some excuse for believing that all were vicious, especially in *la grande société* of that period, from the fact that so very few could be found of whom it could well be believed, even by the most charitably disposed, that they were virtuous.

Unfounded prejudices and irritable temper had raised up a new enemy for the queen, one whose able pen could trace wonderfully piquant portraits, and, without offending good taste, satirise the favourite sports of Versailles, — loto and blind man's buff, with forfeits, in which the king had been prevailed to take part, and had declared he found it amusing; and the romping, boisterous winter games of *Guerre Pan-pan* and *Descampativos*, so grossly vulgar that they would seem to have been designed for the hardy *dames de la Halle* rather than for the delicate *dames du Palais*, with their sentimentalities and their terribly weak nerves. Nevertheless, they were in high favour at Versailles, and in the social circles that took their tone from the château. They are ridiculed, but differently explained, in the letters and memoirs of that day.

But in spite of murmurings and the growing unpopularity of Marie Antoinette, in spite of an empty treasury, — for the money left in it by M. Necker had all been spent, and the queen's contrôleurs-général, MM. Joly and d'Ormesson, had found no way of replenishing it, — the period from 1781 to 1785 was the most brilliant of the French court during the reign of Louis XVI., as it was that of the queen's apparently greatest enjoyment, certainly of her dissipation and extravagance. The lead of the court was generally followed in this reckless plunge into folly, — the rich *bourgeoisie* vieing with the *noblesse* in their luxurious style of living and lavish expenditure. The *grandes dames* of the court could not surpass, and often did not equal, in the magnificence of their dress and splendour of their jewels, the wives of some of the financiers. Never did the looms of Lyons produce, even for Madame de Pompadour, silks of richer quality or greater beauty of design; or Alençon and other lace-making towns more exquisite specimens of their beautiful art. Every article of the *toilette* was of the finest and costliest kind. Elegant equipages became more generally used, and the number of servants increased. Silver plate was more abundant, and inlaid and artistically carved furniture, and the tapestry of Beauvais and porcelain of Sèvres were in unusual demand.

The carpets of Aubusson manufactured during

that period have never, it is said, been equalled for fineness, closeness, and depth of pile. Perhaps this was partly owing to the extraordinary severity of the weather; for amongst other exceptional things of that date, the winter of 1783 was memorable above all the preceding ones for the intense cold of its seventy-six days of frost. Carpets and hangings of unusual thickness were needed for covering the vast *salons*, and draping the lofty entrances and double windows of the hôtels of the wealthy. Most of them were splendid abodes. In summer, with their *parquet* floors, little foot-carpets, and profusion of flowers, they were charming. But in winter there was little warmth or comfort in them, even when the huge logs were piled up high and blazing in those deep recesses, surmounted by the majestic sculptured marble, or carved oak mantelpiece. Warmth was rather seen than felt, as the flames, darting up the spacious chimney, encountered the roaring wind, and were driven back in a cloud of smoke.

But if the piercing cold of this rigorous winter was felt within the dwellings of the rich, what must have been the sufferings of the poor without, — the wretches who dwelt in the squalid streets of old Paris? That network of narrow turnings and windings was even more supremely miserable than usual that year. Over the ordinary stream of black mud lay masses of snow, in some parts several feet deep. It was weary work to wade through it to the open *places*, where crusts of black bread were thrown to the starving creatures to whom hunger gave the strength or the will to struggle for possession of the charitable dole. It was an arduous time for M. Lenoir, the lieutenant-general of police; he and his staff with difficulty suppressed the inclination of the people to resort to violence, and to take of the abundance of others for the supply of their own necessities.

One means of employment he found for those who were willing to undertake it for the sake of the few *sous* promised, was the removal of snow from the entrances of the ministerial hôtels, and the modelling of it into some resemblance of the human form, — intended to represent a statue of the king, beneath which, on a sort of pedestal, complimentary verses were placed. The object of the lieutenant of police was to raise the cry of "*Vive le roi!*" and with it "*Vive la reine!*" But the cry "*À bas l'Autrichienne*" was so much more frequent that the queen, who was most anxious to bring the sledges again into use, was urged not to do so, lest it should provoke unpleasant results from the irritation of the suffering people. The queen hesitated. "Should she in such a matter regard the opinion of the people?" But M. Lenoir had communicated with the duchess, and sledging was deferred to a more favourable occasion.

It was in the course of this winter that the

young Napoleon Bonaparte, then in his fifteenth year, and a student at the military college of Brienne, summoned his fellow collegians to provide themselves with spades, and with the frozen snow to build up a fortress and a platform. This done, "We will now," he said, "divide ourselves into companies, and besiege and defend this fort; and, as I invented the game, I shall lead the attacking party." The ammunition consisted of snowballs, which were weighted with stones and flints, that they might be aimed with more precision, and produce more damaging effects. But not only the destruction of the fortress was effected; both the besieged and the besiegers had a long list of bruised and wounded; but happily in this conflict none were slain.

But while the future conquering hero and idol of the French soldier was energetically engaged in mimic warfare — then, as in after days, in many a hard-fought battle, rewarding and promoting the valorous on the field — a very different course was being pursued by the military department of the government towards the actual army of France. Troops were daily arriving from America, full of enthusiasm for the cause for which they had been fighting side by side with insurgent colonists; aiding them to throw off, as they termed it, the yoke of oppression, and to procure for themselves liberty and equal rights. Proud of their victory in this War of Independence, though in its benefits they are to have no share, they have yet a legitimate right to expect that on returning to their own country, the value of the services they have rendered will be recognised, and their due reward be conferred. There may be men among them who have borne the brunt of the battle; distinguished themselves by their valour; "covered themselves with glory." But can they produce four quarterings? For if they cannot, there is no promotion for them.

A decree to this effect had been issued, when Général Comte de Ségur, nominated by the queen as Minister of War, entered on his office, two years before, making the grade of officer attainable only by the *noblesse*. It had caused great discontent in the ranks at that time. But its ill effects were more particularly observable when, the wars being ended, a general promotion took place, — not, however, directly to reward either officers or men, but simply to enable Madame de Polignac advantageously to place several of her noble *protégés*, who had either bought or otherwise obtained her favour. A similar decree was issued with respect to the lower ranks of the clergy. However well qualified, however worthy, no priest might aspire to a bishopric or other ecclesiastical dignity unless he could show his four quarterings, — these being regarded as the great essentials for preferment in the Church and Army.

Amongst the many causes cited by different

writers as having occasioned or contributed towards the breaking out of the French Revolution, surely there was no more powerful one than the issuing of the above named decrees. The French soldier became insubordinate, full of ill-feeling toward his officers; "the blacksmith king" inspired him with no enthusiasm, and he awaited but an opportunity of freeing himself from bondage. That opportunity came to him on the 14th July, 1789, and henceforth there was no royal army. The inferior clergy, for the same cause, indignant that a strong line of demarcation should thus permanently separate them from their ecclesiastical superiors, and wholly exclude them from the higher dignities of the Church or any extended sphere of usefulness, in many instances attached themselves to the philosophical party, and eventually in the *Assemblée Constituante*, greatly increased the influence of the *Tiers État*, or Third Estate of the realm. Thus the ill-considered measures whose aim was to keep down the people, to resist the encroachments of the *bourgeoisie*, and to strengthen the hands of the king against them, had precisely opposite results. "A king without understanding is also an oppressor," saith the proverb, Louis XVI. was a striking example of its truth.

But the court is going to Fontainebleau. The opera troupe and the "king's comedians" are ordered to follow. *Fêtes* and balls, *grandes chasses*, and some novel festivities on an extensive scale, are in preparation. Pleasure is the order of the day, and sits at the prow of the vessel of state; for the brilliant M. de Calonne has taken the helm (he has charge of the finances), and promises soon to bring her into smooth waters, richly freighted with gold. His system is prodigality; his motto: "*Vogue la galère.*"

The court is enchanted. And if the dull brain of the king fails fully to comprehend the force of the axiom, "Let us be prodigal in order to be rich," and M. de Vergennes confesses to inability to make it clearer, time will surely bring it home to them. At all events, Madame Jules and the queen, with quicker intelligence, have seized its full meaning, and are convinced that the system advocated by the able and *spirituel* M. de Calonne is both wise and practicable.

The fashionable world fully expects that he will promptly supply Léonard or Mdlle. Bertin with some happy idea for a new *coiffure*, the prevailing *mode* being considered to have had almost too long a reign. It is named the "*bonnet à la caisse d'escompte*," being merely a border or wreath of puckered lace and flowers, wanting the *fond*, an essential part of a *bonnet* or cap. Its name was intended as a playful satire on the empty state of the treasury, unhappily destitute of treasure, or *sans fonds*.

CHAPTER XVIII.

Mariage de Figaro. — Private Readings. — "*Détestable! Injouable!*" — Determined to Vanquish. — The Comte and Comtesse du Nord — "*Le Frère Charmant.*" — "Figaro" at St. Petersburg. — Defying the King. — "Oppression and Tyranny." — The King Consents. — The New Censor's Opinion. — "Much Ado about Nothing." — Untrustworthy Memoirs. — A Picture of the Manners of the Day. — First Performance of "Figaro." — A Galaxy of Talent. — A Trying Occasion. — A Charitable Project. — Inaccessible to Reason. — Vanquishing Lions and Tigers. — Beaumarchais at St. Lazare. — Release of the Prisoner. — The King's Atonement. — A Second Triumph. — Causes of the Revolution. — Mirabeau. — An Affair of Time.

MULTIFARIOUS as were the occupations of M. Caron de Beaumarchais during the American war, he yet had found leisure to write his celebrated comedy, "*Le Mariage de Figaro.*" It was finished in 1781, read to the principal actors of the Théâtre Français, and eagerly accepted by the directors. But when submitted to the censor, M. Suard, that functionary pronounced it "offensive alike to good taste and good manners," and its performance was strictly prohibited. It however became whispered about that the prohibited play was a piquant

Beaumarchais.
Original Etching by Gilbert.

P. A. CARON DE BEAUMARCHAIS.

and rather audacious satire on matters political and social. This at once raised curiosity, and a general desire for its production; and it is characteristic of the levity of the French of that day that, in spite of the troubles then pressing on the nation, and the gradual advance of others, the most engrossing subject of conversation and discussion, both in court circles and the Parisian *salons*, was the interdict on Beaumarchais's play.

For nearly three years its removal was sought with the utmost persistency. Not by the author himself; he had locked up his MS., he said, in his *secrétaire*, and vainly did princes, dukes, and court favourites assail him with requests — none more perseveringly than the Comte de Vaudreuil and the Princesse de Lamballe — to allow it to be privately read in their *salons*. Before consenting to private readings he required the necessary authorisation for its public performance. The Comte d'Artois, the Duc de Fronsac, and all who frequented Madame de Polignac's *salon* — actually the queen's — appealed to the king, who was prejudiced against the play by the report of M. de Meromesnil, the Keeper of the Seals. He warned the king that it was a dangerous play. Yet much the same things had for twenty or more years past been written, and said or sung with impunity in prose and in verse. Ministers and the acts of the government had been satirised in many an epigram, and the morals of the court held up to shame and ridicule in the freest language, in couplets and songs innumerable. "But these," it was argued, "were but ephemeral productions, which raised a passing laugh or sneer, and there was an end of them. Nothing of the sort had been produced on the stage." This was scarcely accurate; for Molière had attacked not only social affectations and immoralities, but had aimed many a shaft at abuses of power.

But the king would look into this play. The manuscript being delivered to him, after he had taken a private cursory glance at it Madame Campan was summoned to read it to him and the queen. Occasionally, as she proceeded, he murmured a word or two of approval, but more frequently exclaimed: "*Mauvais goût! immorale! détestable! injouable!*" When, however, she came to Figaro's famous monologue, in the fifth act, and especially to that part in which he inveighs against *lettres de cachet* and prisons of state, Louis could endure it no longer. Hastily he rose from his seat, and impetuously exclaimed: "It shall never be played! never! The demolition of the Bastille," he continued, "would be necessary to deprive the representation of that piece of its dangerous inferences. The man sports with all that should be respected in a government.* "It

---

* Some few months before, the demolition of the Bastille was actually proposed by a member of the government. But it was a proposal too startling to be entertained.

"It will not be performed, then?" said the queen, in a tone of regretful inquiry.

"No," replied the king. "You may be quite sure of that."

But all Paris and Versailles desired to see the "*Mariage de Figaro*" performed, and determined, having numbers on their side, to vanquish their redoubtable opponents. And so ardent and impatient was the curiosity of this indolent and frivolous society, that the desire to see this play became a fixed and absorbing idea, producing a feverish state of excitement, impossible to suppress. Yielding to the repeated entreaties of the Princesse de Lamballe, Beaumarchais, in February, 1782, read his play at Versailles, in the princess's private apartments, — a distinguished company being assembled for the occasion. It appears that the author read his play with considerable effect, and that the audience were highly amused, as well as charmed, by the piquancy of the dialogue, the brilliant flashes of wit, and no less so at the keenness of the satire directed against themselves. Perhaps some ladies may have been conscious of a natural blush now and then heightening the colour of their *rouge*-tinted cheeks; or the passages that should have had that effect may possibly then have been omitted.

Shortly after, the Grand Duke Paul of Russia, with his wife, being ordered by the Empress Catherine to travel, arrived in Paris under the assumed title of Comte and Comtesse du Nord. Grimm, on their behalf, pleaded so earnestly for a reading of "Figaro," that Beaumarchais once more yielded. Again both *grands seigneurs* and *grandes dames* were delighted. The Comtesse d'Oberkirche, who was present, also speaks of the "fine, handsome, open countenance of the author, of his wonderful *esprit*, and his many fine qualities of head and heart." Beaumarchais had always won golden opinions at first sight from the ladies. He was of lofty stature, and finely proportioned figure. His face was handsome, his manners were fascinating, and he had a remarkably winning tongue. The three ladies he married (his third wife survived him) had all fallen deeply in love with him, and thrown themselves and their fortunes at his feet. He was the only son in a family of six children. His five sisters adored him, and were accustomed to speak of him as *le frère charmant*, and he appears to have merited the appellation, and to have been truly a model husband, brother, father, and son.

But at the period in question Beaumarchais was no longer young. He was just fifty years of age; but from all accounts time had laid but a very light hand on him. His great and varied abilities, and attractive personal qualities, must have had some weight also with his own sex, considering the great difference in character of the ministers who consulted him, — MM. de Maurepas, de Vergennes, Necker, Calonne, de Sartines, Lenoir, and others, — and the opinions he was invited on certain occasions, though *incognito*, to furnish on state affairs. Caron de Beaumarchais was doubtless a highly gifted man, — one of the most remarkable of his day. His fellow citizens, at the time of the famous *procès Goezman*, applied to him the epithet *grand citoyen*; and he might certainly have aspired to fill the highest offices of state, had he not been born in days when, in order worthily to serve God and the king, it was necessary to show four quarterings.

The Comte du Nord was so well pleased with the "*Mariage de Figaro*," that he requested to be favoured with a copy of the play for presentation to the Empress Catherine; and on his return to Russia it was performed with great success at the theatre of the palace of St. Petersburg.

As, however, but few persons could be admitted to the private readings, the report of these few intensified the wish of the many to hear the play read or to see it acted. The cabal became more violent, yet MM. Suard and Meromesnil remained firm in their opinions — the one that it was an offensive play, the other that it was both dangerous and offensive. That the king was wavering was evident from his remark that Beaumarchais's credit would eventually outweigh that of the Keeper of the Seals. And so it proved. Some occult influence had prevailed to attempt to defy the king, — the queen's, it was believed, as she was exceedingly anxious to see the play. In consequence, an unexpected command from the château to study the "*Mariage de Figaro*" for representation at Versailles was received in June, 1783, by the comedians of the Théâtre Français. As the king's supposed order could not be contravened, M. de Meromesnil endeavoured to thwart it by urging how dangerous was the precedent of producing at Versailles a play under the ban of the censor.

The king was amazed at this remark. He had sent no order to the actors; he had not commanded the play. Forthwith, however, a second order reaches the directors, naming the Théâtre des Menus Plaisirs, in Paris, for the performance. It was the theatre attached to the Conservatoire, and used for concerts of the pupils of that establishment — therefore private. But the intendant, M. de la Ferté, lent it on this occasion to the actors of Le Français by order of the Duc de Duras, first gentleman of the king's bedchamber. What artifices were then employed, what intrigues resorted to, to obtain a seat or even standing-room, or to squeeze into the building in any way!

Satin playbills, fringed with gold, are distributed to the court. The elegant theatre is filled in every part by a brilliant audience, whose equipages, surrounding the building, attest that few beside the wealthy and noble are assembled within. There is a feverish impatience for the rising of the curtain. It has been waited for at least five minutes. At last it rises, and the celebrated actor, Préville — who, though about to retire from the stage, has, at Beaumarchais's request, taken the part of Figaro — appears; but it is but to announce the arrival of a courier in all haste from Versailles, with an order signed by the king, forbidding the performance of the "*Mariage de Figaro*" "then or at any future time, at that or any theatre whatever."

There was a moment of silence and general consternation, succeeded by murmurs loud and defiant. Then, for the first time, were heard the words "oppression and tyranny," as passionately and vehemently uttered by this assemblage of the *beau monde*, deprived of its evening's amusement, as at any period of the Revolution by the frantic people whom starvation and oppression had hurried into crime. As for Beaumarchais (whom Madame Campan — either misinformed, or from lapse of time her memory at fault — erroneously represents as "swearing that his play should be performed, and perhaps in the chancel of Notre-Dame"), he merely exclaimed: "Well, well! Again, then, I lock up my play in my *secrétaire*, to await a more favourable opportunity of seeing the light."

Three months had not elapsed when Beaumarchais, who was then in England, received several letters from the Duc de Fronsac informing him that "the queen has told him the king's consent was given to his play being performed before the court at the duke's château of Gennevilliers, which has an elegant theatre, and where M. de Vaudreuil proposes to give a *fête* to the Duchesse de Polignac and the Comte d'Artois. The consent of the author, therefore, alone is wanting, and this," the duke continues, "he has undertaken to prevail on him not to withhold." But Beaumarchais now chose to be entreated, and the *fête* was deferred in consequence. His "*fol ouvrage*," as he termed his play (its first title being originally "*La folle journée*" — "A day of folly, or the marriage of Figaro"), had been revised by two other censors since its condemnation by M. Suard. Both had approved his work, changing only, or omitting, a word here and there. Consequently, he considered himself entitled to make his own conditions.

He declined to confirm the king's permission to perform his play for the gratification of Madame de Polignac and the court, unless from that time it became the property of the actors of the Théâtre Français, to be played without let or hindrance whenever the directors might see fit. In any case, he required that it should again be placed in the hands of a censor. This unlooked-for opposition on his part served but to stimulate the efforts of the court party to secure its public performance, in order first to be gratified themselves.

M. Gaillard, the distinguished historian and an academician, was the new censor. He entirely approved the work. "It was a very sprightly play," he said, "and all history taught us that sprightly people were not those who were dangerous to the state. Conspiracies, assassinations, and such like horrors, had invariably been conceived and carried out by the moody, the reserved, and the morose. He could not imagine the intriguing Figaro being dangerous, as an example, to any man in the world. In short, he considered it a well-written play, likely to prove attractive, — a comedy of the kind much needed to increase the receipts of the theatre."

This, by all concerned, was believed to be the last act of the court comedy of "Much ado about Nothing," of which Beaumarchais's play had furnished the subject. True, the king had not actually given any promise that nothing more was to follow; but the lieutenant of police, believing that the play was accepted on the author's own conditions, led him to believe it also. The letters of MM. de Vaudreuil and de Fronsac, so profuse of thanks, seem to have been written under the same impression. Beaumarchais, satisfied with this result, returned to Paris to superintend the performance, and some few days after the whole of the court assisted, with unfeigned satisfaction, as we are told, at the representation of a play which the king had pronounced *détestable, immorale, et injouable.*

His consent had certainly been wrung from him by the queen, who had proposed to be present herself. But for once in his life Louis opposed her wishes, so far as to forbid her presence at Gennevilliers being known. An excuse was made, on that occasion, of indisposition confining the queen to her own private rooms, while she is said actually to have been at that time at the play, but *en cachette.* And it is the more probable that it was so, as the king really intended that once, and once only, to gratify the dear duchess, should this terrible play be performed. The small theatre of Gennevilliers was crowded, so much so that many of the great ladies of the court, who from excessive sensibility were subject to frequent fainting fits, were threatened with fainting, in reality, from the effects of the overpowering heat. According to the pretty Madame Vigée Lebrun — the fashionable and much petted portrait painter of that day — Beaumarchais, when made aware of the languid condition of the ladies, at once let air into the building by driving his cane through the window panes.

He may have done so. But, as M. de Loménie, his only trustworthy biographer, remarks, the reminiscences of Madame Lebrun, like the memoirs of Madame Campan, were written by the aid of imagination, when memory was dimmed by the lapse of years.

After the successful performance of the "*Mariage de Figaro*" at Gennevilliers, the public began to be clamorous for the play. But the king had returned to his first resolve. "Government was held up to contempt; morality was outraged." No doubt there were many speeches in it that one scarcely understands that ears polite, and ladies' ears especially, could have listened to with complacency. Yet M. de Vaudreuil, in rejecting another play as *plus forte*, says of "Figaro:" "The ear is not startled, because of Beaumarchais's choice of words."

Grimm, writing of it, describes it as "a true picture of the manners of that day; of the manners and sentiments," he repeats, "of the best society" (*meilleure compagnie*). "It is certainly not an austere play," he says, "but it is less free and licentious than the plays of Le Sage, Molière, Regnard, and others."

Hitherto submissive to the royal prohibition, Beaumarchais now becomes impatient, pressing, almost imperious. The play is again, by the king's command, twice submitted to new censorship. "This bagatelle, this frivolous play," writes Beaumarchais, "has caused me more worry and annoyance than the most complicated and troublesome business I have ever been engaged in. I am overwhelmed with letters from people in the provinces and in Paris; the actors reproach me with neglect of their interests,—and all this to obtain a decisive reply, whether this trifling piece shall or shall not be acted."

From this time the king was beset with entreaties, and even demands, for the public representation of the "*Mariage de Figaro.*" Of the six censors, five joined the cabal of the court. The comedians, on their part, loudly complained of the injury their theatre was sustaining; while the Parisian public generally were inclined to be mutinous, declaring that unless the concession made to the courtiers of Gennevilliers were speedily made also to them, they would wrest a consent from the king. His obstinacy in this ridiculous contention would, it is asserted, have soon led to serious disturbances in Paris, and were indeed only averted by its being insinuated to him that the failure of the play was *morally* certain. To gratify the public curiosity was therefore to disappoint its expectations. The idea pleased the king, and forthwith he yielded.

On the 25th of April, 1784, the first public performance of the celebrated comedy took place, and survives in writings of the period as one of the most remarkable souvenirs of the eighteenth century. From early dawn all Paris was hurrying towards the Théâtre Français, ladies of highest rank passing in early with the actresses and dining in their boxes, to make sure of their places; *grands seigneurs* mingling with the crowd, *cordons bleus* elbowing Savoyards, — all striving to get nearer the entrances, to which no carriages could approach. The usual guard was driven from its post and dispersed by the impetuous rush of the throng. The iron railings were torn down, and the doors of the theatre forced in. Women were screaming and fainting, and three persons were actually stifled by the pressure of the struggling crowd. Never had any play so roused public curiosity and caused such general excitement.

The cast included the most brilliant talent of the French stage of that period. Mademoiselle Sainval played the Comtesse d'Almaviva, at Beaumarchais's solicitation, and developed a new talent, having won her reputation in tragedy. He displayed equal discrimination in requesting Mademoiselle Contat to take the part of Suzanne, considered rather "out of her line." She had hitherto charmed by her beauty, her extreme elegance, and a certain *espièglerie* in the *rôles* of "*les grandes coquettes.*" But, like the rest of the actors on this memorable occasion, excited by the enthusiasm of the audience, she surpassed herself. Her great celebrity dates from this time. Her acting is said to have been inimitably piquant, and Préville, who watched the performance of his wife's pupil with exceeding interest, at the conclusion of the play embraced her, and kissing her on the forehead, said: "This, fair Louise, is my first infidelity to Mademoiselle Dangeville — you have surpassed her!"

That great actor reserved for himself only the small part of Bridoison. He felt that he then possessed neither the youth nor the agility that was needed to do justice to the vivacious Figaro, therefore gave up the part to the younger but distinguished actor, Dazincourt. Almaviva was played by the celebrated Molé. Larive also took a small part; and Mademoiselle Olivier, a young actress of promise, who died of decline, soon after, at the age of eighteen, was the precocious page Cherubin. This triumphant first representation of his play was witnessed by the author from a *loge grillée*. His companions were two clerical friends, the Abbé de Calonne, brother of the minister, and the critic and *littérateur*, the Abbé Sabatier de Castres. Beaumarchais had invited them to dinner, and afterwards to accompany him to the theatre; having need, he said, on so trying an occasion, of much *spirituel* support.

The "*Mariage de Figaro*" had reached its hundredth performance — an unprecedented run in those days — but the public still continued to flock to it. Renewed after the usual vacation, its attraction remained unabated, and the play-loving Parisians were yet unweariedly running after the Andalusian barber when he made his three hundredth appearance. The play brought a small fortune to the directors of the Théâtre Français, raised the reputation of the actors, and, so far as Beaumarchais's share of the profits, about £13,000, was concerned, served also the cause of charity. He gave the whole of that sum towards founding a benevolent institution at Lyons. Jealousy and ill-will had raised up around him a host of malignant enemies, of whom M. Suard was chief. His charitable projects were therefore thwarted in Paris; but the Archbishop of Lyons gladly carried out his idea, accepting both the money then offered, and the further aid which a man so wealthy and generous as Beaumarchais was in a position to afford him.

Neither M. Suard nor the king were able to forgive the success of the "*Mariage de Figaro.*" The former, an academician, having to address the learned forty, and a number of distinguished guests, on the reception of a new member, contrived to introduce into his discourse some very severe strictures on Beaumarchais and his play; as well as on the depraved taste of those who nightly applauded it, most of those present being of the number. The prince royal of Sweden — afterwards Gustave III. — was among the visitors. On leaving, after having complimented M. Suard on his address, "You have treated us rather severely," he said; "perhaps with reason, but," he added, laughingly, " I am myself so inaccessible to reason, that I am now leaving you to assist for the third time at 'Figaro's Marriage.'" "Fine fruit my sermon has borne, then, *mon Prince*," replied Suard, rather stiffly.

Louis XVI. was also greatly piqued at a success towards which the importance he had given to the play, by so tenaciously withholding it from the public, had largely contributed. One evening, however, in the full tide of "Figaro's" popularity, — when the queen and the ladies of the court had all adopted the "*coiffure à la Suzanne*," or "*à la Comtesse d'Almaviva*," which brought the graceful lace mantilla again into favour; and while still the Comte d'Artois, the French Almaviva, sat in his *loge grillée* gazing night after night at the "*ravissante* Mdlle. Contat," in her Andalusian costume, — the unwieldy person of the wily, slander-loving Monsieur de Provence waddled into the king's apartment. That he had something of moment to impart was evident.

The king was playing his usual game, not for money, as before observed, but perhaps for love, while he never won more than its poor relative — pity. The game is interrupted by the entrance of Monsieur, but it is almost a relief; for it opens wide the sleepy eyes of the players. Monsieur pours a torrent of undertone eloquence into his royal brother's ears. The blood mounts to Louis's face; with all his piety, we know that he can be obstinate and brusque, even brutal. He learns at this moment that the presumptuous Beaumarchais, in the pride of his heart, has been boasting of vanquishing lions and tigers, which Monsieur interprets as evidently designating the king and queen. Really intended to do so, they might have been considered compliments, compared with the epithets employed by himself in the infamous epigrams he had scattered broadcast over France, and of the authorship of which the king was well aware.

But resentment towards Beaumarchais smoulders in Louis's breast. His "Figaro" has been played, and successfully, and in spite of him; and the thought of his having compared him to a lion, perhaps ironically, adds fuel to the fire. His anger rises, and less like the lion than the tiger preparing for his spring, he hastily writes with a pencil on the seven of spades — which he had held in his hand since the suspension of the game — an order for the immediate arrest of Beaumarchais, and his imprisonment at St. Lazare, where it is customary to confine the depraved youth of the capital when guilty of offences against decency and order. This, in itself, is an insult. No reason is given for treating as a dissolute young vagabond a man of fifty-three, — one of the wealthiest men in Paris, a public benefactor, a distinguished dramatist, the head of a great commercial house, and one whom the king had employed in important state affairs.

This occurs in the midst of his triumph in

March, 1785. Of course it is known throughout Paris within a few hours. Notwithstanding the sensation it occasions, the fact of the once gay and brilliant, out now somewhat sobered, Beaumarchais being shut up with disorderly young scamps of the Paris streets, appears so comical to the volatile-minded Parisians, that one general burst of laughter seems to ring through the capital. This is, however, but momentary; and no cause being assigned for Beaumarchais's imprisonment, the arbitrary act is seriously discussed. "People are asking," says Bachaumont, "who can be sure of sleeping in his bed to-night; who can be certain that he is safe from arrest. Every one considers his liberty menaced and his respectability at stake." The fourth day arrives; Beaumarchais is still at St. Lazare, and no explanation yet given of his offence. Indignation becomes general, and the rising effervescence of the people warns the king, and perhaps Monsieur, that it is time to release the prisoner.

But he objects to be released until he has been told what crime is laid to his charge, and judges to determine his guilt or innocence are appointed. His friend, M. Lenoir, lieutenant of police, privately reveals the secret to him: "He is believed to have intended to compare Louis XVI. to a lion or tiger. But that on reflection it seems to the king an offence too ridiculous to bring publicly against him, and he is entreated to leave the prison." Is it not equally ridiculous, he asks, that he should attempt to defend himself from such a charge. It was, however, contrived that the king should know that Beaumarchais, having for a long time been subject to most malicious and slanderous anonymous attacks from the pen of M. Suard and the Comte de Provence, in the "*Journal de Paris*," he had once for all replied, in the same journal, that, "having overcome lions and tigers, he thought it beneath him to slay insects. In other words," as he observed, "he had fought with giants: should he deign to crush pigmies?—mere figurative expression opposing the great to the small."

The king had long since named his brother "Tartuffe." He had now been led by his artifice to do a hasty, arbitrary, and unjust act. He endeavoured to atone to Beaumarchais for his five days' imprisonment by desiring M. de Calonne to write in his name that his explanation was satisfactory, and that he would be glad to avail himself of any opportunity of conferring some mark of his esteem on him. On the evening of the day Beaumarchais left St. Lazare, Grimm states that all the ministers, by the king's desire, attended the performance of " Figaro." Many of the ambassadors, and several of the court party, were also present, and, together with Beaumarchais's friends and partisans, made up so crowded and brilliant an audience that it was regarded as a second triumph.

In further expiation of the king's error, Beaumarchais was shortly after invited to witness the performance of his "Barber of Séville" at the little theatre of Trianon, — the queen playing Rosina; the Comte d'Artois, Figaro; and M. de Vaudreuil, the Comte d'Almaviva. But probably even a greater satisfaction to Beaumarchais was the receipt of an order for the payment of 800,000 *francs*, — an instalment of a large sum long due to him, from the government.

The "*Mariage de Figaro*" has been termed "the lever of the old *régime*." It presented the people with a lively but forcibly drawn picture of the lax morality and dissolute lives of the class that claimed by right of its quarterings of nobility to set its foot upon them. Eleven years before, Beaumarchais had propounded the maxim, "The nation should judge its judges," when, on the occasion of the famous *procès Goezman*, — setting at defiance the iniquitous custom of trying and sentencing accused persons within closed doors, — he published reports of his trial, and as a citizen appealed to public opinion. In this bold step some writers have also seen the first decisive advance towards Revolution. But it has been proved that Beaumarchais, though he may have desired, like many others, the reform of abuses from which he had himself personally suffered, was but very mildly revolutionary. So many causes combined to bring about the great Revolution, that it is difficult to determine which among them was chiefly prominent. Beaumarchais may have been one of the first to hasten the fall of the tottering tree that had long been rotten at the core. But if so, it was without design to bring it to the ground; for no one, and he as little as others — as a French writer remarks — then foresaw or desired a general social and political overthrow such as eventually occurred.

A bandage was over the eyes of the men of that period, and none thought of taking any serious account of the sallies of "Figaro." M. Suard had protested in the interests of good taste and good manners, and one other objector had certainly gone much further than that. It was a man of dissolute life, living on loans from any that would lend, and squandering them in riot and dissipation. That man was Mirabeau. Knowing nothing of Beaumarchais but his reputation for wealth and open-handedness, he called on him and requested that he would lend him 12,000 *francs*. Beaumarchais politely declined. "You can lend it if you choose without any inconvenience," said Mirabeau. "Of course, M. le Comte," replied Beaumarchais. "But a disagreement would certainly arise between us when your note of hand became due. I prefer that it should be to-day — by which I shall be gainer of 12,000 *francs*." Mirabeau immediately became his inveterate enemy; accused him of insulting and outraging all orders of the state, all laws, and all regulations, — of attempting, in fact, with the prickings of pins, what three years later he himself strove to accomplish with the heavy blows of a club.

Yet so little did the minds of men of the most advanced opinions foresee, even in 1787, how near to them or how impetuous was the torrent that was destined to sweep all before it, that General de La Fayette, writing to General Washington, after enumerating all the symptoms of the movement then preparing, says: " These several causes combined will lead us by slow degrees, and without any great commotion, to representative independence, and consequently to a diminution of the royal authority. But it is an affair of time, and its progress will be so much the slower, that the interests of men in power will put spokes in the wheels" (*mettront des bâtons dans les roues*).

If La Fayette could write thus in 1787, it is less astonishing than some writers have thought that the court and official society were in 1784 unconscious of committing an act of suicide when they complacently exposed themselves to the deadly shafts of ridicule aimed at them by "Figaro." *

---

* Louis de Loménie, "*Études sur la société en France XVIIIme Siècle.*"

CHAPTER XIX.

Birth of a Second Son.— Dazincourt.— Arrest of Cardinal de Rohan.— The Mystery of the Necklace.— The Château of St. Cloud.— Jeanne de Saint Rémy-Valois.— Jeanne's Patrons.— Presented to the Queen.— Unfortunate Concealment.— Cagliostro.— The Alchemist's Portrait.— The Comtesse Cagliostro.— The Cardinal's Trial.— The Cardinal Acquitted.— The Sister Superior.— The Queen's Dissatisfaction.— Poor Marie Antoinette.— M. de Bréteuil.— " The Excellent *Abbé*."

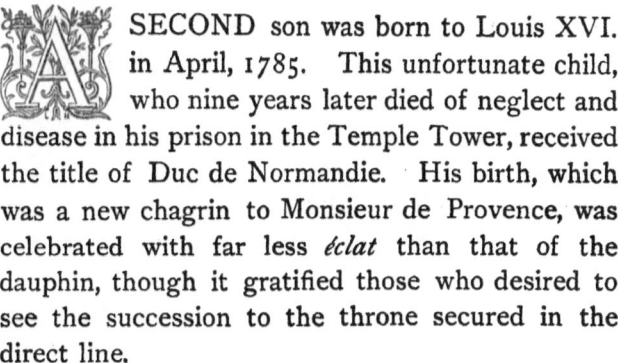A SECOND son was born to Louis XVI. in April, 1785. This unfortunate child, who nine years later died of neglect and disease in his prison in the Temple Tower, received the title of Duc de Normandie. His birth, which was a new chagrin to Monsieur de Provence, was celebrated with far less *éclat* than that of the dauphin, though it gratified those who desired to see the succession to the throne secured in the direct line.

Marie Antoinette was now thirty years of age; but her conduct was still marked by levity and frivolity, as great as when first she arrived in France, an ill-mannered, hoidenish girl of scarce half that age. In May, on recovering from her confinement, she desired the Duc de Duras to convey her commands to the actor Dazincourt to repair to Trianon to instruct her to act Rosina, and other *soubrette* parts in the plays she proposed to produce at her theatre. Dazincourt had a similar reputation to that of his predecessor, Grandval, whom fine gentlemen went to see that they might study his grand manners when he himself played the fine gentleman. Like him, too, Dazincourt was an educated man and of good family. He pleased the queen so well that she appointed him teacher of declamation at Trianon, with a large salary and a pension. Frequent valuable presents were also sent to him. It was the result of his teaching that Beaumarchais was invited to see, when his "Barber of Séville" was performed at the little theatre at Trianon on the 19th of August, 1785.

It was rather an ill-judged exhibition at that particular moment. For the queen had that morning seen the jeweller Boëhmer, to learn from him further particulars respecting the mysterious affair of the necklace. On the 15th the Cardinal de Rohan had been arrested, and on the 17th imprisoned in the Bastille, — an unfortunate resolve on the part of the king, exciting indignation in many, consternation in all, even before it was generally known precisely what he was charged with. For, on being transferred from the episcopal palace to the Bastille, he requested to be allowed to walk. Naturally, therefore, the people were much astonished, and their sympathy greatly excited, by the unusual spectacle of a prince of the Church, surrounded by guards and accompanied by the Governor of the Bastille and the lieutenant of police, proceeding on foot to a prison. The cardinal was a man of imposing presence, and about fifty years of age. Certain redeeming qualities had given him a sort of popularity, notwithstanding the irregularities of his earlier years. When, however, it was ascertained that he was arrested at the instance of the queen, the popular voice, which for some years had gradually been growing more hostile, burst forth against her in railing invective stronger than ever. The issue of the forthcoming *procès* might then have been surely predicted. Who shall tell the "true story of the diamond necklace?" It has probably never been told, and more probable still — as the Cardinal's papers were destroyed — is never likely to be.

Madame Campan, who might perhaps have partly unveiled the mystery, adhered, of course, to a statement in accordance with the queen's. To a certain extent it was probably a true one. But that there were circumstances connected with this singular transaction, suppressed by the queen, and very possibly unknown to Madame Campan, there can be very little doubt. Marie Antoinette did not always give her full confidence to her *première femme de chambre*. Some memoirs state that she doubted her fidelity; though, from the many proofs the queen had received of her attachment and her devotion to her interests, she would seem to have had little, if any, cause to do so.

Boëhmer is said to have first shown his superb necklace to the king, who would have bought it for the queen (its price was £65,000), had she not been unwilling to allow him to spend so large a sum for such a purpose. He had but recently redeemed and presented her with the splendid pearls and other jewelry that had belonged to Henrietta of England, — the first wife of Monsieur, brother of Louis XIV., — and which had long been in the hands of some Amsterdam merchants as security for a loan. M. de Calonne was then borrowing money wherever he could obtain it, and the king, the queen, and the government were carrying out his system of lavish expenditure, while he announced a yearly increasing deficit of many hundred millions. But if the queen had then no fancy to possess more diamonds, she had a fancy for another estate, which was to be more exclusively her own property than Trianon.

She had set her mind on the château and domain of St. Cloud, the property of the Duc d'Orléans, who ceded it for sixteen or seventeen millions, — about the same sum that Boëhmer asked for the necklace. May she not rather have accepted such a present from the king, and afterwards — as M. de Calonne was prepared at all times to advance whatever she required, and frequently pressed offers of large sums upon her — been led to change her mind, and buy the necklace herself, paying for it by instalments? She may have acted on this sudden impulse, and have obtained the jewels secretly, and again, on second thoughts, have sent them back. It is remarkable that she desired Madame Campan to tell Boëhmer "she preferred to spend her money in increasing the extent of her domain of St. Cloud by the purchase of the surrounding estates." Why should she give him this information unless she felt that she had disappointed him? To return the jewels she needed not Madame Campan's aid. There was Madame de Saint-Rémy Valois de la Motte at hand, who, appropriating the necklace entrusted to her, might have accomplished what followed, unknown to the queen.

This Jeanne de Saint-Rémy Valois, with her sister and brother, had some few years before excited great interest at court. The Marquise de Boulainvilliers had met with them asking alms on the road at a village in Burgundy, "for the love of God, and as descendants of the old kings of France." Each child carried a bundle of sticks and branches of trees, — their father being occupied in the adjacent forest as a wood-cutter. They were very pretty children, it appears, and so much interested the marquise that she inquired into their history. Family papers were produced, and placed in the hands of the *juge d'armes*, who confirmed their claim to be descended from Saint-Rémy de Valois — the natural son of Charles IX. — and their right to quarter the arms of France.

A memorial was then presented to the queen and M. de Maurepas, which resulted in a pension being granted to each of the young people. Their father, it appears, died in the Hôtel Dieu at that time. The Duc de Penthièvre interested himself for the brother, who, recognised as the Baron de Saint-Rémy Valois, was placed in the navy. Jeanne was certainly patronised by Madame de Provence, and for some time was in the household of Monsieur. In 1780 she married the Comte de la Motte, a young officer in the *gendarmerie de France*, who was thence transferred or promoted to the *gardes* of the Comte d'Artois. His pay and his wife's pension formed almost, if not quite, the only income the young couple possessed. With the view of soliciting his influence in her favour — with whom does not appear, but perhaps it was M. de Maurepas — for obtaining an addition to her pension, Madame de la Motte was introduced to Cardinal de Rohan.

Cagliostro probably recommended her to him. For the La Mottes then lodged in the Rue Sainte Claude, in the same house as that famous quack.

He was then mystifying Paris, and dividing the attention of the fashionable world with Mesmer and a Comte de Saint-Germain, who pretended to have lived for several hundred years, and told his distinguished auditors wonderful stories of their ancestors. But on referring to family records, they were found so strangely at variance with the tales of this still living familiar friend of the dead of ages long past that it was charitably inferred he had mistaken by a few centuries the date of his own birth, or that, in the long course of years which had rolled over his head, his memory had become rather hazy.

To return to Madame de la Motte, it is asserted, and it may or may not be true, — for except that long, wearisome state documents, relating to the trial of the cardinal, show that certain statements were made, though they elucidated nothing, the true story of the necklace is a doubtful story still, — it is assèrted, then, that Madame de la Motte was presented to the queen, though not formally, by the Princesse de Lamballe. It was probably with a view to obtaining her patronage, as the pretext for introducing her was to submit to her majesty a portrait of herself, painted by, or for, this Madame de la Motte. The portrait, apparently, did not please; but the supposed artist did. The queen is said to have been inclined to make a favourite of her; to have seen her several times; and to have treated her, considering their relative positions, in a manner that would warrant the belief of her having employed her to secretly return the necklace to Boëhmer. That there was some unfortunate concealment on the part of the queen there can be little doubt, and Madame Campan may have been compelled, against her own better judgment, to support her in it.

It would have been a wiser course, perhaps, to have refrained from arresting the cardinal. But poor Marie Antoinette's strong, and often groundless antipathies, generally prevented her from consulting the safest advisers. She had an aversion to M. de Vergennes, the only man then in the ministry who had the interest of the king and the nation really at heart, and who, having no personal ill-feeling towards the cardinal prince to gratify, would not, like the miserable Abbé Vermond, and the queen's injudicious friend, M. de Breteuil, have publicly compromised her for the sake of the poor pleasure of humiliating a man of exalted station, whom, for private reasons of their own, they disliked.

The particulars of the arrest of the cardinal prince on his arrival at Versailles, in full pontificals and wearing the grand cross of St. Louis, to perform mass in the royal chapel on the day of the Assumption; of that of Madame de la Motte, who was preparing to follow her husband to England; as well as that of Cagliostro (denounced by Madame de la Motte), as he was setting out for Lyons — are widely known. No less so is the result of the investigation before the Grande Chambre. Both history and historical romance have made this mysterious incident in the life of the unfortunate Marie Antoinette too familiar to render it needful that any of its details should be minutely entered into here.

Of the five persons placed on their trial (the most guilty as some writers have thought, the most guiltless according to others), the most remarkable and most mysterious was certainly Joseph Balsamo, *alias* Count Tischio, Comte de Melissa, Commander de Belmonte, Chevalier Pelegrini, Count Fénice, and finally, Comte de Cagliostro. The Marquise de Créquy received him several times, for the sake of more particularly observing the renowned necromancer and professed alchemist, whose astonishing cures, magnificent liberality, and strange power of divination, excited so much astonishment and general enthusiasm in Parisian society. Prince Louis de Rohan had a great personal regard for him, as well as the highest admiration of his talents. The marquise describes him as short, rather stout, and of little distinction in his manners. But he had perfectly regular features, a fresh complexion, a superb set of teeth, and two such eyes as she had never seen the like of before. He seemed to have every variety of expression of feature at command, and varied his tone and manners with wonderful facility, according to the persons he conversed with, — having apparently the keenest perception of shades of difference in their character and station.

His usual dress was a blue silk coat, bordered, and trimmed at the seams with silver lace, an embroidered shirt, the collar thrown back, as worn by the children of that time, and without cravat. His hair was abundant, plaited, and gathered up with a riband at the back. His stockings were of mottled silk, with gold clocks; his shoes, velvet, with buckles set with diamonds or other precious stones. He wore a profusion of diamonds — on his fingers, his shirt front, and ornamenting his watches and chains. A plume of white feathers adorned his hat, which he appears never to have put on his head except when arguing with unwonted energy. Then he would snatch it up, place it on his head, and, regardless of his plumes, give it a blow with his hand that sent it down over his eyes. This was probably his mode of clinching his arguments. In winter he covered his finery with a large fur pelisse, of the skin of the blue fox, to which a hood of the same fur was attached. Its form was similar to the carapace, or hollow part of the turtle's shell that covers the upper part of its body. When with this hood over his head Cagliostro went into the streets of Paris, the children are said to have fled before him, shrieking with terror.

He spoke French and other languages fluently;

Joseph Balsamo, Count Cagliostro.
Photo-etching from Engraving by Bartolozzi

but when with persons whom he did not know, he affected to have difficulty in making himself understood, while those who watched him narrowly would sometimes detect a derisive smile hovering on his lips, as if in spite of himself. It answered, probably, to play the charlatan, and excite the wonder of the credulous. He had a very pretty wife, gentle and amiable, who — to please her liege lord, no doubt — wore rose-coloured silk, with diamonds, and a hat with white feathers, from the earliest hours of the morning. An air of greater romance and mystery was at once thrown over the affair of the necklace when so singular a character as Cagliostro was accused of complicity in it.

During the course of the proceedings before the Council of the Grande Chambre, the members composing it were overwhelmed with petitions, memorials, and statements in favour of the cardinal. The Pope also protested against a prince of the Church being made accountable for his acts to any but the highest ecclesiastical tribunal (an assembly of the cardinals at Rome), while the *haute noblesse* generally looked on the cause of the Prince de Rohan as in some sort their own, — considering the rights and privileges of their rank entrenched upon when a near relative of the princes of the blood was put on his trial before the Council of the Grande Chambre. The king's brothers were of the same opinion; also

Mesdames, to whom the old Cardinal de Bernis — then French ambassador at Rome — earnestly wrote, advising that the king should be prevailed on to suppress the proceedings, and, for the queen's sake, to hush up the scandal.

The cardinal was eventually acquitted; also, Cagliostro and the woman Oliva, who had personated the queen. The man Villette, who wrote the letters supposed to be hers, was banished. Madame de la Motte alone was severely punished — by flogging, and branding on both shoulders. Her husband was condemned to the galleys for life; but he naturally kept out of the way, and his wife was soon after allowed to escape in disguise. It is even doubted whether she underwent the branding, as she was not publicly punished. Nor was the morbid curiosity of some ladies of the Palais Royal household gratified, who desired to see her after her punishment had been inflicted. Three of them called at the Hôpital de la Salpêtrière under pretence of going over the establishment. To their remarks and hints respecting Madame de la Motte the Sister Superior gave no reply; but on stating unmistakably that they came to see her, and that they were the ladies of the Duchesse de Chartres, "The greater the reason then for being merciful," replied the nun. "I cannot show you the person you ask for." "But why not, good sister?" said one of these ladies persistently. "Because, madame," said the Sister

Superior, "it is no part of her sentence; she is not condemned to that." The libellous work published under the name of Madame de la Motte in England was said to have been written by the meretricious writer, Louvet de Couvray, the friend of the Duc de Chartres.

The ignominy of this affair fell wholly on the king and queen, but more particularly on the latter. A perfect ovation awaited the cardinal and the *soi-disant* Comte de Cagliostro on their liberation from the Bastille. It had been supposed that the former would be deprived of all the privileges of his rank and his high position in the Church, and delivered over to the shame and contempt which, after a life of extravagance and disorder, had justly overtaken him. But, so far from it, his judges treated him with marked respect and deference, and did not, as in ordinary cases, require him to stand during the lengthened interrogatories to which he was subjected. It fell not within their province to condemn him for the irregularities of his past career, but simply to decide whether he was guilty or innocent of the specific charge brought against him. They saw in him, it appears, only the dupe of an unscrupulous *intrigante:* and such, in all probability, he was, — marvellous and almost incredible as, in some sense, it would seem to be. Nothing, indeed, but extraordinary credulity was proved against him.

But unfortunately, in proving that, the very

light esteem in which the queen's character was held was also proved; for had she commanded the respectful homage and high consideration that should have been paid her, so disgraceful an intrigue could not have occurred. Such a story as La Motte's would have carried with it its own refutation. However, both king and queen were greatly dissatisfied with the decisions of the council. According to their idea, there should have been an interchange of sentences between Madame de la Motte and the cardinal. To equalise them more, the king exiled the cardinal to his Abbaye of Chaise Dieu, banished Cagliostro from France, and facilitated the escape of Madame de la Motte to England. This made matters worse for the queen, — the cardinal and the count being regarded as victims of an act of vengeance, the decree of banishment having emanated only from the king. The escape of Madame de la Motte, and the supposed partial infliction of her punishment, were attributed to the interest the queen took in her, and served to confirm the opinion of the public that she had been leagued with her in defrauding the court jewellers, Boëhmer and Bisange, of their property.

Henceforth, adieu to all respect for poor Marie Antoinette. The news of the cardinal's entire acquittal of any complicity in the robbery of the necklace was received throughout France with an explosion of delight. The part of the woman, De la Motte, seemed to be overlooked in the general satisfaction openly expressed that the supposed vengeful intentions of the queen towards the cardinal had been frustrated.

Both Marie Antoinette and the king were inclined to blame those who had so eagerly advised the cardinal's arrest, and, having advised it, had neither the prudence nor the policy to refrain from displaying their ill-feeling towards him. All the lamentable errors committed in the conduct of the affair were attributed by the excellent Abbé Vermond to his friend, M. de Bréteuil. The latter had been twice ambassador at the court of Vienna, and was one of the plenipotentiaries at the peace of Teschen. He succeeded in persuading M. de Vergennes to consent to the payment of a large indemnity to Joseph II. on that occasion. He was, therefore, in high favour with Marie Antoinette, and was really one of her firmest if not most judicious friends. He has been described as "a man with an enormous voice, a slanderous tongue, and petty ideas." On returning from his embassy he was made minister of state, *sans portefeuille*, and afterwards controller of the king's household.

M. de Bréteuil being immensely rich, the Polignacs were anxious to transfer his wealth to their family by arranging a marriage between a little granddaughter, who was his heiress, and their own son, a mere child. The queen was delighted with the idea; but when the alliance was proposed to M. de Bréteuil, he very respectfully, but very firmly, declined the honour, and thus incurred her majesty's displeasure and her favourite's enmity. The lamentable result of the arrest of the cardinal led to a further loss of royal favour, more grievous still; it led to a cessation of the intimacy that had long existed between him and the "excellent Abbé Vermond;" for as a faithful servant of the queen, those who lost her favour must reckon on losing also the *abbé's* friendship.

CHAPTER XX.

The King Buys Rambouillet. — "*Le Déjeuner de Chasse.*" — "*Il Est Ivre Mort.* — Dining in Public. — The Queen's New Domain. — "*De Par la Reine.*" — Mdlle. Necker's Suitors. — The Accepted Suitor. — Count Fersen Released. — Madame Lebrun's *Étrennes*. — An Ineligible *Ami Intime*. — An Invitation to the Ball. — M. de Calonne's Last Remedy. — Death of M. de Vergennes. — A Lost Friend.

THE brilliant, the gallant, the intrepid M. de Calonne was not yet at the end of his resources, but continued to supply funds without stint for the pleasures and caprices of the court. Even the king could not resist throwing away a few millions. He coveted Rambouillet, though his forests and hunting-grounds were already so numerous, and prevailed on the Duc de Penthièvre to part with that extensive domain and fine château.

In the time of the duke's father, the Comte de Toulouse, when Louis XV. was a shy, handsome youth, what gay hunting parties took place in the well-stocked forest of Rambouillet! What repasts were spread in its shady nooks; how keen were the appetites, sharpened by exercise, with which ladies and gentlemen partook of them; and how hilarious they all were after the champagne. It was the king's favourite wine, and it inspired Vanloo with the idea of one of his prettiest pictures, "*Le Déjeuner de Chasse*," — a share, and a large share, too, of the merit being also due to the exhilaration of the scene, and the joyous and picturesque party before him.

But it was not to revive those gay scenes of bygone times that Louis XVI. sought possession of Rambouillet. He had always been fond of the chase, and, from still increasing obesity, it was the exercise now most congenial to him. Those who accompanied him returned not to the château to dance, as in the days when the charming Comtesse de Toulouse arranged, after the hunt, the *soirées-dansantes* for the young king. The chase ended, they now dispersed, and Louis, thoroughly exhausted, threw himself into his carriage, and sank into deep sleep. Arrived at the palace, it was no easy matter to rouse him. The attendants were obliged very roughly to handle their sovereign to make him conscious that his journey was ended, and that it was time to alight. At last, partly awakened, he would come stumbling out; then reel and stagger, and rub his eyes, before he began with unsteady step to ascend the grand staircase. Often the impression of this scene on those who stood around to see the king return from the chase was expressed in the whispered exclamation: "*Il est ivre mort*" — "He is dead drunk!"

These words were one day uttered at Versailles

by a son or nephew of Voltaire's friend Thiriot, and uttered loud enough to be heard by one of the gentlemen-in-waiting, who ordered his arrest.

He was immediately surrounded by soldiers of the guard, to be escorted to prison. The king, perceiving this, asked what the young man had been doing. When informed of his offence he burst into a hearty laugh. "Do not take him to prison," he said; "conduct him only to the gates, and there tell him that I am going to drink his health in a glass of lemonade." Anecdotes of Louis XVI. are not numerous; there are few, indeed, that do not excite more pity than amusement, and fewer still that reveal anything in his character to admire. His excesses were, however, rather in eating than drinking. Like all the Bourbons, his appetite was enormous; and even when dining in public, publicity imposed no restraint on his gross habits. Those repasts were torture to the queen. It may have been injudicious to have absented herself from them whenever it was possible to do so, but it is not surprising she should have desired it.

The king at this time dined more frequently in public than usual, — hoping, perhaps, by showing himself and family oftener to his subjects, to revive the waning respect for royalty, which even he, since the affair of the necklace, could hardly fail to observe. The public dinners were among the sights of Paris. Country cousins were fond of gazing at those royal feasts, where, to the amazement of many, the monarch appeased his appetite much in the same way as themselves, and without a crown on his head or a sceptre ready to his hand. On the occasion of Louis's first visit to the Hôtel Dieu, the multitude were also greatly astonished to find that in appearance their sovereign was only a fat, ordinary-looking *bourgeois*, wearing a slovenly round wig, a small hat, and a shabby brown coat.

The queen, delighted with her new domain, began to pass much of her time at St. Cloud. It had also become a favourite Sunday excursion with the Parisian shopkeepers and *petite bourgeoisie*. On Sundays the fountains were in full play. But they were not the only attraction. It was "*les eaux et l'Autrichienne*" they went to see. Unhappily at this period everything seemed to concur towards placing the queen's conduct in a more and more disadvantageous light, and increasing her unpopularity. Offence was very generally taken — and not alone by the holiday-making Parisians — at the rules and regulations concerning admission to the royal palace and park of St. Cloud, and which were posted up at all the entrances, being headed "By order of her majesty the queen" — the queen's private livery only being worn by the lodge-keepers and servants employed in the grounds. "Here was a novel pretension indeed!" — an infringement of the king's prerogative that no Queen of France had hitherto attempted.

The length of the queen's visits to Trianon, — where the king was supposed to go only by invitation, — had been often mentioned even by Joseph II. with much disapproval; but the possession of a palace, recognised as exclusively her own, was declared to be "equally impolitic and immoral." When this matter was pressed on her attention by friends sincerely devoted to her and her interests, she declined "to compromise her dignity" by substituting "*De par le roi*" for "*De par la reine*." Poor Louis XVI. was certainly at fault here. It was a case in which there was a double duty on his part to command, and the same on hers to obey. It afforded a proof, if proof had been wanting, that the king was utterly unfit for his high position; and it would not have been surprising if the hopes and expectations of Monsieur, unbrotherly though they were, had then been realised. But Monsieur, wily as he was, inspired no public confidence; the reign of folly and imbecility, therefore, was for a brief space destined to be prolonged.

Marie Antoinette is believed to have been at that time greatly under the influence of her attachment to Count Fersen. Unlike the young Marquis de La Fayette, his sojourn in America had inspired him with no enthusiasm for liberty and independence, but rather had strengthened his aristocratic prejudices. By these he was greatly swayed, and, though strictly honourable in his principles, blinded to much of the danger surrounding the king and queen. His strong antipathy to La Fayette was shared to the full by the latter, and distrust of the popular general was thus communicated to the king.

When Count Fersen returned to Paris in 1783, his father wished him to pay his court to the wealthy heiress, Mdlle. Necker, then just seventeen. But he had no mind for the match; neither had Marie Antoinette a mind that the man between whom and herself a strong feeling of attachment had for some years existed (of which there can be little doubt) should marry into a family she so thoroughly detested. But there were many other suitors in the field. Among them Mr. Pitt is said to have been one of the foremost. The queen, however, suggested to Baron de Staël, the Swedish Secretary of Legation — Count Creutz being the head of the mission — that he should enter the lists. "The baron," she said, "is still a handsome man; mademoiselle is extremely ugly. He is very poor; she is very rich; and as both are Protestants, a better match could not be arranged." She might have added that he was extravagantly inclined, was in the autumn of life, and was of noble and ancient lineage. The younger suitor accordingly withdrew, and left the ground open to his presumed rival.

The offer of the baron's hand and heart was not unfavourably received. The young lady seemed to see in him the kind of husband she could bend to her will, and who in other respects suited her views. The objection of the parents was the suitor's want of any assured income. His noble name was fully appreciated. But even had he claimed to attach Holstein to it, which certainly he did not (it was annexed by madame after his death, though she had no right to it), M. Necker was not so much in love with a name as to give his daughter, with her large dowry and larger expectations, to a man who had not a *sou* of his own to support it with due *éclat*. The "to be or not to be" therefore remained in suspense for three years, until M. de Staël was named minister or ambassador, with a promise from Gustavus III. that he was to hold the appointment permanently, and to receive besides a pension of 20,000 *francs* for past services. This settled, and other hard and stringent conditions laid down by the lady being accepted by the gentleman, Mdlle. Anne-Germaine Necker, in January, 1786, became La Baronne de Staël.

The baron's proposal, when first entertained, served to release M. de Fersen. He wrote to his father: "I am by no means sorry your idea cannot be realised. It was only to please you that I for a moment thought of it. She is not pretty," he continues; "quite the contrary. But she is lively and witty and highly talented." De Staël was instigated by his wife to adhere to the revolutionary party. Gustavus, in consequence, is said "to have been obliged to dissemble his real feelings, and to have desired Count Fersen to explain this to the king and queen." Fersen in the following year accompanied Gustavus on his travels, and returned with him to Sweden. But shortly after we meet him again in Paris.

On the 27th of February, 1786, Madame de Vergennes gave a grand ball at her residence, the magnificent Hôtel de Mêsmes. All the ministers, including, of course, M. de Calonne, were invited. It was carnival time, and in spite of the hunger and cold, and their usual attendant miseries in the poorer quarters of Paris at this season, prosperity seemed to reign elsewhere. Scarcely was a gayer or more brilliant carnival remembered. The reign of M. de Calonne was drawing to a close. But like the sun at his setting, when his golden rays are of deepest hue, and the colouring of the sky most varied and splendid, the fertile brain of the Minister of Finance contrived, when his fall became imminent, still to illumine the atmosphere of the court and society with bright, if deceptive, gleams of apparent prosperity.

The pretty and clever Madame Lebrun had recently painted the minister's portrait, and it was rumoured that, like some others who had sat to that artist, he had fallen a victim to the fascinating beauty of the lady. A story was current that to win her smiles he had availed himself of the custom of offering *étrennes* on the New Year's Day, to present her with a lavishly expensive present — the chief cost of which fell on the state. It consisted of an elegantly ornamented satin bag filled with *bonbons en papillotes* — the *papillotes*, or wrappers, being orders on the treasury for payment at sight of no insignificant sum of money. And this was not all. Besides the bag there was a box — an elegant trifle, but having on the top a groove containing a movable ornament, *en rivière*, of diamonds — the box itself being filled with newly coined *louis d'or*.

The story was told in various ways, as indignation or envy prompted. But Madame Lebrun, who stood high in the queen's favour, declared to her majesty that it was entirely a malevolent exaggeration. The box, she said, was not worth more than 500 *francs*, and its contents were but the price of the portrait, a sum much less than she had expected. M. de Beaujon, the rich financier, had paid her twice as much; or rather he had paid her husband, who appropriated the whole of her large earnings, sparingly doling out to her now and then a few *louis d'or*. The *papillotes*, she asserted, were merely imitations of *billets d'escompte*, supplied by the confectioner as an amusing surprise when opened. This was probably the truth — but no one was disposed to believe it. To the charge that she had accepted him as *un ami intime* she replied — and thought it a sufficient refutation — " M. de Calonne is elderly and ugly, and wears a lawyer's wig."

As rank, wealth, and fashion — French and foreign — flocked to the *atelier* of this, more than in one sense, pretty portrait painter, it is presumable that younger and handsomer men, who wore wigs more *à la mode*, sought her smiles with greater chance of obtaining them. Her *salon* was always full, when aristocratic ones were often empty; and as her suite of rooms was small, her most distinguished guests were willing to sit on the floor if they could find no vacant seat elsewhere. But — to return to M. de Calonne and his *étrennes* — as already observed the Minister of Finance was invited to Madame de Vergennes's carnival ball. The story of the *papillotes*, diamonds, and *louis d'or*, had then become widely known, and the supposed value of the present increased tenfold. On his way to the Hôtel de Mêsmes, as soon as he was recognised, he was assailed by hisses and groans, cries of *voleur des papillotes*, and epithets anything but complimentary. The streets were full of masqueraders, who surrounded his carriage, broke the windows, and attempted to pull him out. His position began to be perilous, when his coachman, vigorously lashing his four horses, then kicking and prancing, sufficiently dispersed the assailants to enable him to wheel about and bear his master home. The minister lost his ball, but got safely into his hôtel before a pursuing hooting mob could come up with him.

This incident appears to have been accepted by M. de Calonne as a warning to retire from the ministry. For soon after he addressed a memorial to the king reminding him of the state of the treasury when the direction of the finances was conferred on him; it contained, he said, just 2,400 *francs*, scarcely £100. "Illusion had since taken the place of reality. France had been supported by artifice. The annual deficit was four hundred millions, and the debt of the state, one milliard six hundred and forty-six millions." Yet there remained a remedy; and his majesty assenting to his plan, he would stake his existence on its success. In six months, or at furthest a year, prosperity should be restored to France, his majesty's anxieties ended, and M. de Calonne, having then done his duty to his king and his country, would — tendering his resignation — say with an approving conscience: "*Nunc dimittis servum tuum, Domine!*"

These grand objects were to be obtained from the Assembly of the Notables. The king consented to the scheme; the assembly was convoked, and opened its session at Versailles February, 1787. No part of the burden of the state was borne by the higher classes. M. de Calonne now informed those privileged persons that the people, unaided, could bear it no longer. He therefore invited them to waive their right of exemption, and contribute towards the needs of the country. They were not disposed to accede to his request; still less were they inclined when, drawing aside the veil, he disclosed to them, in the enormous annual deficit, the heavy national debt, the results of the system he advocated as the true principle of credit and national prosperity. The minister perceived that his hopes were misplaced, — that he had announced his own fate in the revelation he had made. He immediately resigned and fled the country. The assembly separated on the 25th of May, spreading everywhere alarm, by reporting throughout the kingdom: "The throne in need; misery without resource; bankruptcy imminent."

During the session of the assembly, M. de Vergennes, unfortunately for the king, was taken ill and died. His death was believed to be accelerated by extreme anxiety concerning the heavy and ever increasing troubles of the country, and a foreboding of some terrible catastrophe, occasioning a general disorganisation of society. Shortly before his death he endeavoured to impress on the king the danger of his position, and urged him to pursue a more vigorous and firmer line of conduct. Louis was personally attached to him, and perhaps felt the full force of his advice. He had lost a friend on whose support he could rely. He is said to have lamented him bitterly, and to have exclaimed when he died: "I should indeed be happy to repose beside him." Poor Louis!

CHAPTER XXI.

A Lifelong Wish. — The Queen's Advisers. — The New Minister of Finance. — Struggling with Difficulties. — Shovels and Tongs. — M. Necker's Return to Paris. — Paying Court to the Queen. — Agriculture in France. — The Three Estates of the Realm. — The "Plebeian Count." — The Dawn of the Revolution.

TO be minister of state, to succeed to the controllership of the finances, had been the lifelong wish of the Archbishop of Sens, M. Loménie de Brienne, as also it had long been the aim of his former *protégé*, the Abbé Vermond, to raise him to that little enviable but much envied position. The favourable moment at last is arrived. The queen, by the death of M. de Vergennes, is become, uncontrolled, first minister of state, and is present at the council. She dominates in the government by dominating the feeble-minded king, who is incapable of taking, or following up, any resolution. Yet his dissimulation is profound, the result of the evil training he had received in common with all the princes of the House of Bourbon, and to which their misfortunes were largely due.*

The Abbé Vermond is, of course, after Madame

* *Mémoires du Comte Miot de Melito.*

de Polignac, the queen's chief adviser. He is now "the great man of a petty coterie." Hitherto, it has been usual to speak of him familiarly in the household as "the *abbé;*" but now every one bows low as he passes through the anterooms, or along the corridors of Versailles and, as Madame Campan says, salutes him deferentially as "Monsieur l'Abbé." When M. de Calonne decamped, M. de Castries ventured to suggest M. Necker as his successor. But the queen would not hear of recalling the "Genevese charlatan," and the king, rather amusingly, objected to him as a "restless fanatic (*brouillon fanatique*), governed by his wife; a man of talent, no doubt, but who sought to transfer his kingdom into a clamorous republic like the city of Geneva." The queen added that "M. Necker would make a King of France as great a nullity as a King of England."

M. Loménie de Brienne was therefore nominated by the queen Minister of Finance. He had amazing confidence in himself, and believed that he was possessed of far greater financial ability than Calonne, — that he, in fact, was destined to save the sinking ship. His predecessor had fled so suddenly to Brussels — fearing that a day's delay would lodge him in the Bastille — that the Assembly of Notables was not yet dissolved. M. de Brienne, as the antagonist of M. de Calonne, believed that the "Notables" would do for him what they had refused to do for the latter. But on making his appeal — for he perforce adopted Calonne's plan — he found them none the less resolved to make no sacrifices for the state. As M. Mignet observes, they had seconded his attacks on Calonne, which were in their interests, and not his ambition, to which they were indifferent. He could impose no new taxes, for the Parliament refused to confirm his decrees. He could raise no loans, for the credit of the state was exhausted. Whatever measure he proposed failed to succeed.

In the interests of the *fermiers généraux*, who complained of the loss sustained by the smuggling of merchandise into Paris without payment of the *octroi*, M. de Calonne had authorised the construction of new walls round the capital, with barriers of expensive and fanciful architecture, designed by Ledoux. The archbishop, amazed at the enormous sums already expended on this work, and still demanded in order to complete it, in November, 1787, inspected the vast undertaking. His anger, when he perceived that utility had been less considered than ornamentation, and the question of expense utterly disregarded, is described as excessive. In a paroxysm of rage he ordered the demolition of the portion already completed, and the sale of the materials. But the council, assembled on the 25th of the same month to consider the matter, ordered only the suspension of the works.

The archbishop continued ineffectually to struggle with the difficulties of the position he had accepted. The ardent support of the queen and Monsieur l'Abbé availed him nothing. "He tried intrigue and oppression; he banished the rebellious Parliament, but found obstacles only where he looked for aid. Weakened and wearied by contention, he at last succumbed, falling by the faults of Calonne, as Calonne had supported himself by the confidence inspired by Necker, but being chiefly to blame for presumption in accepting a position from the difficulties of which he knew not how to extricate himself." * Having given in his resignation (August 25th, 1788), the archbishop forthwith proceeded to Rome, where a cardinal's hat rewarded his ministerial trials and troubles.

A perfect explosion of joy hailed his departure, and both he and his friend and colleague, M. de Lamoignon, were burned in effigy on the Place de Grève to the music of shovels and tongs, kettles and pans, and cries of "*Vive Henri Quatre!*" "*Au diable Lamoignon et Brienne!*" The queen at this time was so ill-advised as openly to express regret at the forced resignation of a minister whose fall was hailed by the whole nation with joy. She presented him at his departure with her portrait set in diamonds, and named his niece *dame du palais.* "He was sac-

* Mignet's "*Révolution Française.*"

rificed," she said, "to the factious spirit of the nation." Yet, "upwards of a hundred couriers set out from Versailles on the day he quitted office to carry the welcome news to the provinces." The unpopularity of the queen is at its height, and Monsieur and the Duc d'Orléans are more opposed to her than ever. Her portrait is removed from the *salon* because of the insults of the people. They call her Madame Déficit, accuse her of stealing the necklace, and of treason in state affairs. The king is pitied, advised, and remonstrated with on all sides.

All respect for the monarchy is gone. The revolution is inevitable, and step by step it is preparing. "Young France wears the portraits of General de La Fayette and Admiral d'Estaing on its waistcoats. The *États Généraux* are demanded as the only means of government, and the last resource of the throne. M. Necker is recalled, and is informed of his reappointment by the queen herself, — though it is the public voice and no suggestion of hers that reinstates him. His return to Paris is a triumph, the king having but recently ordered him to reside at a considerable distance from the capital. Fourteen medals are struck in his honour, and waistcoats, buttons, snuff-boxes, neckties, are adorned with his portrait — if such a portrait could be said to adorn anything. Madame de Staël is almost beside herself with joy, and can scarce be restrained from displaying her eloquence in a complimentary harangue to the enthusiastic mob."

It happened that Madame de Canisy and Madame de Staël, some few days after, paid their court to the queen at the same time; the former attired with elegance, and observant of customary etiquette, as befitted a lady of the palace; the latter dressed with all her known bad taste, and regardless of the *convenances*, as befitted a woman of republican principles and a genius. Under the circumstances it was ill-judged to make any difference in her manner of receiving the ladies. But the queen was impetuous, and had no command of her temper; and, according to the report of Madame de Staël, "all the graciousness of the sovereign's reception was for the niece of the outgoing minister; all the ungraciousness for the daughter of the incoming one."

In the interval between M. Necker's return to power and the opening of the States General — fixed for the 5th of May, 1789 — much sickness and misery prevailed throughout France. Heavy storms, violent winds, and an unusual quantity of hail destroyed the crops. The imperfect system of agriculture had also much to do with this constantly recurring famine in the land. According to the report of Mr. Arthur Young, who visited France for four successive years, from 1787 to 1790, for the purpose of inquiring into the state of agriculture in France, it was miserable in every respect. He says, also, that where he expected to find farms and farmers, he found only monks, monasteries, and state prisons. There was general gloom and dissatisfaction in the country, and a looking forward to the assembling of the States for great changes in the system of government, though none seemed to have any definite idea of how those changes were likely to be brought about.

Beside the wretchedness of the people, the thoughtless prodigality and luxury of the rich formed a striking and painful contrast. The carnival was brilliant; Longchamps superb. The ladies had resumed their lofty head-dresses; and the favourite vehicle was the newly introduced whiskey.

The election of the deputies for the States General occasioned much agitation and even serious disturbances, both in Paris and several of the provincial towns. Meanwhile, the costume of the different orders and the etiquette to be observed at their installation occupied the attention of the court. The 4th of May arrives. In the evening a religious ceremony in the Church of St. Louis precedes the opening of the States on the 5th; and as the procession winds its way along the vast streets of Versailles, the public observe with pain how strikingly marked are the distinctions of rank and costume that divide these three different bodies of men on whom their destiny depends, and who, therefore, should have equal rights. To the episcopal purple, the crosiers, and grand mantles of the dignitaries of the Church, succeed the long black robes of the "inferior clergy." There are two hundred and five of them, in two divisions, separated by a band of music. Next appear the vests and facings of cloth of gold, the lace ruffles and cravats, the Henri IV. hats, floating plumes, and mantles of state of the nobles, making up a brilliant show. Following after, in the humble, antiquated guise of the "*vilains*" of 1614, come the modest Third Estate of the realm. Their costume is a close-fitting black dress, with short black woollen mantle, plain muslin cravat, a small round black hat that not only has no feather, but is without either band or cord of any kind.

The absence of finery in their humble garb is atoned for in the eyes of the populace — who received them with hearty cheers and acclamations refused to the higher grades — by the resolute expression of countenance, the firm step and undaunted air, observable in most of them. One only is generally known; and all eyes are fixed on that face whose power is in its wonderful ugliness, whose life has been a life of tempest and storm — it is the "plebeian count," De Mirabeau. The *cortège* of the princes, who are surrounded by courtiers, is allowed to pass by in silence. The king appears; his face expresses no emotion, no interest in the scene. As usual, he moves without dignity, and appears as though he were simply acquitting himself of some ordinary duty of etiquette.

Monsieur is more grave and pensive, and apparently more impressed by the importance of the occasion. He walks with difficulty, owing to his extreme corpulency. The Comte d'Artois shows evident signs of *ennui* and bad temper, and casts disdainful glances to the right and left on the crowd that lines the streets. The queen has an anxious look. Her lips are closely pressed, as if in a vain effort to dissemble her trouble and to give an air of satisfaction to her countenance, promptly suppressed by inquietude of mind and bitter thoughts.*

No really hostile sentiments can be said to have then animated that vast throng. Nevertheless, alike among those who formed the procession and those who were only its spectators, there was a lurking latent feeling that something strange, something hitherto unknown, coming from the past and pressing on to the future, was moving onwards towards France. It was the Revolution, to be decreed by the *États Généraux*.

* *Mémoires du Comte Miot de Melito.*

END OF VOL. I.

www.ingramcontent.com/pod-product-compliance
Lightning Source LLC
Chambersburg PA
CBHW022046160426
43198CB00008B/142